WILD DENVER

WILD DENVER

EXPLORE THE AMAZING NATURE IN AND AROUND
THE MILE HIGH CITY

Felicia Brower

TIMBER PRESS • PORTLAND, OR

Dedicated to the people, plants, and animals that make Denver an incredible place to live; to those who have nurtured the city's natural beauty over the years; and to those committed to protecting its parks, gardens, and wildlife for generations to come. Thank you.

Timber Press
Workman Publishing
Hachette Book Group, Inc.
1290 Avenue of the Americas
New York, New York 10104
timberpress.com

Timber Press is an imprint of Workman Publishing, a division of Hachette Book Group, Inc.
The Timber Press name and logo are registered trademarks of Hachette Book Group, Inc.
Printed in Shenzhen, China (APO), on responsibly sourced paper
Text design by Laura Shaw, based on a series design by Anna Eshelman
Cover design by Leigh Kaisen
Illustrations by Alec Backhus
The publisher is not responsible for websites (or their content) that are not owned by the publisher.

ISBN 978-1-64326-493-6
A catalog record for this book is available from the Library of Congress.

CONTENTS

INTRODUCTION

Whispers of the Wild West echo through the streets of Denver. Discreet plaques and markers on the sidewalks and historic buildings remind modern-day residents of the memorable events and places that have withstood the test of time.

But this area's history didn't begin there. It started millions of years ago, under a sea. As time went on and the landscape of the world changed, Denver did too. Dinosaurs roamed and eventually died out. The area's first human inhabitants lived their lives to fit the seasonality of the land. When European settlers forced them out, the land was altered to fit the lives of these new residents. As time went on, the city shifted and grew and eventually became the place we know today.

Denver is a city of change, but one thing has stayed eternal: the stunning natural beauty of the area. Nestled at the foot of the Rocky Mountains, Denver and the Front Range offer easy access to world-class outdoor recreation. Places like City Park and Denver Botanic Gardens offer serene escapes within the city, and even simply watching the sun set over the mountains from the right road or rooftop can give you butterflies. It's an incredible place to call home.

Before we dive in, I want to be clear that I'm not a scientist. I'm just a person who loves learning and can't get enough of the outdoors. I wrote this book because it's the guide I wish I had when I first moved here. I've spent the past decade getting to know the ins and outs of the city's natural places, and I want to share some of them with as many people as possible. Bringing more folks to the trails can be a touchy subject in a city grappling with growth, but there *is* enough room for all of us to recreate responsibly and connect with the spaces that keep our hearts wild. The more people love and respect the outdoors, the better our odds are for protecting these cherished places.

This book is essentially a field guide to Denver and the surrounding suburbs of Aurora, Golden, Lakewood, and Littleton. It's split into three sections: Wild Denver, 99 Species to Know, and Field Trips.

'Wild Denver' dives into the natural history and ecology of the city. This section is broken into ten chapters that cover everything from fossils to weather to water to citizen science you can do to help wildlife.

The '99 Species to Know' section highlights some of the plants, animals, insects, mold, and mushrooms that you can see on the Field Trips. Common names can vary depending on the species, so if you want to take your research to the next level, rely on the italicized scientific names. The first word (or genus) is always capitalized, and *spp.* in lieu of a second word (the species name) means that there are several species, and that the entry relates to them all. All of the common names in this guide are lowercase for

consistency (e.g.,mountain lion and black-footed ferret), except for the ones named after a place or a person (e.g., Rocky Mountain elk and Steller's jay).

Finally, 'Field Trips' is a selection of 25 parks and trails within an hour of the city. These trips are a mix of easy, paved walks to more challenging hikes with elevation gain. There are different habitats on these hikes—some are open prairies, some are mountain forests, and some are a mix. Many trips are accessible or have at least one accessible trail, and most are easy for first-time hikers to attempt. All have descriptions of what you can expect during your visit.

This book covers the basics and should give you a good foundation to feel comfortable going out on the trails. The information is geared toward beginners, and this is only a sampling of some of the interesting things you can see and expect. *Wild Denver* is a good place to start if you're new to your ID journey, and it can easily fit into most packs.

Humans are an important part of the natural world. We belong in it. May this book inspire you to explore and appreciate the wonders that surround us.

WILD DENVER

Discovering Denver's Wild Side

At a Colorado Rockies game, you'll probably spot a purple triceratops making its way around the stadium to get the crowd pumped up. Upon first glance, it seems like a random choice for a mascot, but Dinger the Dinosaur is actually a nod to a discovery made during the construction of the home of Denver's Major League Baseball team.

When ground was broken for Coors Field, there was a high probability that fossils would be found. Every few years, the discovery of a fossil from somewhere in or around the city makes the news, and as the site at Blake and 20th was excavated, what was eventually determined to be the ribs of a triceratops were unearthed.

When news got out, the owners of the field even debated naming the ballpark Jurassic Park to lean into the discovery. They went a different direction but were adamant about paying homage to the fossils, and Dinger was born. (Literally—there are videos of him breaking free from his egg at a game in 1994.)

While we now think of Colorado as a landlocked state, millions of years ago, it was under a sea. During the late Cretaceous Period, this shallow sea was rich with marine life, leaving behind sedimentary rock layers such as limestone and sandstone, which are now part of Denver's geology. As tectonic forces uplifted the Rocky Mountains and it receded, the ancient seabed was pushed to the surface. Today, fossils and sedimentary layers provide valuable insights into what Denver has looked like throughout history and all the dramatic geological changes that have occurred over millions of years.

◀ Paleontologists carefully excavating the future Coors Field site

◀◀ Dinger the Dinosaur at Coors Field

► See the biggest bear in Colorado without leaving the city: "I See What You Mean" by Lawrence Argent is a 40-foot blue bear looking in the windows of the Colorado Convention Center

WILD DENVER

Nature Is All Around You

Denver is a city for all types of life—you just have to know where to look. With more than 280 parks and 850 miles of trails in the city alone, you don't have to go far to feel immersed in the natural world. Even downtown Denver, with its skyscrapers and traffic, is home to plants and animals that have excelled at adapting to life alongside humans.

Birdlife is particularly diverse in the city. Tall buildings and green spaces serve as habitats and feeding grounds, making it easy for birdwatchers to spot mourning doves, hawks, and house sparrows. Permanent avian residents quickly learn which streetlights are the best to hang near to snatch bugs out of the sky. More recently, peregrine falcons have returned to the city to nest on skyscrapers, utilizing the city's high-rise structures as artificial cliffs for their nests. Denver is also a perfect place for birds to stop and rest their wings during long cross-country migration journeys.

Insects and spiders occupy cracks and crevices all around the city. Swallowtails flutter around and visit the flowers in pocket parks, and miller moths become inescapable for a few weeks each year. Eastern fox squirrels dart between the old-growth trees that line the streets, which turn blazing hues of yellow and gold every fall. Residents in neighborhoods plant flowers and shrubs to provide beauty and serve as food sources for birds, bugs, and other animals.

Once you leave the city limits, the habitats and wildlife change. The suburbs and lower foothills of the Front Range are home to birds of prey like red-tailed hawk and American kestrel, as well as larger mammals like mule deer grazing in open fields.

As you venture farther into the foothills, wildlife really starts to diversify. You might even spot a black bear or mountain lion in more forested areas. Birdwatchers have a better chance of spotting birds that only live at higher elevation or are more elusive, like Steller's jay and great horned owl. Reptiles

▲ Mule deer are
common in the
foothills and on
hiking trails

◄ Squirrels are
everywhere in
Denver

▲ Asters bloom at the end of summer

► People often set out peanuts as treats for crows and squirrels

like prairie lizard and gopher snake also become more common. More specialized animals like bighorn sheep have adapted to the cooler, rocky environments found farther away from the city.

Denver is called the "Mile High City" because it's 5280 feet above sea level—1 mile. Because of the elevation, the weather feels a little different here. We're physically closer to the sun than many other cities in the country, so the heat is often described as more intense. Our winters are mild, but we do get hard freezes and snowstorms that make it a tough place to survive outdoors.

The flora and fauna (plants and animals, respectively) of Denver have to be tough to make it through the year and have evolved in response to the city's climate and geography. Plant species native to the Denver area are low water and drought tolerant with roots that reach down inches or even feet to access moisture that isn't lost to evaporation from sun and wind. Blue grama grass, sagebrush, and various species of wildflowers like columbine, aster, and sunflower are just a few species you'll find in yards in the city and out on the trails.

Mule deer, black bear, mountain lion, raccoon, skunk, and fox all call this region home. Bird species in the area include American robin, red-tailed hawk, and various species of songbird. Insects such as butterflies and bees play a crucial role in pollinating the region's flora.

The People Before the Place

It's estimated that 48 or more Indigenous tribes occupied Colorado for some amount of time, including Arapaho (Hinono'ei), Cheyenne (Tsistsistas), and Ute (Nuuchu or Nuu-ciu) tribes. The Ute people inhabited much of southwestern Colorado, traveling to the Denver area seasonally to hunt. The Arapaho and Cheyenne were nomadic Plains people who lived east and north of Colorado but would also set up seasonal camps in the area as they followed bison herds and other resources.

Colorado was admitted to the Union as the 38th state on August 1, 1876, exactly 100 years after the Declaration of Independence was signed in 1776, earning it the nickname the "Centennial State."

Like many places in the United States, the official incorporation of the state into the Union marked the end of a way of life for Indigenous peoples who had called the area home for generations. The displacement of these people involved a combination of unfulfilled treaties, military force, and settlement policies that had devastating impacts on Indigenous communities as well as the environment.

◄ "The Closing Era," outside Colorado State Capitol, was created by Preston Powers and represents the end of the traditional lifestyle of Native Americans in Colorado

A Commitment to Greener Growth

Between water demands and increased pollution, Denver has had some struggles as a city trying to maintain a connection to the natural world. Urbanization has led to habitat fragmentation and the loss of natural areas. The expansion of the city has encroached on or altered habitats for plants, animals, and insects.

Our population increase is going to continue, so if we want to make sure we have green spaces that can help us combat some of these issues, we have to set aside space intentionally. Creating an extensive network of parks and open spaces has been a priority since the city's formation and continues to be one today.

Water in the West

You can't survive without water. For a city set in a semi-arid climate with a history and predisposition to drought, that can sometimes be a major issue. Finding a way to provide water for both consumption and irrigation and maintain a balance between both is a struggle we've been dealing with since the early days of Denver.

Before the official establishment of Denver, the Indigenous peoples of the region utilized the area's natural water sources for their sustenance and daily needs. The arrival of European settlers in the mid-19th century introduced new challenges and demands on these water sources. The city's location along the South Platte River was advantageous for initial settlement, but the river's seasonal fluctuations and unreliable flow made it impossible to depend upon the river as a consistent water supply. The challenge of securing water made farming and daily life tough, pushing pioneers to adopt clever irrigation systems and establish laws around water rights.

In 1868, Sloan's Lake served as a key reservoir and helped manage the water supply in the growing city. In 1900, the Denver Water Company (now Denver Water) was established to manage and improve the city's water supply. They carved out a citywide ditch and began digging reservoirs to store water.

As the population continued to grow, the city invested in infrastructure to divert water from nearby mountain streams and rivers, including the construction of pipelines and tunnels to transport water from higher elevations to the city. The state's complex water-rights system—based on "first in time, first in right"—has led to historical and ongoing conflicts and legal disputes. Due to the state's limited water resources and high demand, surrounding communities have grown concerned about providing water to their residents too.

Big Floods and Devastating Droughts

Cherry Creek, a tributary of the South Platte River, runs through the heart of Denver, and its watershed reaches urban and suburban areas around the city. Many early Denver neighborhoods were built around it because residents and farmers needed easy access to water.

One night in May 1864, heavy rainfall caused the Platte River and Cherry Creek to overflow their banks, leading to Denver's first major flood. People were killed, infrastructure and homes were completely destroyed, and the event prompted efforts to improve flood management and infrastructure, laying the groundwork for future flood-control measures in the growing city.

While floods were a major concern in Denver, especially after the Cherry Creek disaster, early Denver also faced significant hurdles due to its challenging drought conditions, which were a stark reminder of the region's arid climate.

Droughts aren't just bad for people. For plants, the lack of water leads to reduced growth, stressed vegetation, and increased vulnerability to diseases and pests. Gardens and natural landscapes suffer as soil moisture dwindles, leading to browning, die-off, and a decline in biodiversity. Many native and nonnative species struggle to survive, affecting the overall health of local ecosystems. Vegetative stress disrupts food chains, leading to declines in animal populations and changes in behavior as wildlife adapts to the harsher conditions.

▲ Houses and commercial buildings destroyed by flooded Cherry Creek

The city was also impacted by America's most catastrophic drought. The Dust Bowl had a profound environmental impact on Denver and the surrounding region, particularly in terms of air quality, agriculture, and landscape degradation. As severe droughts and relentless dust storms ravaged the Great Plains in the 1930s, the city occasionally found itself blanketed in dust, with thick clouds of dirt carried by strong winds from the east. These dust storms—some lasting for days—compromised air quality, making it difficult for residents to breathe and causing widespread health issues, particularly for those with respiratory conditions. Outside the city, the drought decimated crops and left the land parched and barren.

Droughts since then haven't been as intense, but they have resulted in water restrictions and a general shift in how we think about water in Denver. The threat of drought always looms and agencies are tasked with making sure we have enough to go around.

Denver's Water Demands

Denver's water supply is sourced primarily from two major river basins: the Colorado River, with key contributions from reservoirs like Gross and Dillon, and the South Platte River. These sources are managed through an extensive network of infrastructure, including the Moffat Tunnel, to channel mountain water into the city's system.

Eighty percent of Denver's surface-water supply comes from melting snow on the mountains sent to the city primarily by river.

Managing Denver's water supply comes with its own set of challenges. One significant issue is sedimentation, which can accumulate in reservoirs and reduce their storage capacity over time. Sediment from runoff and erosion—as well as from wildfires and human activities like construction, deforestation, and land development—can also affect water quality, making treatment more complex and costly. As a result, Denver Water continuously invests in water treatment and reservoir maintenance to address these challenges and ensure a consistent and clean water supply for its residents.

Summer water restrictions are an attempt to help manage the city's limited water resources and ensure sustainable use, especially during periods of drought or high demand. These restrictions typically include guidelines on when and how often residents can water their lawns, limiting irrigation to certain days of the week or specific times of day to minimize evaporation. There may be limits on using water for nonessential purposes like washing vehicles or filling swimming pools during critical dry periods.

As water restrictions become more common, homeowners are transforming their hellstrips (the patch of grass between the sidewalk and the street) into low-water landscapes, making it easier to see native plants like

yarrow, blanket flower, asters, and prairie coneflower without heading out of the city.

Population growth, urban development, and the impacts of climate change—including shifting precipitation patterns and increased evaporation rates—continue to strain existing water infrastructure and pose risks to the city's water supply.

To address these challenges, Denver Water is focusing on adaptive water-management strategies that emphasize resilience and sustainability. This includes investing in water conservation, exploring alternative water sources, and enhancing infrastructure to withstand changing climate conditions. The city is also engaged in collaborative efforts with other water users and stakeholders to address regional water issues and ensure a reliable water supply for future generations.

▼ Blanket flower is a drought-tolerant perennial

▲ Prairie cone-flower is a late-season bloomer

► During a blizzard, 28 inches of wet snow hit Denver, making it extremely difficult to get around

Weather

Colorado has three distinctly different regions: the plains (east of the city), the mountains (north and west), and the Western Slope (far west). Denver is located where the mountains and the plains meet. Known as the foothills (of the Rocky Mountains), these little pockets create interesting microclimates—smaller areas with distinctive climates—that support different species.

"ONE MILE ABOVE SEA LEVEL" is engraved on the 15th step of the capitol building, but the actual one-mile measurement has changed multiple times over the years.

Changes in elevation can drastically impact the weather. Denver is 5280 feet above sea level. Higher elevations get colder first, so it's possible to get heavy snow in Golden and not a flake in downtown Denver.

Westerly winds blow smoke from wildfires in California and Canada in summer, leading to severe air pollution as inversions form and trap pollutants in a layer of cold air. In winter, strong mid-latitude jet streams known as polar jet streams pass through, which can result in heavy, wet snow deposited all over the area.

Breath of Semi-Fresh Air

Denver struggles with having some of the worst air-quality rankings in the country and, on some days, the world. A significant issue is ground-level ozone, a harmful pollutant formed when sunlight reacts with emissions from vehicles, industrial sources, and other pollutants. This photochemical reaction typically occurs on hot, sunny days (Denver's specialty!), leading to elevated ozone levels. In 2008, the Environmental Protection Agency (EPA) set the National Ambient Air Quality Standards for ozone at 70 parts per billion (ppb), which translates to 0.07 parts per million (ppm). This means that for every million parts of air, no more than 70 parts should be ozone to avoid adverse health effects.

Air inversions happen when a layer of warm air sits above a layer of cooler air, trapping the cooler air and anything in it close to the ground.

During warmer months, Denver frequently exceeds this standard, posing significant health risks for vulnerable populations such as children, the elderly, and individuals with respiratory conditions. Factors contributing to elevated ozone levels include heavy traffic, which increases emissions of nitrogen oxides and volatile organic compounds (the precursors to ozone formation) and wildfires that introduce additional particulate matter and pollutants, further degrading air quality. Some of these fires occur in Colorado, but sometimes smoke travels all the way from Canada, making the air hazy and hard to be out in.

If you're hiking in summer, always check the air-quality warnings before you go for advisories about days and times to avoid being outdoors.

To combat these challenges, city and state officials have implemented a range of mitigation strategies. Stricter emissions regulations for vehicles and industrial sources; public-awareness campaigns encouraging residents to adopt alternatives to driving, such as using public transportation, biking, or carpooling; and air-quality monitoring by EPA and local agencies helps track pollution levels, allowing for timely public-health advisories when ozone levels are high.

It's Always Sunny in Denver, Too

Denver gets more than 300 days of sunshine annually . . . or so the story goes. In the late 1800s, rail companies needed to convince people to visit and live in Denver, so they bent the truth about our sunshine count to make it more appealing. The true number of sunny days Denver has each year is up

◄ Some days you can see a layer of pollution settled over Denver from far away; it's known as the "brown cloud" and it's visible from spots like Mount Falcon or William F. Hayden Park on poor air-quality days

► An advantage of planting native flowers like asters is that they grow well in Denver's dry, clay soils

for debate based on what is considered a full day of sun, but it is rare to have more than one fully cloudy day in a row.

Having so much sun feels good for the soul, but it can make it harder for plants to grow well. Strong UV rays and high levels of solar radiation can lead to increased evaporation rates, causing faster soil moisture loss and stressed vegetation. This intense sunlight can also result in sunburn on plants, leading to damaged leaves and reduced photosynthesis. As a result, plants may become more susceptible to drought and pests, impacting their overall health and growth.

"We Needed the Moisture"

You'll hear someone say it every single time it rains, but that's because it's true. While our semi-arid climate stays on the drier side, Denver does get rain; the annual precipitation level is just relatively lower compared to other regions. Moisture from the Pacific Ocean must cross the Rocky Mountains, and moisture from the Gulf of Mexico has to travel a considerable distance before reaching the city, with much of it dissipating along the way. Consequently, Denver averages around 15 to 20 inches of precipitation per year.

Caused by Climate

As of this writing, September 2024 was our hottest September in history.

Climate change has intensified existing weather threats, leading to more extreme conditions. El Niño and La Niña patterns are contributing to some of the hottest and coldest days on record, while droughts are becoming more prolonged.

In 2024, the USDA updated its agricultural growing zones, moving Denver from Zone 5 to Zone 6. Although this change might not have a significant impact on farmers and gardeners who were already used to the shifting season, it has notable consequences for migratory birds and insects that depend on specific native plants for food and reproduction. When these birds arrive along their migration routes and find that their food sources are not yet available, they face increased risks, potentially leading to higher mortality rates or forcing them to continue their journey with inadequate nourishment. This has even led to some birds altering their diets or relying more on feeders for survival.

▲ A coyote walks up a road on a sunny snowy day at Rocky Mountain Arsenal National Wildlife Refuge

◀ Black-capped chickadees are familiar sights at bird feeders in winter

Denver Through the Seasons

Our climate is changing and weather can vary drastically, but typically, you can expect the seasons to follow a pattern. January is usually the coldest month, while July or August is the hottest.

WINTER

Denver's winter weather can be a wild ride, swinging from sunny and mild to snowy and frigid in the blink of an eye. With temperatures often ranging from the 30s to 50s during the day and an average snowfall of around 60 inches each year, Denver's winter can feel like a roller-coaster.

Many plants go into hibernation to survive the cold, but random warm days can trick them into budding too early, leaving them vulnerable to late frosts. Wildlife, on the other hand, must adapt to unpredictable conditions by growing thicker coats, changing their diets, or migrating to find more reliable food sources. Birds seek out feeders and native plants with berries that persist through winter, while insects either die or find cozy spots to hunker down for the season.

Winter is a great time to hit the trails if you want to avoid the crowds. Make sure you have the proper gear (microspikes are a must on any trail with ice) and bring warm clothes.

SPRING

Spring in Denver is a time when flowers burst into color and trees leaf out, while the chance of a late freeze keeps everyone on their toes. One day,

you might be soaking up the sunshine in a T-shirt, and the next, a surprise snowstorm might have you reaching for your winter coat again. Flowers like crocuses, snowdrops, and pansies that bloom in spring are especially hardy and can survive chilly temps. Meanwhile, wildlife wakes up from hibernation and starts gearing up for breeding and migration.

It might seem late, but it's best to wait until after Mother's Day to plant anything in the garden. Late frosts and unpredictable spring weather can harm tender plants.

Thawing snow and melting ice turn trails into muddy messes in spring. The shifting weather means that each outdoor adventure can come with a bit of unpredictability. If you're going on the trails during mud season, be prepared to walk through it. Walking around mud contributes to erosion and widening of the trails. If it's a really muddy day, choose another trail.

SUMMER

Denver's summer weather is a dream. Temperatures often climb into the 80s and 90s accompanied by plenty of sunshine and low humidity. It's perfect for outdoor activities, from hiking the scenic trails of state parks to enjoying a day paddleboarding on a reservoir or birdwatching in one of Denver's many parks.

Peak summer can get hot, with streaks of hotter days becoming the norm. Animals like mule deer and red-tailed hawks adjust their behavior by becoming more active during cooler parts of the day and seeking shade to avoid overheating. Plants are also challenged, with natives like blue grama

▲ Hardy pasque-flowers are usually one of the first blooms in spring

► Blue grama grass is also called eyelash grass

WILD DENVER

grass thriving by growing deep roots to access underground water and conserve moisture efficiently. Unfortunately, while the weather feels amazing, the air is not. Smoke becomes an issue outdoors every summer. Check the air quality before heading to the trails.

FALL

Fall in Denver is a time of vivid transformation, with cooler temperatures ranging from the 50s to 70s triggering a breathtaking display of foliage in reds, oranges, and golds. The season's cooler, crisp air signals plants and animals to prepare for winter. Trees like the quaking aspen and sugar maple put on a spectacular show of color before shedding their leaves, while grasses like blue grama turn a rich golden hue.

Mule deer and elk begin their migration to lower elevations in search of more accessible food, while black bears enter a phase of hyperphagia, eating excessively to build fat reserves for hibernation, affectionately known as

▲ Denver neighborhoods explode with color each fall

◀ A bald eagle's nest in fall leaves

"Fat Bear Fall." Red foxes and coyotes become more active, foraging for food to prepare for the coming winter. Meanwhile, birds like American kestrel and golden eagle can be seen hunting in the cooler air, and smaller birds such as chickadee and nuthatch start to combine flocks to make the most of the resources and prepare for the frosts of winter.

Finding Fossils

During the Mesozoic Era millions of years ago, the area now known as Denver was at the bottom of the Western Interior Seaway, an inland sea that stretched from the Gulf of Mexico to the Arctic Ocean and divided North America into two landmasses. It was a shallow marine environment, teeming with diverse life, evidenced by the fossils of ancient sea creatures like ammonites and crocodiles that have been discovered in the rocks of the Denver Basin.

As the sea receded, it left behind thick layers of sediment. The uplift of the Rocky Mountains, which began around 75 million years ago, reshaped the landscape, pushing the seafloor sedimentary rocks to the surface, creating dramatic mountain ranges and rugged terrain.

These layers of rock contain fossils and traces of ancient marine life and provide valuable insights into the geological and biological evolution of our region.

Geological Formation

Denver lies, unsurprisingly, within the Denver Basin—a sedimentary basin that formed during the late Mesozoic Era 70 to 100 million years ago. It's a series of sedimentary rock layers, primarily composed of sandstone, shale, and limestone deposited over time by the ancient sea, as well as rivers and lakes, that covered the region.

The most notable geological feature in this part of the state is the Rocky Mountains, which began to form about 75 million years ago during the Laramide Orogeny. This mountain-building event resulted in the uplift of the Rockies, beginning to shape the rugged terrain that often serves as the backdrop of the Denver skyline.

► Map of North America with the Western Interior Seaway during the Campanian (Upper Cretaceous Period)

The Morrison Formation

The Morrison Formation is a geological wonder lying right beneath Denver, holding secrets from 150 million years ago. This rock formation runs through Colorado (starting in Morrison), Utah, Wyoming, Montana, and Arizona and is a fossil treasure trove from the Late Jurassic Period. Because of the Morrison Formation, scientists are able to piece together the prehistoric environment of North America using fossil evidence.

Remarkable discoveries from the Morrison Formation include the stegosaurus, known for its distinctive row of bony plates and spiked tail; diplodocus, a long-necked herbivore with a whip-like tail; apatosaurus, a massive, long-necked dinosaur once mistakenly identified as brontosaurus; allosaurus, a skilled predator with sharp teeth and claws; and brachiosaurus, known for its long legs and towering height.

▶ *Allosaurus fragilis* and *Stegosaurus stenops* at Denver Museum of Nature and Science

Dinosaur Ridge

Twenty minutes west of the city is a special spot for dinosaur fans. Dinosaur Ridge in Morrison is an iconic national natural landmark that features an array of fossil tracks and bone beds, transporting visitors back to the Late Jurassic Period. As you walk along the paved Dinosaur Ridge Trail, you'll pass more than fifteen fossil and geologic sites, including a world-famous tracksite. See hundreds of well-preserved footprints of dinosaurs like diplodocus and allosaurus captured in rock over 100 million years ago, providing a tangible connection to giants that once roamed the region.

The Dinosaur Ridge Exhibit Hall has fossil replicas and educational displays that detail the history and significance of the finds. Take a guided tour (they have walking and bus options) to learn about the creatures that left these fossils behind.

Plants and Mammals

For even more fossils, head to Triceratops Trail—a 1.5-mile gravel trail located a block east of 6th Avenue and 19th Street in Golden. Along the trail, you'll pass interpretive stops that highlight the area's rich geological history and fossilized tracks from dinosaurs, birds, mammals, insects, invertebrates, and plants.

Noteworthy finds include a large, three-toed tyrannosaurus track and several four-toed triceratops prints from 68 million years ago.

One cool thing about Triceratops Trail is that it also features plant fossils, including large palm fronds. These are from a time when the area was a delta-like environment with palms, magnolias, and low-lying ferns that characterized Colorado's Late Cretaceous ecosystem. Near the end of the trail by Fossil Trace Golf Course's thirteenth hole, you can see these ancient plant impressions preserved in sandstone.

► A palm frond fossil in sandstone on Triceratops Trail

▼ Footprints from the past at Dinosaur Ridge in Morrison

The Bone Wars

The Bone Wars was a fierce and dramatic period of scientific rivalry in the late 19th century, primarily between two paleontologists: Othniel Charles Marsh and Edward Drinker Cope. The first Stegosaurus fossil was unearthed in Colorado in 1876 by Marsh. Driven by the race to uncover and describe the most dinosaur fossils, Marsh and Cope engaged in a heated competition that spanned over a decade, from roughly 1877 to 1892. Their rivalry was marked by aggressive tactics including the use of spies, theft of fossils, destruction of dig sites, and intentional misinformation.

This intense competition led to a flurry of fossil discoveries and publishing of scientific papers. Unfortunately, the two were sometimes more concerned with competition than they were with the facts or preserving history. Despite discovering many new species, their tactics created a mess that took paleontologists more than a century to sort out. At the end of it all, many of the species were not valid and it turned out that Marsh and Cope destroyed one-of-a-kind specimens that have yet to be seen again. It's not all bad though. The men did grow a collection of thousands of fossils and fragments, which helped paleontology progress.

Biodiversity

Biodiversity is vital for keeping Denver's natural spaces resilient. A rich variety of plants and animals helps maintain a healthy ecosystem, ensuring everything from air and water quality to pest control runs smoothly. When our ecosystems are diverse, they're better able to bounce back from environmental changes and challenges, like climate shifts or invasive species. If something targets a species, it's better that that species doesn't make up the entire ecosystem. If it's lost, others can fill that void.

The blend of the high plains, foothills, and the montane regions just beyond the city limits lends itself to a naturally diverse landscape. The city's parks, greenbelts, and waterways serve as crucial refuges for many species. Places like City Park, Washington Park, and the Denver Botanic Gardens provide guaranteed habitats for numerous birds (both year-round and migratory residents), mammals, and insects that might have a harder time surviving in the city without them.

During the day, you'll see squirrels and rabbits, and you might come across a raccoon, skunk, or opossum if you're out at night. In more natural areas a little farther away from Denver, species like coyote and fox are more common. The nearby foothills and open spaces offer habitats for larger mammals and provide migration corridors for deer and elk moving between the mountains and the plains.

Insects might be small, but they're a critical component of Denver's biodiversity. They're our pollinators, decomposers, and serve as food sources for other wildlife. Native bees pollinate our native low-water and drought-tolerant plants, ladybugs help control aphid populations, and dragonflies hunt mosquitoes and other small insects.

► City Park offers a respite for migrating birds and resident animals in the city

◄ Monarch butterfly on a coneflower

. . . .

A host plant provides food, shelter, or a suitable environment for a particular animal, insect, or parasite during part or all of its life cycle.

. . . .

WILD DENVER

In Denver's urban parks and gardens, you can find a mix of native and non-native plants. Rocky Mountain columbine, Indian paintbrush, currant, American plum, and sagebrush thrive in these environments, providing essential food and shelter for local and migratory wildlife.

Threats to Diversity

Denver faces several challenges related to urbanization, habitat loss, and environmental change. The expansion of the city and its infrastructure have led to habitat fragmentation, which makes it nearly impossible for movement to new areas and reduces available resources for many species. Efforts are being made to address these challenges through urban planning that includes wildlife corridors and conservation initiatives.

••

Bees pollinate 70 of the around 100 crop species that feed 90 percent of the world. If we lose bees, it would be catastrophic for everyone.

••

Organizations like Denver Audubon and local conservation groups are actively involved in protecting and enhancing the city's natural habitats. Their work includes habitat restoration projects, educational programs, and advocacy for wildlife-friendly policies.

Losing biodiversity is like pulling out threads from a carefully sewn patchwork quilt. When species disappear, ecosystems become less stable and resilient. Without a diverse mix of plants, animals, and microorganisms, natural systems can't work as effectively, leading to problems like reduced soil fertility and less-efficient nutrient cycling. This can make ecosystems more vulnerable to pests, diseases, and ever-increasing extreme weather events.

Keeping our planet's diversity intact isn't just good for nature—it's crucial for our own well-being and future. We all rely on these ecosystems for clean air and water, fertile soil for farming, and climate regulation. Losing biodiversity means losing these critical benefits, which can hit our food supply and overall health hard.

Native and Invasive Species

Native species are the locals of an ecosystem; they've adapted over time to thrive in their specific environment and play key roles in keeping things balanced. They interact with other local species in ways that help maintain a healthy, functioning ecosystem. For example, native plants provide food and habitat for local wildlife, and native pollinators help those plants reproduce.

On the flip side, invasive species are the newcomers who don't always play nice. They can quickly take over an area because they don't have natural checks and balances to keep their population from doing so. This can lead to big problems like blocking out native species, disrupting local food chains, and management that costs a lot of money. While not every non-native species causes issues, the invasive ones can really shake up the local environment and hurt biodiversity.

Native Species

Native species are essential for maintaining the intricate ecosystems around Denver. Evolved to thrive in our conditions, these species have developed unique relationships with their environment that help sustain ecological balance. The Rocky Mountain columbine (Colorado's state flower) and Rocky Mountain bee plant draw a variety of pollinators like (unsurprisingly) bees, wasps, hummingbirds, and swallowtails. Sagebrush and saltbush are particularly suited to the semi-arid environment of the Denver area, requiring far less water and minimal maintenance compared to nonnative species.

Each native species plays a specific role—whether it's the white-tailed prairie dog, which creates burrows that provide shelter for other wildlife like

burrowing owls and black-footed ferrets, or the Colorado River cutthroat trout, which maintains aquatic health in high-altitude streams by serving as both predator and prey. Native plants such as penstemon and Indian paintbrush not only add to the beauty of Denver's natural areas but also have deep roots that help stabilize soil and prevent erosion.

An endemic species is a plant or animal that is native and restricted to a specific geographic area, such as a particular country, region, or habitat. This means that it doesn't naturally occur anywhere else in the world outside of this defined area. While Denver doesn't have a lot of endemic species, Colorado has quite a few. Rocky Mountain columbine is not only native, it's considered endemic to the region. Colorado four o'clock, black-footed ferret, and Colorado River cutthroat trout are also endemic to the state.

It's important to note that just because a plant isn't native doesn't mean it's bad. In fact, nonnative plants can actually be quite beneficial as long as they aren't invasive. Many nonnatives are introduced to landscapes for their aesthetic appeal, adaptability, or utility without causing harm to local ecosystems. The European cranberry bush is valued for its beautiful foliage and berries, which can enhance garden diversity and support wildlife, and nonnative ornamental grasses such as feather reed grass can add visual interest to gardens and serve as groundcover without spreading and displacing native species. As long as these plants don't outcompete local flora, they can coexist harmoniously with native species, contributing to a rich and varied landscape.

▼ Cheatgrass is an invasive grass causing a lot of problems in the west

▲ Pollinators like sweat bees rely on native plants like rubber rabbitbrush for pollen

Invasive Species

Invasive species often disrupt the local balance and make it hard, if not impossible, for native plants to survive. Russian olive was initially brought to the area for its ornamental value and erosion control, but it has turned into a troublesome invader, forming dense thickets that outcompete native plants, altering soil conditions, and disrupting local wildlife.

The problems invasive species cause are not just about losing a few plants or animals. They lead to serious ecosystem disruptions by preventing native species from accessing essential resources like food, water, and habitat. Cheatgrass is one of the most notorious invaders in the Denver area. It can intensify wildfires, devastate native plant communities, and cause erosion; you'll see it in every park.

In addition to the ecological problems caused by invasive species, there are also often hefty economic costs associated with them, whether it's the expense of managing and removing them or the damage they cause to agriculture and natural resources.

NOXIOUS WEED LIST

If a plant is invasive enough, it's added to the Colorado Department of Agriculture's Noxious Weed List. This list identifies plants that threaten agriculture, natural resources, and ecosystems and classifies them into three categories based on how they need to be managed. List A includes weeds that are not yet widespread in the state but pose a significant threat if they spread farther. These are targeted for eradication efforts and include plants like giant hogweed and bohemian knotweed. List B is for weeds that are

more common but still require management to prevent further proliferation, like Russian knapweed and purple loosestrife. List C features weeds that are already widespread across Colorado and are typically managed at the local level, such as common tansy and field bindweed. This classification system helps guide landowners, farmers, and land-management agencies in prioritizing control measures to protect Colorado's diverse landscapes and ecosystems.

▲ Cheatgrass has fueled major wildfires in the west, like this one in Idaho

Movers and Shakers

Migration, or the mass movement from one place to another, happens for a myriad of reasons. Some animals move to follow available food sources, some move for better weather, and some move because of shifts in the magnetic forces of the planet.

Birds, bugs, and mammals are the top migrators in Denver. Different species move during different times of the year, but most follow their food sources, so their migration times and paths are historically based on when different plants grow and bloom in our region.

Birds

For many birds, Denver is the perfect stopover destination during their hundred- to thousands-mile journey crossing our continent. Each year, more than four billion (with a b!) birds make the cross-country trek for survival.

There are four North American bird migration flyways: Atlantic, Mississippi, Central, and Pacific. These flyways serve as general guidelines for the paths that birds take on their voyages from Canada to Mexico and back again. Colorado is in the Central Flyway, with the Rocky Mountains serving as the border.

Birds will travel from Montana through Texas and the Gulf of Mexico shoreline, continuing down to Mexico, Costa Rica, and Panama before resting in the warm weather of Argentina. Most birds in the western hemisphere migrate two times a year: moving south to north in spring and moving from north to south in fall.

The exact path depends on the bird. More than 50 percent of waterfowl use the Central Flyway, stopping at Denver's larger lakes such as Ferril Lake and Duck Pond at City Park, Crown Hill Lake at Crown Hill Park, and Barr Lake at Barr Lake State Park in Brighton, located 27 miles northeast of Denver. Songbirds like swallows and thrushes use Denver's ample green spaces for stopover spots.

◄◄ Spotted tow-hees are birds that migrate in spring and early fall

◄ Eastern kingbirds utilize the Atlantic, Mississippi, and Central flyways

▲ Mallard ducks wearing their bird bands

The flyway can also shift depending on environmental factors. In recent years, we've seen the impact on migration pathways due to wildfires, which clog up the air with particulate and destroy spots that birds would typically use to rest, as well as the food sources they need to keep their metabolisms running well.

While they don't stop in Denver, the most well-known Central Flyway migratory bird is the sandhill crane. These massive birds gather in massive numbers in the Nebraska sandhills every year. On their way, they pass through the San Luis Valley in Colorado, often stopping for rest at the Monte Vista National Wildlife Refuge in early spring or San Luis Lakes State Wildlife Area in fall.

Bird tagging and tracking data has told quite the story of the changes and challenges over the years. By catching and weighing birds and then comparing them to previous years, researchers can determine whether or not the birds are going to survive their journeys. If they can't get their weight up before it's time to leave, they end up staying behind or trying to complete the journey and perishing along the way.

Lights Out

If someone shines a flashlight in your eyes on a dark night, you're going to feel disoriented. Birds are no different. As human expansion and development leads to more light pollution, birds are becoming increasingly more confused on their journeys. This confusion can lead to collisions with buildings and vehicles, but it can also guide them away from their paths, using up valuable energy they might not be able to spare in order to recalibrate and get back on track. Even if they do make it to their destination, they might not be able to breed, which threatens future populations.

The majority of bird flights during migration actually take place at night. Efforts like Audubon's Lights Out programs are working to keep birds safer by convincing building officials nationwide to turn off excess lighting during the months birds migrate. It sounds simple enough, but minimizing light pollution in a city is a challenge, not only logistically but also in the way of public opinion. For many, lights mean safety, and walking down dark city streets isn't a feasible ask.

Insects

Butterflies, dragonflies, and moths migrate annually, but we typically only notice it when they become a nuisance or if we're really looking for them. The notorious miller moth is one of Denver's most anticipated migrations because of how many of these moths make their way into our homes, cars, and any crevices that offer them shelter during the day. Though harmless, it can be alarming to suddenly see one flapping and flitting around or toward you, so their annual migration is often met with more negative feelings.

On the flip side, monarch butterflies are one of the more beloved migratory insects. Monarchs rely on milkweed for survival. It's the only plant their larvae can feed on, and they lay eggs on it so the larvae have a food source immediately. Of the more than 100 different types of milkweed species native to the United States, two are common and found in Colorado: showy milkweed (*Asclepias speciosa*) and common milkweed (*Asclepias syriaca*). Once endangered, the monarch butterfly population has now stabilized thanks to nationwide conservation efforts, including the mass planting of milkweed plants.

The nectar or foliage of plants often serves as food sources for insects, so you can usually track insect migrations based on plant blooming times. Many bird migrations end up following the same path because they rely on the insects as food. It's a connected web.

◀ Showy milkweed

► Common milkweed

Mammals

Mammal migrations are tougher to track, save for Denver's most visible migrating mammal: elk. If you want to see an elk without traveling too far, head 15 minutes west. Every fall, they come down from the mountains to Golden. There's even a residential heard that hangs around the South Table Mesa and can be seen on the football field at Golden High School, meandering around on the green at Fossil Trace Golf Club, or crossing US-6 between the Heritage Road and 19th Street exits at their designated crossing section. Colorado Parks and Wildlife has begun an effort to put GPS collars on

◄ Rufous humming-
birds migrate
through Colorado
and rely on plants
like Rocky Mountain
bee plant

▲ Elk during
rutting season

40 female elk in the herd to study them over the next five years. The hope is they'll be able to learn more about the herd's movements throughout the year and track population trends.

Most of the mammals that live in the city itself don't migrate, as the roads and human development make it too hard to navigate safely and they've found ways to adapt to the climate.

Climate Change and Other Challenges

As climates change and plants bloom earlier or later, it messes up the cycle for insects and birds that rely on them to survive.

The United States Department of Agriculture (USDA) hardiness zones divide the United States into regions based on average lowest temperatures. Each zone, from the warmest (Zone 13) to the coldest (Zone 1), guides gardeners in choosing the perfect flowers, shrubs, and veggies. The USDA hardiness zone for Denver recently switched from Zone 5B to Zone 6A. This zone is a guideline for where and when certain plants can grow. While it's only a change of a few degrees, it's a signifier of the temperatures that certain plants can grow in. If plants or blooms are delayed by a week, that can mean insect eggs don't hatch on time for birds who need them during their visit to Denver. These birds won't have enough food to make the trip when they head back out on the road, which also impacts breeding sites.

Urban sprawl and development in Denver have led to the loss of natural habitats that are crucial for migratory species. As open spaces become apartments, homes, and businesses, there's a greater risk for human-animal conflict, which often ends poorly for animals. Prairie dogs are a prime example of this. They can cause a lot of damage to properties near dens, and they are sometimes killed for removal.

One of the best things a city can do to protect migrating species is to make sure that they're preserving and creating as many green spaces as possible. Denver already has a lot of great green spaces, but building new wildlife corridors and public-education initiatives go a long way. Creating corridors connects fragmented habitats, allowing animals to move safely between different areas, and planting more native plants in public parks and yards provides reliable food and habitat for birds, mammals, and insects.

Our Animal Neighbors

Living in the city doesn't mean you're separated from nature. Urban areas are home to an array of animals who've adapted to city life in fascinating ways. Take the raccoons that have become adept at navigating our trash cans or the foxes that can be spotted darting through green spaces and city parks. There's always a bird close by, from the familiar house sparrow to red-tailed hawks soaring above the skyline. Even the elusive coyote has made an appearance in some parts of the city and surrounding suburbs.

Even in the midst of bustling streets and towering buildings, these animals carve out niches and thrive, and taking time to observe these city-dwellers not only adds a touch of nature to our daily lives, it highlights the incredible adaptability of wildlife.

A Different Look at Denver

Every neighborhood in Denver has a wild side if you're patient and know what to look out for. Look up to the sky at City Park, Washington Park, or the Denver Botanic Gardens, and you might spot a majestic peregrine falcon or a hawk cruising high above the cityscape. These birds of prey are pros at navigating urban life, hunting for pigeons, rats, and mice amid the high-rise buildings.

Confluence Park, Civic Center Park, Cheesman Park, and City Park are small mammal havens. Eastern fox squirrels and smaller rock squirrels are often seen scampering up trees and darting across lawns, busy collecting nuts and seeds. Monarch butterflies, bees, and dragonflies buzz around the city's gardens, pollinating flowers and contributing to the health of urban green spaces.

Oak trees like those found in Sloan's Lake, Berkeley Lake Park, and along Cherry Creek Trail attract pollinators such as bees and butterflies. Honeybees and native bumblebees are especially drawn to the oaks for their pollen and nectar. Maples and cottonwoods, with their catkins and flowering structures, are pollinated by insects like bees and small flies, while their seeds provide food for birds such as finches and chickadees.

Backyard Buds

Many Denver backyards are teeming with wildlife, offering a slice of nature right at home. The northern flicker, a striking woodpecker with a distinctive call and colorful plumage, is known for its knack for finding ants and other insects underground. The incessant sound of a flicker drumming on an old-growth tree or calling loudly to other flickers is sometimes annoying, but these birds do a lot for our ecosystem.

The spotted towhee can often be seen foraging through leaf litter for seeds and insects. With their rust-colored feathers and bright red eyes, these birds are known for the unique scratching behavior they use to find food. Magpies, with their striking black, blue, and white plumage, are also a common sight around town. These highly adaptable birds are known for their complex social structures and curiosity.

Common eastern cicadas and lively grasshoppers add to the sounds of summer. Cicadas, with their distinctive buzzing sound, play a role in the decomposition of organic material, while their larvae feed on plant roots. Grasshoppers, with their impressive jumping abilities and varied colors, feed on grasses and other plants, contributing to the natural cycle of growth and decay in your backyard ecosystem—though they're sometimes the bane of the home gardener's existence.

Get More Green Spaces

Advocating for green spaces and protecting backyard habitats must happen if we want to maintain the health of our environment and support local wildlife. Green spaces such as parks and urban forests serve as refuges for a variety of species, providing essential food, shelter, and breeding grounds. They help maintain ecological balance by supporting biodiversity and offering crucial migration pathways for animals. These areas also play a significant role in mitigating urban heat islands, improving air quality, and managing stormwater runoff, which helps to regulate local temperatures and reduce flooding.

Similarly, creating and protecting backyard habitats extends these benefits right into our neighborhoods. Backyard gardens with native plants, bird feeders, and supplemental water sources offer food and shelter for local wildlife, species that might otherwise struggle in an urban environment. By fostering both public green spaces and private backyard habitats, we can enhance biodiversity, improve our quality of life, and create a more resilient environment that benefits all species, including humans.

▾ House sparrows are everywhere in Denver

▴ Black-billed magpies are pretty, noisy birds

◂ A red-tailed hawk watches dutifully in a tree after a fall snow

▸ Having large open lakes is important for ducks and geese to rest between flights

WILD DENVER

Bring It Home

Taking small steps at home to protect local wildlife can make a big difference to the health of our ecosystems. Simple actions, like planting native species, creating bird-friendly spaces, or setting up a water feature, provide crucial resources for animals that live in your area. For example, native plants like coneflower and golden currant offer food and shelter for pollinators like bees and butterflies. Be mindful that how you interact with your environment can have significant benefits for nearby species, and by making your yard a welcoming haven, you're not just enhancing your own outdoor space—you're also giving a helping hand to the creatures also trying to survive.

Keeping outdoor lights dim or using motion-sensor lights can help protect nocturnal animals like bats and moths from disorientation. Reducing pesticide use helps maintain a healthy population of beneficial insects and keeps the local food chain balanced. Every action, no matter how small it may seem, contributes to a larger effort to create a harmonious environment where wildlife can thrive. So, by making thoughtful choices in your own backyard, you're helping to sustain the natural world right outside your door.

Xeriscaping

The word xeriscaping is derived from the Greek word *xeros*, meaning dry. Essentially, it's all about designing gardens and landscapes that thrive on minimal water, making it a perfect fit for Denver's dry climate. This method focuses on using drought-tolerant plants and smart gardening techniques to create a lush, low-maintenance yard that doesn't need a lot of water to look nice.

· ·

The term "xeriscaping" was coined by Denver Water in the early 1980s. It was developed as part of an initiative to promote water-efficient landscaping in response to water scarcity issues that were already becoming evident.

· ·

Xeriscaping can involve swapping out entire lawns and replacing them with resilient groundcovers like buffalo grass or adding succulents like sedum to your garden beds. These plants are built to handle Denver's arid conditions while still providing beauty and texture.

The benefits of xeriscaping extend beyond just conserving water—it also supports local wildlife. By incorporating native plants such as Maximilian sunflower or little bluestem, you're providing vital resources for native bees, moths, butterflies, and other pollinators that help sustain our ecosystems.

Animals After Dark

As dusk settles over Denver, places like the Rocky Mountain Arsenal National Wildlife Refuge and Eldorado Canyon State Park become playgrounds for bats. These nocturnal flyers are nature's pest control, zipping through the night sky to feast on mosquitoes and moths, with some bats able to catch and eat up to 1000 mosquito-sized insects in an hour. There are also bats in more suburban neighborhoods. If you want to roll out the welcome mat for these beneficial creatures, consider installing a bat house. They'll appreciate the cozy roost, and you'll enjoy fewer insects buzzing around.

When night fully falls, the action doesn't stop. Over in Denver's foothill parks, you can catch the hoots of owls such as the great horned owl and eastern screech owl. These impressive raptors are nighttime hunters that help keep rodent populations in check.

Even the urban fringes of Denver are alive with nocturnal critters. Parks like Crown Hill and Cherry Creek State Park are frequented by coyotes, raccoons, and foxes. Coyotes might patrol the edge of the city, while you could find raccoons and foxes exploring your suburban yard. These animals help maintain the balance of the ecosystem by managing small mammals and waste.

If you want to make your yard a welcoming spot for nighttime visitors, try planting flowers that bloom after dark, like moonflower and evening primrose. Also make sure to add a water source and dial down your outdoor lighting.

Be a Good Neighbor

Our actions can have a big impact on wildlife around us. Keeping your cats indoors is a simple yet effective way to protect local wildlife. Outdoor cats can be a significant threat to birds like northern flicker and small mammals such as American deer mouse. By keeping your feline friends inside, you help safeguard these native species while also protecting your pets from dangers like traffic and disease.

Keeping bee boxes can be great for honey and supporting honeybee colonies, but there are other, smaller native bees you can help out too.

Like their name suggests, solitary bees don't live in large colonies. Unlike hive-dwelling bees, bees like leafcutters and mason bees rely on a few simple things to thrive. By leaving some leaf litter and allowing a few areas of your garden to stay a bit unkempt, you provide them with natural nesting sites and safe spaces to hibernate. Adding a bee hotel—a small structure with tubes or holes for nesting—and planting native flowers like western

▲ Great horned owls are a sight to behold in the woods

▲ Backyard bee hotels are great habitats for solitary bees

◄ Walk through coyote habitat at the Crown Hill Park wildlife refuge

coneflower or golden currant will offer them the nectar and pollen they need to survive.

Another way to be a considerate neighbor to these creatures is by reducing your use of pesticides. These chemicals can harm beneficial insects like ladybug, which helps control aphid populations, and bees such as honeybee, which are essential for pollinating plants. Instead, consider using natural pest-control methods or planting native species like pearly everlasting and wild bergamot, which attract these helpful insects and reduce the need for chemical interventions. Making eco-friendly choices helps create a safer environment for all urban wildlife and supports a more balanced and healthier city ecosystem.

Up on the Rooftop

Green roofs are a game-changer for urban biodiversity, providing valuable green spaces in otherwise concrete-dominated environments by introducing a layer of vegetation atop buildings. Rooftop gardens can support an array of plants, from hardy grasses and wildflowers to shrubs and even small trees. In Denver, green roofs often feature native species like blue flax and yarrow, which are adapted to local conditions and offer food and shelter to native pollinators. This helps to restore some of the natural ecosystems lost to urban development and provides essential resources for wildlife that might otherwise struggle to find habitat in the city. These elevated green spaces offer a refuge for birds, insects, and small mammals in the urban landscape.

The plants on green roofs can also help moderate temperatures and provide shade, reducing the urban heat-island effect. This effect can turn cities into sweltering hotspots, where heat-absorbing surfaces raise temperatures

significantly higher than in surrounding rural areas, impacting energy use, the environment, and public health, as well as making cities inhospitable for some species. Additionally, green roofs can incorporate water features such as rain gardens or small ponds, which offer drinking water and habitat for amphibians and insects. By blending vegetation into the fabric of urban architecture, green roofs help integrate nature into city life, benefiting both local wildlife and residents alike.

▲ This green roof in Denver was one of the first of its kind in Colorado

Citizen and Community Science

Sometimes, scientists need a helping hand to make their research more effective and expansive, and that's where citizen and community science come in. These collaborative efforts invite people from all walks of life to contribute to scientific projects, adding valuable local insights and expertise. By partnering with local organizations and the community, scientists can gather data more affordably and on a larger scale than if they worked alone. This teamwork not only makes research more feasible but also enhances its accuracy and relevance.

Citizen science often casts a wide net, focusing on broad topics like climate change or species tracking, and involves people from all over participating in large-scale studies. On the other hand, community science hones in on local issues, such as monitoring air quality, tracking wildlife, or addressing urban-planning concerns. These projects are tailored to specific communities, allowing residents to address issues that directly impact their everyday lives and environments. While citizen science might involve large datasets and broader research goals, community science is more about solving local problems through targeted, grassroots efforts.

Getting involved in these projects can be as simple or as complex as you like. Some initiatives might only require a few minutes of your time and a notebook, while others could involve more specialized tools and training. Whether you're tracking wildlife in your backyard or participating in a local cleanup effort, your contribution helps scientists gather data and insights that would be impossible to collect otherwise.

When you take part in these projects, you're not just helping scientists; you're also spreading awareness about local environmental issues and fostering a sense of community responsibility. By becoming active participants, residents can influence positive changes in their environment and make

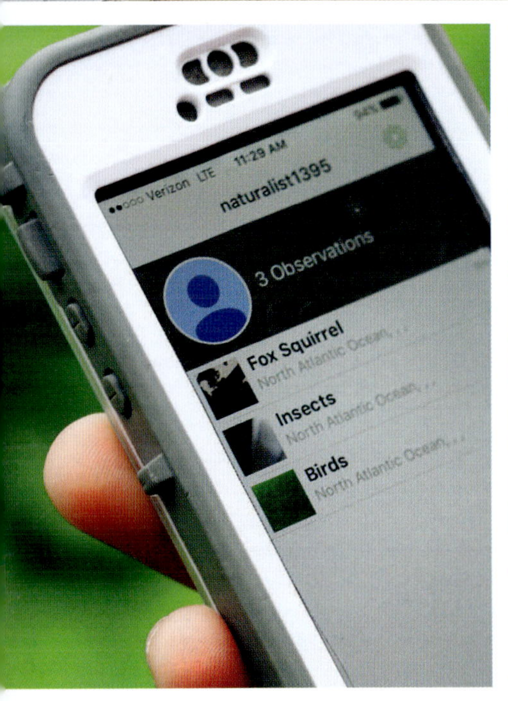

▲ The Colorado Rare Plant Conservation Initiative is made up of 23 statewide and regional agencies working to conserve 121 rare plants in Colorado

◄ Use iNaturalist to record the plants and animals around you

more informed decisions about their well-being. Volunteer contributions play a crucial role in advancing scientific knowledge, monitoring changes, and making new discoveries that benefit everyone.

How to Get Involved

Getting started with citizen science in Denver is easier than you might think. If you're fine with trying it out on your own, apps like eBird and iNaturalist make it simple to track birds and identify local species right from your smartphone. You can take photos and share your observations, all while learning more about the incredible biodiversity in your area. Plus, with online training available, you can become a citizen scientist from the comfort of your home.

For those who prefer hands-on involvement, Denver Parks and Recreation offers a variety of volunteer opportunities. You can participate in plant restoration, invasive-species removal, and habitat monitoring, all of which help improve local parks and natural areas. If you're passionate about birdwatching, check out opportunities with Denver Audubon. They offer programs focused on bird monitoring, including annual counts and nesting surveys. Joining local environmental groups like the Greenway Foundation can also be rewarding. They run various citizen science projects that include habitat restoration and wildlife monitoring. Your contributions can support conservation efforts and influence local environmental policies.

Engaging in these activities not only helps the environment, it builds a sense of community and fosters a deeper connection to nature. Whether you're volunteering in the field or participating in local events, you get to know your city on a deeper level and help protect a place we all love.

99 SPECIES TO KNOW

Common Stinkhorn

Phallus or *Clathrus* spp.

SLIMY CAP ◆ **TALL** ◆ **SPONGY TEXTURE**

In some European folk traditions, the phallic shape of certain stinkhorn species has been associated with fertility and the supernatural. Their striking resemblance to a particular body part and their offensive smell have also led to their use in traditional remedies and rituals to ward off evil spirits or address other mystical concerns.

The distinctive, pungent odor and . . . intriguing appearance of the stinkhorn mushroom offer a fascinating glimpse into the stranger side of nature. If you can guess from the name, stinkhorns are famous for their foul smell, which is often compared to rotting meat or excrement. This unpleasant odor serves a practical purpose: it attracts flies and other insects that are essential for the mushroom's reproduction. The flies are drawn to the smell and inadvertently pick up spores from the mushroom's surface, carrying them to new locations where the spores can germinate and produce new fungi.

The stinkhorn mushroom often appears as a tall, spindly structure with a cap that looks like a grotesque, slimy, or egg-like mass. The fruiting body of a stinkhorn typically emerges from an egg-like structure called a gleba, which is buried in the ground.

As the mushroom matures, it breaks through the gleba and extends upward, sometimes reaching heights up to 10 inches. The cap is often covered in a sticky, dark spore slime, which is the part that emits the characteristic odor and attracts insects. These mushrooms can grow from an underground egg to a mature, spore-dispersing structure in just a matter of hours.

A Sign of a Strong Ecosystem

In Denver, stinkhorn mushrooms can be found in a variety of habitats, from damp, wooded areas to decaying organic matter like logs and leaf litter. Their presence is often a sign of a rich, decomposing ecosystem where organic material is breaking down.

Different Species, Different Smells

There are numerous species of stinkhorns, each with their own unique appearance and odor profile. In Colorado, you might encounter species like common stinkhorn (*Phallus impudicus*) or devil's claw stinkhorn (*Clathrus archeri*).

Where to See Them

You can find stinkhorns in mulched yards and in damp, wooded areas with decaying logs and leaf litter like at Rocky Mountain Arsenal National Wildlife Refuge and Cherry Creek State Park (Trips 9 and 15).

Dog Vomit Mold

Fuligo septica

BRIGHT YELLOW OR ORANGE GOOP ◆ SPONGY TEXTURE ◆ UNEVEN EDGES

This slime mold's vivid coloration is not just for show; it serves a practical purpose. The bright hue helps attract insects, which play a crucial role in dispersing its spores.

Despite its unappealing common name, dog vomit mold is a marvel of natural adaptation. It's a type of slime mold, part of a group of organisms that exhibits characteristics of both fungi and amoebae.

When it first emerges, it resembles a bright yellow or yellow-orange mass of goo that looks remarkably like scrambled eggs or vomit (hence the name). As the slime mold matures, it turns a darker color (eventually dark brown or black) and dries up, leaving behind a powdery mass of spores ready to be spread by wind or animals.

This mold thrives in moist, shady areas such as forests, woodlands, and gardens. It often grows on decaying mulch and leaf litter. Highly adaptable, it can survive in a range of environmental conditions, making it a common sight in the mulch of yards and parks all over Denver. Its presence is often an indicator of a healthy, decomposing ecosystem where organic matter is breaking down and contributing to nutrient cycling.

Movers and Shakers

Dog vomit mold is capable of amoeboid movement, which means it can shift its shape and "crawl" across surfaces. This movement is facilitated by the slime mold's ability to form a network of protoplasm that flows and reconfigures, allowing it to explore its environment in search of nutrients. Slime molds are studied for their unique biological processes, including their movement, feeding mechanisms, and spore dispersal strategies.

Where to See Them

Dog vomit mold thrives in moist, shady areas such as forests, woodlands, and gardens. It's also found in more manicured environments on decaying wood and organic matter in places like Denver Botanic Gardens and City Park (Trips 2 and 1).

Common Orange Lichen

Xanthoria parietina

ORANGE OR YELLOW-ORANGE   ◆   SPRAWLING   ◆   FLAT LOBES

The bright yellow-orange pigment produced by common orange lichen, known as parietin, was historically used as a textile dye. This natural dye was valued for its vibrant color and used to create garments and artifacts.

Common orange lichen can be found clinging to rocks, tree bark, and artificial structures along trails, adding a splash of color to the often stark, rocky terrain of area parks.

It's a foliose lichen, meaning it has a leafy or lobed appearance, which differs from the crusty texture of other lichens commonly found in the area. Its lobes are flat and can spread out from the central attachment point, giving it a somewhat rosette-like form. This

structure allows it to capture moisture and nutrients efficiently, even in arid conditions.

Look on the Bright Side

The eye-catching hue of the common orange lichen is the result of pigments in the lichen's cells, particularly carotenoids, which help it absorb sunlight while also protecting itself from harmful UV radiation. In Denver and surrounding areas, we're a mile closer to the sun, so light can be intense and conditions harsh. This pigmentation is an adaptive advantage, allowing the lichen to effectively harness light for photosynthesis while minimizing damage from UV rays.

Air-Quality Test

Unlike other lichens that are more limited by their habitats, orange lichen can pop up in several, from the dry, exposed surfaces of rocks to the sheltered bark of trees. It's known for its tolerance to pollutants, including sulfur dioxide, making it a useful bioindicator of air quality. Its ability to withstand pollution makes it a valuable species for monitoring environmental health, particularly in areas affected by industrial activities or urbanization.

Where to See Them

Common orange lichen can be found on rocks and tree bark at Eldorado Canyon State Park (Trip 25).

Gold Cobblestone Lichen

Pleopsidium flavum

YELLOW OR ORANGE ◆ **THIN** ◆ **CRACKED SURFACE**

This lichen absorbs moisture from dew and rain.

Gold cobblestone lichen adds a vibrant splash of color to the rocky landscapes found in the foothills. Its vivid yellow hue is the result of pigments in the lichen's cells, which help absorb sunlight and protect against UV radiation. In sunlit rocky outcroppings, this coloration actually maximizes its ability to photosynthesize and survive in conditions where other plants might struggle.

Gold cobblestone lichen is a crustose lichen. It forms a thin, crusty layer that sticks to surfaces such as rocks and tree bark. This growth form is an adaptation to its environment, allowing it to cling securely to substrates while withstanding harsh weather conditions. The lichen's surface is often covered in small, scaly, or granular patches that give it a textured appearance.

Soil Creator

As a pioneer species, gold cobblestone lichen is among the first organisms to colonize bare or disturbed rock surfaces. Through its growth and eventual decomposition, it helps to break down rocks into smaller particles, contributing to the gradual formation of soil. This process is crucial for creating a more hospitable environment for other plant and animal species to establish themselves over time.

Where to See Them

Spot gold cobblestone lichen on the rocks at Eldorado Canyon State Park, North Table Mountain, and Lookout Mountain (Trips 25, 17, and 16).

Mica Cap

Coprinellus micaceus

BELL-SHAPED CAPS ◆ BROWN ◆ CLUSTERS

As with all mushrooms, be careful if you forage mica caps. They can easily be confused with scaly ink cap or toxic Galerina mushroom.

Mica cap mushrooms usually grow in clusters. Their dainty caps are a light brown or tan color with a glistening, almost-sparkling appearance—hence the name mica. This shimmer comes from the tiny scales that cover the cap, resembling mineral flakes. Mature caps can reach 2 to 4 inches in diameter, starting off as rounded before gradually flattening out as they grow. The edges of the cap often remain slightly curled inward.

The gills of mica caps are closely spaced and free from the stem, turning from white to black as the mushroom matures. This unique feature is part of a process called autodigestion, where the mushroom digests its own gills, causing the cap to eventually dissolve into a dark, inky substance. This process is not just a visual spectacle but also a fascinating adaptation that helps the mushroom disperse its spores effectively.

Mica caps' affinity for decaying wood makes them excellent decomposers, breaking down complex organic materials and returning vital nutrients to the soil.

Where to See Them

Mica cap mushrooms thrive in a variety of habitats, often appearing in clusters on decaying wood, particularly stumps, logs, and other organic matter. Look in overirrigated residential areas and parks like City Park, Sloan's Lake, and Chatfield State Park (Trips 1, 6, and 21).

Broadleaf Arrowhead

Sagittaria latifolia

BROAD, ARROW-SHAPED LEAVES ◆ AQUATIC ENVIRONMENT ◆ LIGHT GREEN

The arrowhead plant produces edible tubers, which can be boiled, roasted, or ground into flour, providing a nutritious food source.

Broadleaf arrowhead can be found in pretty much every lake in Denver. It's a native aquatic perennial named for the distinct arrow-like shape of its leaves that can be spotted floating on the water's surface. In late summer and early fall, delicate white or pinkish flowers rise above the water on tall stalks like a mini floral firework, attracting bees, butterflies, and other pollinators.

Whether it's a shallow pond, a marsh, or the edges of a slow-moving stream, this plant seems to grow effortlessly. Its resilience and adaptability make it a valuable species for wetland restoration projects, helping to stabilize the soil and improve water quality.

Arrowhead is also an important food source for wildlife. Ducks and other waterfowl munch on its tubers, which grow underground and are rich in nutrients.

Where to See Them

If you're near a shallow pond, lake, or the edges of a slow-moving stream, keep an eye out for this aquatic plant. You're guaranteed to spot it at Crown Hill Park, City Park, Washington Park, Belmar Park, and Sloan's Lake (Trips 11, 1, 3, 12, and 6).

Burdock

Arctium lappa

TRIANGULAR LEAVES • SPIKY GREEN SEED HEADS • PURPLE, THISTLE-LIKE BLOOM

Burdock's unique seed-dispersal mechanism was the inspiration for the invention of Velcro.

Burdock sports large, heart-shaped leaves and thistle-like purple flowers. The plant grows up to 6 feet tall, with leaves up to 12 inches long. Its flowers, which appear in late summer, are clusters of small, purple blooms that eventually develop into bur-like seed heads. These seed heads are notorious for their hook-like bur structures that easily attach to clothing and animal fur.

Burdock is a hardy plant that thrives in disturbed soils and can grow in various conditions, from full sun to partial shade. Its adaptability to various soil types makes it a common sight in parks and along the trails in Denver. Burdock also provides habitat and food for wildlife. Its flowers attract pollinators like bees and butterflies, while its seeds offer nourishment to birds.

Rooting for You

One of burdock's most notable characteristics is its deep, spindle-shaped root system, which has been used for centuries in traditional medicine. The root, often harvested in its first or second year of growth, is valued for its purported health benefits and is used in culinary applications, especially in Asian cuisine, where it's added to soups, stir-fries, and pickles for its crisp texture and mildly sweet flavor.

Invasive Tendencies

Although it's beneficial in many ways, it can become invasive in areas with less competitive plants. Burdock's robust root system can cause it to outcompete native vegetation, which may disrupt local ecosystems. This makes management of burdock important in areas where it is not native or where it poses a threat to local plant communities.

Where to See Them

Burdock is particularly prevalent in disturbed soils. You can often find it thriving in areas that have been disturbed by human activity like near the trails at Red Rocks Park, Chatfield State Park, and Cherry Creek State Park (Trips 19, 21, and 15).

Cattail and Bulrush

Cattail

Typha latifolia

BROWN, CIGAR-SHAPED SEED HEADS ◆ TALL GREEN STALKS ◆ CRISP GREEN BLADES

Bulrush

Scirpus spp.

TALL GREEN OR BROWN STALKS ◆ SLENDER GREEN LEAVES ◆ TINY FLOWER CLUSTERS

Fluffy cattail seed heads, when dried, were once used as insulation in clothing and bedding.

If you're walking near a marshy wetland, you might be quick to call all the plants you see there cattails (*Typha latifolia*). But you might be wrong. Bulrushes (*Scirpus* spp.), often mistaken for cattails, are also probably present. An easy way to tell them apart? Cattails have the hot dog at the top of their stalks, while bulrushes have tiny clusters at the tops.

Both plants are several feet tall with long, sword-shaped leaves, but the tops are where things switch up. Cattails have a distinctive flower spike that looks like a fuzzy brown cigar standing tall above the foliage. These seed heads are not just for show; they are crucial for reproduction and dispersal. In late summer, the seeds inside these spikes are released and can float away on the wind, helping the plant spread to new locations. Bulrushes are sedge plants, so they have small flower clusters at the top of the plant.

You'll spot both in a variety of wetland environments, from shallow ponds and marshes to slow-moving streams. They're incredibly resilient, able to tolerate fluctuating water levels and varying soil types.

▲ Cattail

▲ Bulrush

These plants' dense growth provides crucial habitat for a variety of animals. Birds like red-winged blackbird and marsh wren build their nests in the foliage, and insects like dragonfly and damselfly use them as perches and hunting grounds. The dense root systems help stabilize the soil and prevent erosion and filter out pollutants and excess nutrients from the water, effectively acting as a natural water purifier. This is especially important in areas where water quality might be compromised by runoff or pollution. Both are equally important players in maintaining the health of wetland environments.

Where to See Them

You'll spot cattails on any trips near lakes or slowly moving rivers, including Crown Hill Park, Sloan's Lake, and Berkeley Lake Park (Trips 11, 6, and 7).

Cheatgrass

Bromus tectorum

DROOPING CLUSTERS • LONG, POINTY AWNS • GREEN, BROWN, OR REDDISH

Cheatgrass is a winter annual, meaning it germinates in fall, overwinters as a seedling, and resumes growth in spring before maturing and setting seed in early summer.

Cheatgrass has a reputation for rapid growth and adaptability, which allows it to thrive in both disturbed soils and stable landscapes. One of its most distinctive features is its seed heads, which are covered in long, bristly awns. These awns can easily catch on clothing or animal fur, helping the seeds to disperse widely. This characteristic makes cheatgrass invasive, as it can quickly spread across large areas, choking out the resources for other plants.

Super Seeder

Cheatgrass appears on the Colorado Department of Agriculture's Noxious Weed List—a list of plants considered harmful or invasive due to their ability to aggressively spread and disrupt native ecosystems, agriculture, or other land uses—and the impact of cheatgrass is significant. It's listed on the state's C list, which means that control is recommended.

Ramping Up Wildfires

One of the primary concerns with cheatgrass is its fire risk. It can outcompete native grasses and plants, forming dense mats that dry out quickly. These mats are highly flammable, which can increase the frequency and intensity of wildfires. In Colorado, where wildfires are a common natural occurrence, cheatgrass can make these fires spread faster, leading to more frequent and severe burns.

Negatives and Positives

While it can be invasive, cheatgrass does serve as a food source for wildlife, including mice, squirrels, and birds. It can also serve as a temporary groundcover in areas where other plants struggle to establish themselves.

Where to See Them

Cheatgrass thrives in disturbed soils and open grasslands. You'll spot it next to the trails at Rocky Mountain Arsenal National Wildlife Refuge, Bluff Lake Nature Center, and Chatfield State Park (Trips 9, 8, and 21).

Columbine

Aquilegia spp.

BLUE-AND-WHITE PETALS ◆ LONG SPURS ◆ EAGLE'S CLAW FLOWER

While the Rocky Mountain columbine (Aquilegia coerulea) pictured here is the most iconic in Colorado, there are over 70 species of columbines worldwide. Each species has its own unique color and shape variation.

The Rocky Mountain columbine, the state flower of Colorado, has blue-and-white blossoms with long, slender spurs extending from the petals, making it instantly recognizable. These spurs are not just for show; they play a crucial role in attracting pollinators like hummingbirds, bees, and butterflies, which feed on the flower's nectar. They also protect the nectar from rain, keeping it available even during unpredictable mountain weather.

The flower's name is derived from the Latin word *aquila*, meaning eagle, due to the shape of the flower petals resembling an eagle's claw.

Colorado's Columbine

The columbine became the state flower in 1891 when groups of schoolchildren participated in a vote. Of the 22,316 votes cast, 14,472 went to

▲ Columbine

▲ Another columbine variation

the Rocky Mountain columbine, and it became the official bloom of the Centennial State.

In 1925, the Colorado's General Assembly enacted a law that made it illegal to uproot the flower on public lands and limit the gathering of blossoms and buds to 25 per day.

Where to See Them

In Colorado, you'll find columbines thriving in moist, well-drained soil in forested areas, alpine meadows, and along stream banks. They can be found in the wild at Golden Gate Canyon State Park and Red Rocks Park (Trips 24 and 19) and in the city at City Park and the Denver Botanic Gardens (Trips 1 and 2).

Creeping Mahonia

Mahonia repens

DENSE MATS ◆ YELLOW CLUSTERS OF FLOWERS ◆ GLOSSY HOLLY-LIKE LEAVES

The rhizomes of creeping mahonia, also called creeping Oregon grape, contain berberine—an alkaloid that is used to treat stomach, liver, and digestive issues.

Creeping mahonia is a low-growing, native evergreen shrub that often forms dense, short thickets or mats on the forest floor. It only reaches a height of 1 to 2 feet and spreads outwards considerably, making it an effective groundcover in shady and semi-shady areas.

In spring, creeping mahonia produces small, bright yellow flowers that appear in clusters and attract pollinators drawn to the plant's nectar. The flowering period lasts from April to June, adding a splash of color to the undergrowth of Colorado's woodlands.

Following the flowering period, the plant develops small, dark blue berries. These are often consumed by various wildlife, including fox, grouse, pheasant, squirrel, and other small mammals.

Creeping mahonia's blue-black berries resemble small grapes, giving the plant its other common name. The berries are edible but can be tart, so they are often used to make jelly with other juices.

Where to See Them

Creeping mahonia prefers shaded to partially shaded areas and it's adaptable to various soil types. You'll find it in residential areas like Denver Botanic Gardens and City Park (Trips 2 and 1) as a popular ornamental bush and forested areas at Mount Galbraith, Mount Falcon, and Waterton Canyon (Trips 18, 20, and 22).

Eastern Cottonwood

Populus deltoides

40 TO 100 FEET TALL • BROAD, ROUNDED CROWN • TRIANGULAR SERRATED LEAVES

Cottonwoods are some of the fastest-growing trees in North America. They can grow several feet per year under prime conditions.

Mature eastern cottonwood trees are huge—like up to 100 feet tall, huge. They typically grow in stands (groups), and their broad, triangular leaves flutter in the breeze and create a serene rustling sound. In spring and summer, the leaves are a vibrant green, but come autumn, they turn a brilliant yellow, adding splashes of color to Denver's streets and nearby forests.

Cottonwood trees are bustling ecosystems, offering shelter, food, and nesting sites to animals and insects. Cottonwood moth, great horned owl, northern flicker, woodpecker, chickadee, and other species find homes in the tree's bark and cavities. Cottonwood leaves and seeds are a food source for deer and other small mammals, and beavers use cottonwood branches for building their lodges and dams.

Summer Snowfall

Its name hints at another of its unique features: cottony seeds. In late spring and early summer, cottonwoods produce fluffy, white seeds that float through the air, resembling cotton. These are an adaptation that helps the tree spread and colonize new areas. If you've ever seen a snowfall of white fluff on a warm day, you've likely witnessed the cottonwood's seeding process in action.

Roots for the Win

The trees have an extensive root system, which helps them access water and nutrients from a wide area. In our riparian zones—areas adjacent to rivers and streams—cottonwoods

play a crucial role in stabilizing the soil and preventing erosion. Their roots also help maintain the health of waterways by filtering runoff and providing habitat.

Where to See Them

Cottonwoods were planted in residential areas and parks in the early days of Denver. Take a drive through neighborhoods in fall, and you'll get to see them with their golden glow. If you're looking to spot some cottonwoods out in the wild, look for large stands of trees near moist areas like creek beds or lakeshores at Crown Hill Park, Bear Creek Greenbelt Park, and Cherry Creek State Park (Trips 11, 13, and 15).

Gambel Oak

Quercus gambelii

SINGLE-TRUNKED TREE OR A MULTI-STEMMED SHRUB ◆ **3- TO 6-INCH DEEPLY LOBED LEAVES DARK GREEN AND GLOSSY**

Unlike many oaks, Gambel oaks don't reproduce well from acorns. They rely on their rhizomes to spread instead.

The Gambel oak is a relatively small species compared to other oak varieties. Maxing out at 30 feet in height, it exhibits a bushy and compact form. Its leaves are deeply lobed and resemble those of other oaks but shrunken down. In autumn, the foliage transforms into a range of colors, from golden yellow to deep red.

Gambel oaks thrive in rocky, well-drained soils and can tolerate the relatively dry climate of our region. The tree's robust root system enables it to access water even in less-than-ideal soil conditions. Its leaves are adapted to withstand strong winds and variable temperatures, and the tree is noted for its resistance to

common oak pests and diseases, such as oak wilt and insect infestations.

Gambel oak acorns are an important food source for wildlife, including squirrels, deer, and birds, and the tree's dense foliage provides cover and nesting sites for birds and small mammals.

Fire Friendly

Gambel oak often resprouts readily after fire. Oak rhizomes are 4 to 20 inches deep in the soil, so the density of Gambel oak thickets often increases after fire. When fires clear out competing vegetation, reducing competition for resources like light, water, and nutrients, newly germinated oak seedlings can establish themselves more effectively.

Where to See Them

Gambel oaks can be spotted at Mount Falcon, Waterton Canyon, and Fairmount Cemetery (Trips 20, 22, and 5).

Kinnikinnick

Arctostaphylos uva-ursi

TINY, ROUNDED EVERGREEN LEAVES ◆ GLOSSY ◆ WHITE OR PINK FLOWERS IN CLUSTERS

The name "kinnikinnick" is said to be derived from an Algonquin word meaning smoking mixture.

Kinnikinnick, an evergreen shrub also referred to as bearberry, has a low-growing, spreading form. It typically reaches a height of 6 to 12 inches but can spread up to 3 feet wide. The plant's small, leathery, evergreen leaves are oval-shaped and have a glossy appearance. These leaves are usually green but can turn reddish or purplish in fall.

The small flowers of kinnikinnick appear in spring and are typically white or pink, clustered in dense groups. Following the flowering period, the plant produces red berries that are about the size of a pea and stay on the shrub through winter. These berries are edible and often consumed by birds and small mammals.

Kinnikinnick is commonly found in open, sunlit areas or under the canopy of coniferous forests, where it benefits from the dappled sunlight that reaches the forest floor. The shrub plays a role in stabilizing soil and preventing erosion, thanks to its spreading root system that holds the soil in place. It also provides cover and food for wildlife, which is especially important in high-altitude environments where resources can be scarce.

Where to See Them

Kinnikinnick can be found trailside at Golden Gate Canyon State Park, Eldorado Canyon State Park, and Waterton Canyon (Trips 24, 25, and 22).

Mountain Ball Cactus

Pediocactus simpsonii

1 TO 4 INCHES • SMALL, GLOBULAR SHAPES • SOFT PINK OR WHITE FLOWERS

Mountain ball cactus is known for its longevity and slow growth rate. This cactus can live for several decades, slowly expanding its size over time.

Mountain ball cactus, also known as Simpson's pincushion cactus, is native to the southwestern United States and has a small, globular shape that makes it look like (as the common name suggests) a pincushion with spines. This cute cactus only reaches a height of 1 to 4 inches, and its body is covered with a dense array of white to yellowish spines that radiate from the areoles (small, cushioned clusters on the cactus surface). These spines not only add to its distinctive look but also provide protection against herbivores.

From late spring to early summer, the cactus produces delicate, funnel-shaped flowers that are a soft pink or lavender color. These blossoms, though small, stand out beautifully against the cactus's spiny surface. The flowers are a vital part of its life cycle as they attract pollinators, which play a crucial role in fertilizing the plant and aiding in seed production. After flowering, the cactus produces small, cylindrical fruit that contains seeds, continuing the cycle of life.

The slow growth rate of the mountain ball cactus is a reflection of its ability to adapt to harsh environments where resources are limited. Its compact form and minimalistic water needs also make it an ideal candidate for cultivation in xeriscaped gardens, where low-water, drought-tolerant plants are preferred.

Where to See Them

The mountain ball cactus thrives in dry, rocky soils and can be found in desert scrublands, rocky outcrops, and high-altitude grasslands across the Denver region, including at North Table Mountain, Mount Falcon, and Golden Gate Canyon State Park (Trips 17, 20, and 24).

Mountain Mahogany

Cercocarpus montanus

3 TO 10 FEET ◆ **CORKSCREW FEATHER-LIKE SEED HEADS** ◆ **SHRUBBY**

Historically, mountain mahogany wood was valued by Indigenous peoples for making tools and weapons due to its density and hardness.

Mountain mahogany is one of the first shrubs to turn green in spring, but it really shows off in summer. After flowering, the shrub produces small, reddish brown fruits, each with a long, corkscrew-shaped, feather-like tail. These tails, which can be up to 2 inches long, help the seeds disperse by catching the wind and carrying them away from the parent plant. This adaptation ensures that the seeds can spread over a wide area, and mountain mahogany is often one of the first plants to colonize disturbed areas.

You'll often find it growing near trails with limited water, where many other plants struggle to survive. Its ability to thrive in harsh conditions allows it to establish itself in places where other plants might not yet be able to grow, making it an important pioneer species. Its deep root system helps it access moisture and nutrients from the soil, while its tough, waxy leaves minimize water loss.

Its dense, shrubby growth provides valuable cover and nesting sites for wildlife, including mountain bluebirds and rodents, and the seeds with their feathery tails are also an important food source.

Let It Go

Mountain mahogany engages in a form of natural pruning: the shrub gradually sheds entire branches over time. This self-pruning mechanism helps it conserve resources and manage its growth more efficiently. By shedding older branches, the shrub can focus its energy and nutrients on younger, more productive parts of the plant.

Where to See Them

Look for mountain mahogany on rocky slopes and hillsides, open woodlands, and scrubby areas, especially at Mount Falcon, Red Rocks Park, and Roxborough State Park (Trips 20, 19, and 23).

Mullein

Verbascum thapsus

UP TO 6 FEET TALL ◆ STAR-SHAPED YELLOW FLOWERS ◆ LARGE, SOFT LEAVES

Mullein is also referred to by nicknames such as velvet plant, Aaron's rod, king's candle, flannel leaf, Roman's candle, and cowboy toilet paper.

With its towering flower spires and distinctive foliage, mullein is a familiar sight out on the trails. Part of the reason for that is because it's simply easy to spot. Its floral spikes can reach heights of up to 6 feet, making it one of the tallest wildflowers in the region. The plant produces dense clusters of small, star-shaped yellow flowers that bloom from midsummer to early fall.

Mullein leaves are also easy to recognize. They've got a soft, woolly texture thanks to the dense hairs that cover their surface. The leaves form a rosette at the base of the plant during its first year of growth. In the second year, the plant sends up its tall flower spike, completing its life cycle.

Mission (Seemingly) Impossible

Mullein thrives in a wide range of soil types and conditions, from sandy soils to rocky outcrops, which allows it to establish itself in disturbed areas such as roadsides, vacant lots, and open fields. Its rapid growth and prolific seed production make it an aggressive spreader, which can impact native plant communities in some areas. It's no surprise that it's on Colorado's Noxious Weed List as a List C species, but removing it from the landscape is quite the task. One plant can make up to 180,000 seeds, which can stay viable for 120 years.

Where to See Them

Because mullein seeds so heavily and easily, it thrives pretty much anywhere. See if you can spot the spikes at North Table Mountain, Waterton Canyon, and Cherry Creek State Park (Trips 17, 22, and 15).

Penstemon

Penstemon spp.

TALL STALKS ◆ **EVERGREEN FOLIAGE**
TUBULAR FLOWERS

The stamens that make up penstemon's "beard" are sterile and are not involved in pollen production.

There are more than 250 species of penstemon spread across North America, but they really come into their own in Colorado—Rocky Mountain penstemon (*Penstemon strictus*) is shown here. The Centennial State is home to more than 60 native varieties that come in an array of colors, including deep purples, bright pinks, fiery reds, and cool blues. Some are only a few inches high while other reach toward the sky and can be several feet tall. The one thing that stays the same (for the most part) is the flower shape.

Boasting Beards

The tubular shape of the penstemon blossom is adapted for pollination by hummingbirds and bees, which are attracted to their bright colors and nectar. The flowers have a distinctive beard-like structure inside the throat, which gives rise to the common name "beardtongue." The beard's bristly, hairy texture helps direct pollinators toward the pollen-producing parts of the flower, acting as a landing strip. When a pollinator visits the flower, it must navigate through this beard to reach the nectar. In the process, the pollinator comes into contact with the flower's pollen, which is then transferred to other flowers, aiding in cross-pollination.

Where to See Them

If you're interested in spotting penstemons in the wild, keep an eye out during spring and early summer months, when they are in full bloom. They often grow in clusters, creating patches of color that can brighten up any hike or nature walk at Cherry Creek State Park, Washington Park, Bear Creek Greenbelt Park, and Mount Galbraith (Trips 15, 3, 13, and 18).

Ponderosa Pine

Pinus ponderosa

TALL, STRAIGHT TRUNK ◆ THICK, DEEPLY FURROWED BARK ◆ CINNAMON AND DARK BROWN BARK ◆ LONG, SLENDER NEEDLES IN CLUSTERS OF THREE

Ponderosa pines can reach up to 150 feet in optimal conditions.

The distinctive bark of ponderosa pine makes it one of the easier trees to identify on hikes. It's thick and deeply furrowed, with a rich, orange-brown color that provides a striking contrast against its green needles. The bark's appearance changes as the tree matures, evolving from a smooth, reddish brown in young trees to the more rugged, plated texture seen in older specimens.

Ponderosa pine provides habitat and food for a variety of wildlife like chickadee, squirrel, and western pine beetle. The seeds from its pinecones are an important food source for many animals, and the tree's large branches offer nesting sites for birds.

Go Sniff a Tree

When you scrape or break the bark of a ponderosa pine, you might notice a sweet, vanilla-like aroma. The sweet scent comes from the tree's resin and essential oils, which are more pronounced in ponderosas compared to many other pines. This aroma is most noticeable in the inner, lighter-colored bark.

Colorado Tough

Ponderosa pine can endure the challenges of drought and rocky soils. This resilience is partly due to its extensive root system, which allows it to access water deep in the ground. Additionally, its thick bark provides a degree of protection from fire, enabling it to withstand and recover from occasional wildfires.

Fancy Furniture and Resin

Ponderosa pinewood is strong and durable, making it a popular choice for construction and furniture. The tree's wide range of uses extends beyond timber; its resin has been historically used in various applications, from medicinal applications to adhesives.

Where to See Them

Find ponderosa pine trees where prairies and shrublands transition into open pine forests at Lookout Mountain, Eldorado Canyon State Park, and Golden Gate Canyon State Park (Trips 16, 25, and 24).

Prairie Pasque Flower

Pulsatilla patens

CUP-SHAPED FLOWERS ◆ **LIGHT PURPLE EXTERIOR PETAL-LIKE SEPALS WITH WHITE INTERIOR**

FINE LEAVES

Pasque flower is derived from the Latin word for Easter, Pascha, because its bloom often coincides with the Easter season. This connection to the Easter holiday underscores the flower's role as a symbol of renewal and new beginnings.

Pasque flower, also called a prairie crocus, is a resilient wildflower that is one of the first to grace our landscapes in the late winter and early spring when most other plants are still in dormancy. Its presence is a welcome sign that spring is on its way, and its vibrant blooms provide a nice contrast of color against the muted brown backdrop of a Denver winter.

Pollinator Favorites

Early spring bumblebees and solitary bees are among the first pollinators to visit these flowers, collecting nectar and pollen essential for their survival and feeding their developing larvae. The delicate blooms also attract mourning cloak, anglewing butterfly, longhorn beetle, and other flower beetles. Hoverflies, which mimic bees, also visit pasque flowers to feed.

Tough, Yet Delicate

Pasque flowers thrive in prairies and open grasslands, where they endure the cold of early spring and the heat of summer without much protection. The plant's leaves are finely divided and covered in delicate hairs, which help reduce water loss and protect it from the cold.

Where to See Them

Spot prairie pasque flowers at Lookout Mountain, Mount Galbraith, Eldorado Canyon State Park (Trips 16, 18, and 25). You can also see them at Denver Botanic Gardens (Trip 2) if you want to avoid the mud of an early spring hike.

Quaking Aspen

Populus tremuloides

HEART-SHAPED LEAVES WITH SERRATED EDGES ◆ **WHITE BARK WITH BLACK KNOTS THAT LOOK LIKE EYES**
STRAIGHT TRUNK

One 100-acre aspen grove in Utah, known as Pando, is estimated to be over 80,000 years old.

If you walk through a quaking aspen grove at night, you might get the feeling you're being watched. The white bark is smooth and white with black knots, and while it helps to reflect sunlight and reduce water loss, the knots can also look a little like eyes. The leaves are heart-shaped or rounded with finely serrated edges, and they tremble or "quake" in the wind because of their flattened petioles. This quaking effect creates a shimmering effect in the forest and is one of the tree's most distinctive features.

Quaking aspens provide habitat and food for birds, mammals, and insects. The leaves and bark are consumed by deer and elk, while the dense groves offer shelter and nesting sites for birds. Additionally, aspen forests create important ecological spaces for various species of fungi and lichen.

All for One

Aspen trees propagate both sexually and independently. They produce small, greenish catkins that contain seeds and are dispersed by the wind. They also reproduce through root sprouts and form clonal groves. A single aspen tree can give rise to a vast network of genetically identical trees, all connected through an underground root system. Aspen groves can cover large areas and result in some of the largest living organisms on the planet.

Where to See Them

Aspen trees thrive in well-drained soils and are commonly found in mixed forests. Golden Gate Canyon State Park (Trip 24) is known for its aspen leaf peeping in fall.

Rubber Rabbitbrush

Ericameria nauseosa

YELLOW FLOWERS AT STEM END ◆ **BUSHY, SPRAWLING** ◆ **SILVERY GRAY NEEDLE-LIKE LEAVES**

"Nauseosa" in rubber rabbitbrush's scientific name refers to the foul smell given off when the leaves or flowers are crushed.

Rubber rabbitbrush isn't picky about what it grows in; it can thrive in sandy, rocky, or clay soil. The plant is remarkably tolerant of dry conditions, which makes it a common sight in scrubby open sagebrush areas. Its ability to thrive in low-water environments is partly due to its root system, which goes deep into the ground for moisture. These deep roots also allow rabbitbrush to stabilize soil and prevent erosion in hillside areas prone to it.

In late summer and early fall, the shrub explodes with small, bright yellow flowers that form dense clusters at the ends of its branches. Bees, butterflies, and other insects are drawn to the nectar-rich flowers.

Resin and Resources

The plant's leaves have a distinct, resinous smell that comes from its essential oils and serves multiple purposes, including acting as a deterrent to herbivores, reducing the likelihood the plant will be grazed.

Rabbitbrush has historically been used for its medicinal properties, crafting baskets, and as chewing gum. During World War II, there were efforts to use rabbitbrush to make a commercial rubber substitute. (It's occasionally used as a small commercial rubber source today!)

Where to See Them

You can spot rubber rabbitbrush on many open area hikes in the Denver area, but it's especially easy at Crown Hill Park, Berkeley Lake Park, Rocky Mountain Arsenal National Wildlife Refuge, and Bluff Lake Nature Center (Trips 11, 7, 9, and 8).

Soapweed Yucca

Yucca glauca

LONG 4- TO 6-FOOT FLOWER SPIKE ◆ **1- TO 3-FOOT-LONG LEAVES** ◆ **ROSETTES**
CREAMY WHITE, BELL-SHAPED FLOWERS

Soapweed yucca leaves contain natural saponins, which can be used to produce a soapy lather when mixed with water. This property led to its common name.

Soapweed yucca, also known as Great Plains yucca, is a hardy plant that thrives in the rugged terrain of Colorado. It has a rosette of long, sword-like leaves that radiate from a central point. These leaves are stiff and narrow with sharp tips and a blue-green to grayish color. The edges of the leaves are often lined with small, white, fibrous threads that give them a spiky appearance. Indigenous tribes historically used the plant's fibers for making textiles, ropes, and other tools.

Soapweed yucca's deep taproot allows it to access groundwater and survive prolonged periods of drought. Additionally, the yucca's tough leaves and spiny edges reduce water loss and provide shelter and protection for small mammals, ground-nesting birds, and lizards.

During late spring to early summer, soapweed produces a tall, central flower spike. At the top of this spike, clusters of creamy white to pale green flowers bloom. These flowers are tubular and bell-shaped, attracting various pollinators, including bees and moths.

Where to See Them

Soapweed yucca thrives in dry, sandy, or gravelly soils, and can be found in desert scrublands, foothills, and prairie regions. Look for it at Red Rocks Park, Rocky Mountain Arsenal National Wildlife Refuge, and North Table Mountain (Trips 19, 9, and 17).

Western Chokecherry

Prunus virginiana

SMALL WHITE FLOWER CLUSTERS • SHRUB-LIKE • BRIGHT GREEN LEAVES

Western chokecherries look similar to chokeberries, but they are different plants. Chokeberries are members of the Aronia genus, while chokecherries are from the genus Prunus.

If you spot a shrubby-looking tree covered in clusters of small, fragrant white or pinkish flowers in late spring to early summer, you're probably looking at a western chokecherry. These blossoms, which appear in dense, elongated clusters, give way to small, dark red or black cherries by late summer.

The chokecherry tree also has beautiful foliage, which changes colors throughout the year. In spring, its leaves emerge as a bright green, turning to a deep green in summer. As autumn arrives, the leaves transform into stunning shades of yellow, orange, and red.

Forage Friendly

The fruit is where the plant gets its common name—chokecherry. While the berries are edible, they are quite tart and can be astringent, making them less enjoyable to eat raw but perfect for making jellies, jams, and syrups. The high pectin content in the fruit makes it ideal for preserves, and its tart flavor can add a unique kick to various culinary creations.

The nectar and pollen found in chokecherry flowers attract pollinators like bees and painted lady butterflies, while the fruit serves as a food source for birds like American robins, cedar waxwings, and song sparrows, which flock to the trees in late summer and fall. Mammals like white-tailed deer, mice, and mountain squirrels also rely on chokecherry fruit and foliage.

Where to See Them

Chokecherries are often planted as residential trees, so you can probably spot one in your neighborhood if you look hard enough. You can see them in their natural environment at places like Eldorado Canyon State Park, Red Rocks Park, and Roxborough State Park (Trips 25, 19, and 23) along woodland edges, forest clearings, and riparian zones near streams.

Yarrow

Achillea millefolium

LACY OR FEATHER-LIKE FOLIAGE • GREEN OR GRAY GREEN LEAVES • TINY, FLAT CLUSTERS OF FLOWERS

Yarrow's scientific name, Achillea, is derived from the Greek hero Achilles, who was said to have used it to treat wounds during the Trojan War. The plant's ability to stanch bleeding and promote wound healing made it a staple in herbal medicine cabinets throughout history.

Yarrow has finely dissected, fern-like leaves which give it a soft, lacy appearance. These leaves are typically green, though they can sometimes take on a silvery or grayish hue, particularly in dry or sunny conditions. Its blooms are known for attracting pollinators like bees and butterflies, and it can grow in a range of soil types, from sandy to rocky to the tough Colorado clay this region is known for.

In the Wild and at Home

Beyond its practical uses, yarrow adds visual appeal to Colorado's home landscapes. It can endure both drought and the hot summer sun, and its flowers bloom from late spring through summer, providing a splash of color and attracting beneficial insects. It can often be seen flourishing in the wild, despite the harsh conditions.

In our challenging climate, where temperatures can fluctuate dramatically and water availability can be limited, yarrow's ability to survive without a lot of extra effort makes it a popular choice for home landscapes of gardeners looking for low-maintenance, hardy plants.

Where to See Them

Look for yarrow at Mount Falcon, Roxborough State Park, Red Rocks Park, and Eldorado Canyon State Park (Trips 20, 23, 19, and 25). It's usually included in any low-water landscape, so you'll probably spot it in a hellstrip or two as you walk around the city's neighborhoods.

Invertebrates

Banded Garden Spider

Argiope trifasciata

BLACK-AND-YELLOW-STRIPED ABDOMEN ◆ **ZIGZAG PATTERN IN WEB** ◆ **UP TO 2.5 INCHES**

Banded garden spiders are harmless to humans and prefer to avoid confrontation. The spider's bright coloration serves as a warning to potential predators, signaling that it might be toxic.

Aptly named, the banded garden spider has a distinctive black-and-yellow-striped abdomen (its bands) and is found in Denver gardens at the end of summer into fall. The females are notably larger than the males, with bodies reaching an inch in length and leg spans extending up to 2.5 inches. Adult banded garden spiders die off at the end of fall while the eggs overwinter and hatch in spring.

Web of Wonders

This spider makes large, intricate orb-shaped webs that can span several feet and feature a reflective zigzag pattern called a stabilimenta. This highly visible design reinforces the structure and lets birds and other big flyers know there's something to maneuver around. There's a chance it might also alert insects to the trap, but the spiders will relocate if they aren't successfully catching enough prey to survive.

Banded garden spiders are sit-and-wait predators, relying on their webs to capture flying insects like flies, mosquitoes, and beetles. They actively maintain their webs, regularly repairing any damage to ensure efficiency.

Once an insect becomes trapped in the web, the spider swiftly subdues it before wrapping it up for later consumption.

Where to See Them

The banded garden spider prefers sunny, open habitats with plenty of plants to hide in. They can be found in gardens, meadows, and open fields and are commonly encountered in late summer and fall when web-building is at its peak. You'll spot them at Chatfield State Park, Bluff Lake Nature Center, Belmar Park, and Denver Botanic Gardens (Trips 21, 8, 12, and 2).

Bold Jumping Spider

Phidippus audax

BLACK-AND-WHITE PATTERN ◆ **IRIDESCENT** ◆ **FURRY BODY** ◆ **LARGE EYES**

Bold jumping spiders are so docile and friendly that they're sometimes kept as pets.

The bold jumping spider stands out not just for its striking appearance but also for its intriguing behavior. People who come across them say it feels like the spider is watching them back, and oftentimes, they're right! These spiders are harmless to humans, and while they might be curious and wander your way, they tend to avoid contact with people whenever possible.

One of the most distinctive features of the bold jumping spider is its vibrant coloration. Males have striking black-and-white patterns with iridescent green or blue highlights. These bright colors and patterns are not just for show; they are crucial in courtship displays and territorial behavior.

Jump on It

Unlike spiders that spin webs to catch their prey, the bold jumping spider relies on its sight and jumping abilities. The spider's excellent vision helps it spot potential prey from a distance, and its refined jumping technique ensures a successful capture.

Where to See Them

The bold jumping spider can be found on city stoops or in grassy fields, garden beds, and forested areas. They prefer habitats that offer plenty of cover and ample prey. Look for these curious creatures at Mount Galbraith, Golden Gate Canyon State Park, and Washington Park (Trips 18, 24, and 3).

Boxelder Bug

Boisea trivittata

BLACK BODY WITH RED LINES ◆ WINGS ◆ HALF AN INCH LONG

Boxelder bugs emit a faint but funky alarm smell that can be unpleasant if the bugs are smashed. If you have an infestation inside, vacuuming them is the best way to contain the problem.

Whether or not you see boxelders depends on if you're near a host tree (a tree that supports a specific species). Unsurprisingly, for boxelder bugs, it's the boxelder tree, but they can also set up shop around maple and ash trees. Their favorite food is boxelder seed pods, which are only found on female boxelder trees, so go for a male tree if you want to plant one in your home landscape but don't want to deal with the bugs. Adults are about a half-inch long and have black bodies with three red lines on the thorax, a red line along each side, and a diagonal red line on each wing. Juveniles are wingless and have red abdomens.

These bugs are harmless to humans and usually go unnoticed until breeding time, when they appear in swarms. Despite their numbers, the bugs don't do any noticeable damage to plants. Instead, they're just annoying, especially if they find their way into the cracks and crevices of your home to stay warm during winter.

Where to See Them

Boxelder bugs can be found all over Denver, particularly in areas where their host trees are present. In spring and fall, you might spot masses of them grouped together on south-facing buildings or at the base of the trees. Parks with a significant number of boxelder trees like Bear Creek Greenbelt Park, High Line Canal, Fairmount Cemetery, Bluff Lake Nature Center (Trips 13, 14, 5, and 8) are likely habitats, as these areas provide an abundant food source.

Colorado Hairstreak

Hypaurotis crysalus

LIGHT BLUE OR GRAY UNDERSIDE OF WINGS ◆ **SPOTS OF ORANGE** ◆ **PALE BLUE STRIPES** ◆ **PURPLE WINGS WITH DARK BORDER** ◆ **ORANGE TIP OF ANTENNAE** ◆ **TAIL-LIKE STRUCTURE BEHIND HIND WINGS**

Colorado hairstreaks live within a few yards of their hatching place for their entire lives.

The Colorado hairstreak is the state insect of Colorado! Adult hairstreaks can be seen June through August, fluttering among stands of Gambel oak and occasionally resting on leaves. They're quite the sight to behold with their purple, orange, and black wings, and the tiny tail beneath their wings. These fast fliers are often in motion, so it can be challenging to observe them for long periods of time.

State Insect

The Colorado hairstreak became the official insect of Colorado on April 17, 1996. (Colorado was the 37th state to have a state insect/butterfly.) The path to establishing the Colorado state insect was long but successful, thanks to fourth-grade classes throughout the state using the bill proposing the nomination as a civics lesson and actively lobbying for it.

Only the Oaks

The Colorado hairstreak is entirely dependent on the Gambel oak for survival. The adults lay their eggs on twigs where they'll remain throughout winter until they hatch in the late spring. The caterpillars eat the young leaves of the oak until they pupate, and the butterfly eats sap and sugary secretions from oak galls and aphids. Only one generation hatches each year.

Where to See Them

Look closely at groves of Gambel oaks at Roxborough State Park and Mount Falcon (Trips 23 and 20).

Dragonfly

Various species

BRIGHT BLUE, GREEN, OR PURPLE ◆ **FOUR TRANSPARENT AND IRIDESCENT WINGS** ◆ **LONG SLENDER ABDOMEN** ◆ **BIG EYES**

More than 80 species of dragonfly have been recorded in Colorado.

Dragonflies, with their iridescent wings and swift aerial maneuvers, are one of the most mesmerizing insects in Denver. Visit a lake at any park in the city and you'll spot them darting along the shores on the hunt for prey and mates.

They thrive in environments with still or slow-moving water where their larvae, known as nymphs, can develop. These aquatic nymphs are voracious predators and feed on small invertebrates and small fish once they're big enough.

With four wings that can beat independently, adult dragonflies are agile fliers, capable of hovering, rapid acceleration, and flying backward. This agility is crucial for their hunting strategy, as dragonflies prefer to catch their prey mid-flight. Their compound eyes provide nearly 360-degree vision, allowing them to spot and capture fast-moving insects. Their diet consists mainly of mosquitoes, flies, and other small insects, making them pros at controlling pest populations in lakes and backyards.

Dragonflies are more active in Denver on sunny days during the warmer months, typically from late spring through early fall. Different species prefer different temperatures and elevation levels, so identification is easier when you factor in time of year and elevation. Species to be on the lookout for in our area include the twelve-spotted skimmer (*Libellula pulchella*) pictured here, widow skimmers (*L. luctuosa*), black saddlebags (*Tramea lacerata*), blue dashers (*Pachydiplax longipennis*), and eastern or western pondhawks (*Erythemis simplicicollis* and *E. collocata*).

Don't Mistake Them for Damselflies

Biologically, dragonflies and their cousins the damselflies make up the Odonata order. The two groups differ primarily in their wing structure, resting posture, and flight pattern. Dragonflies have broad, robust wings that are held outstretched when at rest, while damselflies

93

have slender wings that are held together above their bodies. Dragonflies are known for their powerful and fast flight, often seen darting rapidly, whereas damselflies have a slower, more delicate flight pattern. Dragonflies prefer open, sunny habitats and are usually found patrolling over water, while damselflies are more likely to be seen in shaded, vegetated areas near water.

Where to See Them

You'll spot dragonflies at ponds, lakes, and reservoirs in and around Denver. The exact species will vary depending on whether you're at a higher altitude area like Golden Gate Canyon State Park or enjoying a walk around City Park or Washington Park (Trips 24, 1, and 3).

European Earwig

Forficula auricularia

FLATTISH BODIES ♦ RED-BROWN COLOR ♦ CURVED PINCHERS

The European earwig has only one natural enemy in the United States: the tachinid fly (Bigonicheta spinipennis).

The European earwig came to the United States around 1907 and rapidly spread across the country, making its debut in Colorado during the 1950s.

Its distinctive feature is a pair of prominent forceps at the back end of its body. The ones on males are more curved than those of females, but neither can use their pincers to attack. Other than an occasional weak pinch (if mishandled or sat on), earwigs are harmless to humans. They mainly use their pinchers to grab prey and hold them in place.

Earwigs are often found in the same hiding places as their crustacean buddy the pillbug. From mid-July through mid-September, they like to hunker down in moist, dark spaces during the day, coming out to explore once the sun goes down. Some of their favorite spots are under rocks, stacked wood, and leaf litter.

A Damaging Reputation

Earwigs feed primarily at night. They are scavengers and will eat almost anything, including plants and insects. While they occasionally chow down on plants like lettuce and flower blossoms, they don't do much damage in gardens if the population is balanced. Not one to forgo a good spot to take cover, they'll hide in damage done by other insects and end up being blamed for it.

Many people are uneasy or afraid of earwigs because of the untrue tales that have been told about them. Contrary to popular belief, they don't crawl into your ears, and their forceps don't cause a painful pinch.

Where to See Them

You'll find earwigs in almost every Denver garden. Check under mulch, stones, and boards or curled up at the base of damaged flower petals. Look for them in the underbrush at Mount Galbraith, Cherry Creek State Park, Sloan's Lake, and Berkeley Lake Park (Trips 18, 15, 6, and 7).

Garden Snail

Cornu aspersum

BROWN, GRAY, OR YELLOW ◆ **DARK STREAKS OR BANDS ON SHELL** ◆ **SOFT, SLIMY BODY**

Latin names of species occasionally change based on biological discoveries. The common garden snail was originally known as Helix aspersa, and stayed that way for over 200 years until it was reassigned to the genus Cornu and renamed Cornu aspersum.

Originally native to the Mediterranean region, common garden snails have become an invasive mollusk in the United States. These small to medium-sized land snails have rounded and somewhat flattened shells with a texture that ranges from smooth to slightly ribbed. Their brown, gray, or yellow coloration, with darker streaks or bands, provides camouflage in their natural habitat.

The high altitude and varying temperatures of Colorado present a challenge for its survival and reproduction, but the common garden snail has managed to establish populations in suitable microhabitats like gardens, parks, and other areas with adequate moisture.

As an herbivore, the snail feeds on crops, ornamental plants, and native vegetation. This feeding behavior can significantly damage plants, leading to huge headaches for gardeners and farmers. They can also outcompete native snail species for food and habitat.

The snail's reproductive strategy contributes to its invasive reputation. Common garden snails are hermaphrodites, meaning each snail possesses both male and female reproductive organs. This allows for high reproductive rates, as individuals can mate with any other mature individual. The ability to produce large numbers of eggs, which are laid in moist soil or leaf litter, facilitates rapid population growth and establishment in new areas.

Where to See Them

Common garden snails live in urban and suburban areas, particularly where moisture is present, such as in gardens and parks. Look closely at the leaf litter at Washington Park, City Park, and Mount Galbraith (Trips 3, 1, and 18).

Grasshopper

There are 548 species of North American grasshoppers. Around 145 of them live in Colorado, and 72 call the Front Range home. Most are relatively uncommon and don't become noticeable pests.

Grasshoppers can be a real problem in Colorado. Population numbers can vary drastically depending on the weather early in the year. If there's a mild winter and moist spring, grasshoppers can decimate plant populations. This area's most commonly encountered species can be split into three subfamilies: Gomphocerinae, Melanoplinae, and Oedipodinae.

Gomphocerinae (Slant-faced Grasshoppers)

These small grass specialists are the grasshoppers you often hear chorusing in meadows during the day. (The chorusing isn't them singing; it's the sound of the male grasshoppers rubbing their legs together.) The slant-faced pasture grasshopper (*Orphulella speciosa*) is a medium-sized early-emerging species easily recognized by their green or gray bodies, distinctive club-shaped antennae, and slanted faces.

Melanoplinae (Spur-throated Grasshoppers)

These are the most commonly encountered grasshoppers and are primarily forb feeders. (Forbs are herbaceous plants that are not grasses.) Melanoplinae are small and short-winged, making it so they can't actively fly. They have a spur on their throats, and the male cercus (found at the end of the abdomen) is an easy ID trait.

Differential Grasshopper Migratory Grasshopper

The differential grasshopper (*Melanoplus differentialis*) is one of the largest in the genus *Melanoplus* and often one of the first grasshoppers found in the garden, while the migratory grasshopper (*Melanoplus sanguinipes*) is really destructive to crops.

Oedipodinae (Banded-winged Grasshoppers)

These grasshoppers are grass and forb feeders and are commonly found in open areas basking in the sun and displaying their colorfully patterned hind wings. They vary considerably in size and are all active fliers that use their wings to make loud clicking sounds. They come in all sizes, so an easy way to ID them is to listen for these sounds when they fly.

Green-striped Grasshopper

The green-striped grasshopper (*Chortophaga viridifasciata*) is a grass specialist with a penchant for mid-sized grasses and disturbed habitats. Most are recognized by the stripe that runs across the top of the body from their heads to the top of their wings.

Where to See Them

There's no shortage of grasshoppers in our grassland areas, especially along trail edges. You'll see them hopping out of your way at Bear Creek Greenbelt Park, Chatfield State Park, and Rocky Mountain Arsenal National Wildlife Refuge (Trips 13, 21, and 9).

Slant-faced

Spur-throated

Migratory

Differential

Green-striped

Japanese Beetle

Popillia japonica

METALLIC GREEN HEAD AND THORAX ◆ COPPER-COLORED WING COVERS ◆ WHITE PATCHES OF HAIR ON SIDES

Japanese beetles were first found in the United States in 1916 and were officially brought into Colorado in the early 1990s on nursery stock purchased in the Midwest. They've since become one of the biggest foes of home gardeners in the Mile High City.

Japanese beetle grubs spend winter underneath the soil of lawns and parks. The nondescript grubs look like other white grubs and can only be positively identified by looking closely at the pattern of spines and hairs on the underside of their abdomen. In spring, the grubs rise to the surface to feed before pupating into adult beetles, which start to emerge from the ground in late June or early July. Once July and August roll around, they're actively feeding, sometimes flying several miles for their meals.

Japanese beetles skeletonize leaves—they eat the tissue between the veins, leaving a lace-like pattern behind. Beetles leave a feeding-induced odor on the leaves they eat that attracts other beetles, so once you spot one, be prepared for more. Healthy, mature trees and shrubs can usually handle damage from the beetles without long-term injury, but young or unhealthy plants might not survive the wrath of a beetle feeding.

Slowing the Spread

Japanese beetles feed on the leaves, flowers, or fruit of more than 300 species of plants. They're major turfgrass pests, chewing the grass roots and causing the turf to brown and pull up easily from the soil, like a loose carpet.

While backyard chickens have been known to enjoy a bucket of beetles picked by gardeners, there are a few other natural defenses. Ants and ground beetles feed on their eggs and young larvae, and moles, skunks, and raccoons prey on the grubs. Two species of tiphiid wasps,

Tiphia vernalis and *Tiphia popilliavora*, have also helped reduce the population. *T. vernalis* feeds on overwintering grubs, and *T. popilliavora* target young grubs in late summer. A type of tachinid fly, *Istocheta aldrichi*, kills adult Japanese beetles by laying eggs on them, and after the larvae hatch, they burrow into the beetles' shells and eat them from the inside out.

Where to See Them

Japanese beetles are found in residential areas and any area with concentrations of broad-leafed plants that they love like Fairmount Cemetery, High Line Canal, and Denver Botanic Gardens (Trips 5, 14, and 2).

Leafcutter Bee

Megachile spp.

SMALL TO MEDIUM-SIZED ◆ THICK FURRY BODIES ◆ DARK METALLIC GREEN OR BLUE COLORATION WITH CONTRASTING BANDS OR SPOTS ◆ STRONG MANDIBLES

Leafcutter bees have tiny but robust, furry bodies adapted for collecting pollen.

Unlike their more adored honeybee cousins, leafcutter bees are a solitary species. Each female operates independently, creating her own nest and gathering everything her offspring need to survive.

The name "leafcutter" comes from their remarkable ability to precisely cut out circular pieces of leaves. These leaf discs are then used to line the inside of their nests. The process is not just for aesthetics; the leaves provide a protective barrier and help to keep the nests moist, ensuring the larvae have the best chance of thriving.

Their nests are often built in pre-existing cavities such as abandoned beetle holes, hollow stems, or even the nooks of human-made structures. A section of Denver Botanic Gardens (Trip 2) is dedicated to solo pollinators like leafcutter bees.

Pollination Pros

As leafcutters forage for nectar and pollen, they visit a wide range of flowering plants, inadvertently transferring pollen from one bloom to another. This not only aids in plant reproduction but also supports the broader ecosystem by helping plants produce seeds and fruits.

Where to See Them

Leafcutter bees are active from late spring to early fall, during the warm months when flowers are plentiful. They're found in gardens, meadows, and forest edges like the ones found at Lookout Mountain, High Line Canal, and Cherry Creek Trail (Trips 16, 14, and 4).

Leopard Slug

Limax maximus

MILKY YELLOW OR GRAY ◆ LEOPARD-LIKE SPOTS ◆ SMOOTH

The leopard slug is one of the largest terrestrial gastropods, reaching lengths of up to 8 inches.

You'll know a leopard slug when you see one. An introduced European native, its body is typically a translucent yellow or grayish color, adorned with dark, leopard-like spots that give it its name.

It has a single, retractable pair of tentacles on its head, which are used for sensing the environment and locating food. The slug moves using a muscular foot that secretes mucus, allowing it to glide over various surfaces.

Leopard slugs have been observed primarily in moist urban and suburban areas where they can find adequate food and shelter. As a generalist feeder, the slug consumes a wide variety of organic materials, including decomposing plant matter, fungi, and occasionally live plants. This feeding behavior can lead to competition with native gastropod species for food resources and may cause damage to garden plants and crops.

Where to See Them

The leopard slug hangs around moist areas of gardens, parks, and other environments with abundant organic matter and shelter. See if you can find one at Eldorado Canyon State Park and Roxborough State Park (Trips 25 and 23).

Mason Bee

Osmia spp.

DARK OR METALLIC GREEN COLORING ◆ IRIDESCENT SHEEN ◆ DENSE, FUZZY HAIR

Mason bees get to work in early spring before other pollinators are active. They are vital for fruit production of many early-blooming plants.

A favorite of backyard beekeepers, mason bees are solitary bees easily recognized by their dark, sometimes metallic blue or green bodies. Their small, compact bodies are covered with hair, perfect for collecting and spreading pollen.

These bees are named for their ability to construct nests out of mud. They use specialized mouthparts to create individual cells within the nest, filling each one with an egg, nectar, and pollen before sealing it off. After hatching, the larvae feed on the provisions until they mature and leave the nest.

Proficient Pollinators

Mason bees are particularly effective at pollinating fruit trees such as apples, cherries, and plums. This is due in part to their methodical foraging behavior. As they move from flower to flower, their bodies pick up and transfer pollen more effectively than many other pollinators. This makes them incredibly valuable for both wild and cultivated plants, ensuring that many of Colorado's fruit-bearing plants and wildflowers thrive.

Cool Bees

Mason bees are in a special group of bees that can tolerate the unique climate of Denver, emerging early in spring when temperatures are still quite chilly. Their resilience and timing help support a range of plant species that rely on early pollination to fruit.

Where to See Them

Mason bees prefer areas rich in flowers and suitable nesting sites. This includes gardens and natural areas with bare soil or deadwood. Look for their well-protected nesting sites at Denver Botanic Gardens and North Table Mountain (Trips 2 and 17).

Milky Slug

Deroceras reticulatum

SOFT AND SLIMY • 2 TO 3 INCHES • CREAMY OR GRAY • 2 PRONOUNCED TENTACLES

While you might only think of shells when you think of snails, many slugs have them too. They're flatter and located under a fleshy part on their backs.

The milky slug, also called the mountain slug, is part of the larger family of terrestrial slugs. It has a creamy, translucent body, varying from white to pale gray, giving it its common name. Its body is soft and pliable, covered with a slimy mucus that helps it retain moisture and move across surfaces. The milky slug is a slow-moving creature that prefers damp and cool environments. It is primarily nocturnal, emerging at night to feed on various types of organic matter. Its diet consists of decomposing plant material, fungi, and occasionally algae.

Slug Central

Milky slugs lay eggs in moist soil or leaf litter. After a few weeks, the eggs hatch into juvenile slugs that are miniature versions of adults. These young slugs undergo several growth stages, gradually increasing in size until they reach maturity. The milky slug's life cycle is closely tied to its habitat, with its survival depending on the availability of suitable moist environments for breeding and feeding.

In Denver, milky slugs are commonly found in shaded, tree-filled areas and under fallen leaves, logs or in the damp soil of garden beds. They thrive in these environments because they provide ample moisture and organic material. This preference for shaded and moist conditions helps them avoid desiccation and extreme temperature fluctuations.

Where to See Them

Look under leaf litter at Eldorado Canyon State Park, Chatfield State Park, and City Park (Trips 25, 21, and 1).

Miller Moth

Euxoa auxiliaris

1 TO 2 INCHES ◆ GRAY OR LIGHT BROWN ◆ DARK WING MARKINGS

Swallows and house sparrows gather at intersections to feed on miller moths during their migration. The stoplights and headlights from cars attract the moths, and the birds enjoy an all-you-can-eat buffet.

Miller moths aren't specific types of moth. The term refers to a locally abundant moth with scales that dislodge from the wings. In Colorado, ours start out as army cutworms. Army cutworms are active in spring and can be seen moving in massive bands. They only have a one-year life cycle, but they make the most of that time.

Harmless Home Invaders

Miller moths are the migrating adult stage of the army cutworm, and every year they swarm the city. They're harmless, but keep your windows, doors, and vents closed, or you'll end up with them fluttering around your home.

During their annual migration, miller moths fly from the eastern plains all the way to the mountains in early summer. The adults then return to the plains in September and October.

Miller moths feed almost exclusively at night, and during the day, they hide in small cracks and crevices, which are unfortunately in homes, under cars, and in door frames. Before you rush to crush them, know that miller moths are important pollinators, and they don't reproduce or feed on anything within the home.

During outbreak years, miller moth flights last five to six weeks, generally starting between mid-May and early June. However, they tend to cause most nuisance problems for only two to three weeks.

The number of miller moths in late spring depends entirely on the number of army cutworm caterpillars earlier in the season. Wet weather, frigid winter conditions, or natural predators like parasitic wasps and birds may kill many of the caterpillars, which results in smaller migratory moth populations.

Where to See Them

If you want to see a miller moth in May and June, you won't have to look hard. They can be spotted everywhere in the city. Try Washington Park, City Park, or Bluff Lake Nature Center (Trips 3, 1, and 8).

Pillbug

Armadillidium vulgare

BLUE-GRAY ◆ **PLATED BODY** ◆ **7 PAIRS OF LEGS** ◆ **2 PAIRS OF ANTENNAE**

Sowbugs and pillbugs are the only crustaceans that have adapted to life on land.

Pillbug, roly-poly, woodlouse, and potato bug: it goes by many names, but one thing this creature is not is a bug. Surprisingly, this common garden and leaf-litter critter is a land-dwelling crustacean!

Pillbugs are scavengers, primarily feeding on moist, decaying plant matter and occasionally tender garden seedlings. They excel at recycling nutrients by shredding dead plant material, breaking it down, and returning the nutrients to the soil. Feeding usually occurs at night; they normally spend the day under cover unless it's overcast or there was recent rain. Despite their rugged, armored appearance, pillbugs are harmless and will not bite.

Under the Sea No More

Pillbugs breathe with gills—thin, membranous areas on the underside of their bodies. You'd think that Denver's semi-arid climate wouldn't be a good match for anything that depends on water to survive, but pillbugs adapted to our ecosystem by seeking out moist microclimates (tiny pockets with different environments). Uropods, their tail-like structures, help them wick up water and allow them to drink from both ends of their bodies. Curling into a ball is not only for defense, it also helps them retain water.

Where to See Them

Pillbugs need moisture, so they are primarily nocturnal and live in damp spaces, including leaf litter, mulch, and under stones. Lift a few logs and scout shorelines at Sloan's Lake, Berkeley Lake Park, Crown Hill Park, and Belmar Park (Trips 6, 7, 11, and 12) to catch a glimpse of them.

Western Paper Wasp

Mischocyttarus flavitarsis

THIN WAIST ◆ BROWN, YELLOW, AND/OR BLACK BODY ◆ TRANSLUCENT BLACK WINGS

A paper wasp nest takes two to four weeks to make, but sometimes they keep building them for months, making elaborate communities.

Wasps have a scary reputation, but they're important pollinators and offer humans natural pest control if left alone. As opportunistic foragers, they feed on various insects, including caterpillars, beetle larvae, and flies.

Unlike bees, which are hairy and more robust, paper wasps have smooth yellow-and-black bodies and long legs that dangle while flying. Their wings are transparent and delicately veined. Although their presence may cause concern due to the fear of stings, western paper wasps are generally nonaggressive and will only sting when they feel threatened or if you stumble upon the nest.

Western paper wasps are social insects, living in colonies that can range from a handful to several dozen individuals. Queens lay eggs and worker wasps take on the tasks of foraging for food, maintaining the nest, and caring for the larvae. There can be multiple queens in one colony.

Paper Wasps Make Paper-like Nests

One of the most fascinating traits of these wasps is their ability to produce a unique paper-like substance from chewed plant fibers mixed with saliva. This material is used to construct their umbrella-shaped nests. Each nest houses multiple hexagonal cells that house larvae.

Where to See Them

Western paper wasps can be found all over Denver. Look for their nests hanging from tree branches or attached to eaves or fences, especially in areas with plenty of flowering plants, which provide the nectar they need for sustenance.

Western Widow Spider

Latrodectus hesperus

BLACK BODY ◆ "HOURGLASS" ON UNDERSIDE OF ABDOMEN ◆ THIN, LONG LEGS

Widow spiders get their common name from the shiny black bodies of adults, and black is associated with mourning widows.

Several types of widow spider can be found in the United States, but the western widow is the most frequently found species in Colorado. (The infamous black widow spider is more common in eastern and southern areas of the country.)

Adult females are the easiest to spot. Their glossy black bodies have the signature red hourglass mark, and they can grow to about 1.5 inches when you include their legs. The males are much smaller (usually a third of the size of females), have banded (striped) legs, and come in a range of colors from light orange to gray. Some have the hourglass marking while others don't, making them more difficult to identify.

Western widow spiders make their homes in quiet, undisturbed places like basements, sheds, or under rocks and logs. Their webs are not your typical, neat spider silk constructions but rather a chaotic, tangled mess designed to trap unsuspecting insects.

Misconceptions and Myths

Despite their fearsome reputation, western widow spiders are generally shy and only bite when they feel threatened. If you get bitten, it's usually more of an inconvenience than an emergency. The bite can cause pain, muscle cramps, and nausea, but severe reactions are rare. While most bites end at irritation, they can be fatal to young children and older adults. Seek medical attention if you have concerns about any spider bite.

Black widows also have a reputation for killing their partners after they've mated, but that isn't how it plays out (most of the time). At any time during the mating process, the female could interrupt and attack the male, but males usually make it through just fine if the female is well-fed. In fact, the males often live around the periphery of the female web and may even feed on food that she has captured.

Where to See Them

Western widow spiders are often found in wooded, enclosed, dark, and cool places, including under logs at Bear Creek Greenbelt, City Park, Roxborough State Park, and Eldorado Canyon State Park (Trips 13, 1, 23, and 25).

Western Yellowjacket

Vespula pensylvanica

YELLOW BODY WITH BLACK STRIPES AND SPOTS • DARK TRANSLUCENT WINGS • THIN WAIST, THICK ABDOMEN

Yellowjacket stingers are barbless, which means the same insect can sting you multiple times.

The slender, smooth bodies of western yellow-jackets with yellow and black markings serve as a warning to potential predators and humans alike. Yellowjackets are a little on the aggressive side, especially when defending their nests. This behavior is often misunderstood; while they might fly around you more than other wasps, they typically only sting when they feel threatened. Their stings can be painful and may cause allergic reactions, so be careful if you find yourself near a yellowjacket nest.

The life cycle of western yellowjackets begins in spring when the queen emerges from hibernation. She starts building a nest, often in underground burrows, hollow trees, or sheltered areas. Once the nest is estab-lished, she lays her eggs, and the first gener-ation of workers emerges in late spring. As the colony grows, so does its need for food, leading the wasps to scavenge for protein- and sugar-rich resources, often resulting in unwanted encounters with humans, especially during picnics and outdoor gatherings. The colony usually reaches its peak in late summer before dying off in fall, leaving only queens to hibernate.

Yellowjacket nests are typically built under-ground or in sheltered spaces like wall cavities, tree hollows, or abandoned buildings. These nests can range in size from small to quite large, accommodating anywhere from a few dozen to several thousand wasps.

Where to See Them

Yellowjackets can be found all over the city and in wooded areas. They're especially active during late summer and fall, often seen scavenging near food outside, hovering around trash bins, and visiting flowering plants for nectar.

Wolf Spider

Hogna carolinensis

BROWN OR GRAY ◆ STRIPES OR SPOTS FOR CAMOUFLAGE ◆ LONG NARROW BODY

COVERED IN DENSE HAIRS

Wolf spiders, among the largest spiders found in Colorado, are often mistaken as tarantulas.

Wolf spiders live up to their names. Unlike many of its eight-legged counterparts, these big arachnids don't rely on webs to catch their prey. Instead, they use speed, agility, and sharp predatory instincts to find and pounce on their prey.

They are ground hunters and actively hunt insects and other small invertebrates, relying on their keen sense of sight and swift movements. Wolf spiders have excellent vision thanks to their eight eyes, arranged in three rows. The two largest eyes, located at the front, provide them with incredible depth perception crucial for stalking and capturing prey.

One of the most striking features of the wolf spider is its size and appearance. They are typically covered in a dense layer of hair that can give them a somewhat fuzzy appearance.

This fur serves multiple purposes: it provides sensory information about their surroundings and helps them blend into their environment. The color patterns of wolf spiders also help them camouflage effectively, with hues ranging from brown and gray to more striking patterns of stripes and spots.

Despite their impressive hunting skills and somewhat intimidating appearance, wolf spiders are not aggressive and usually only bite in self-defense. Their bites can cause minor irritation, similar to a mosquito bite, but they are not venomous to an extent that poses a serious threat to humans.

Where to See Them

These spiders thrive in diverse conditions, ranging from the moist soil of a forest floor to dry, rocky crevices. See if you can spot them at Lookout Mountain, Red Rocks, Golden Gate Canyon State Park, and North Table Mountain (Trips 16, 19, 24, and 17).

Woodlouse Spider

Dysdera crocata

PALE ORANGE OR REDDISH BROWN ◆ BULBOUS ABDOMEN ◆ LONG, SLENDER LEGS

Woodlouse spiders are a gardener's best friend. They've been shown to greatly reduce the number of pillbugs and destructive pests found in gardens.

Often mistaken for something more aggressive because of its bulbous body, red features, and slender legs, the woodlouse spider only has eyes for one thing: pillbugs, also known as woodlice. Well, mostly one thing. Despite their name, their diet also includes silverfish, earwigs, millipedes, burying beetles, and crickets.

Pillbugs make up nearly all of the spider's diet, and the woodlouse spider has evolved to be particularly adept at preying on them. With strong fangs capable of piercing the hard exoskeleton of its prey, this spider is a skilled hunter.

Woodlouse spiders are not aggressive toward humans and pose no threat, though they can be off-putting to those who encounter them. They are shy and reclusive, preferring to stay hidden and only emerging to hunt or to move to a new location.

Where to See Them

Woodlouse spiders thrive in cool, damp environments that offer ample cover. They are commonly found in basements, under rocks, in leaf litter, or among decaying wood in places like Eldorado Canyon State Park, Roxborough State Park, and City Park (Trips 25, 23, and 1).

Bullfrog

Lithobates catesbeianus (Rana catesbeiana)

OLIVE-GREEN OR BROWN ◆ SMOOTH SKIN ◆ LARGE HEAD ◆ VOCAL SAC UNDER CHIN

There's some debate about which scientific name is correct. Lithobates is widely accepted, but some believe bullfrog should still be under the Rana genus.

The common bullfrog is one of the most recognizable amphibians in North America thanks to its enormous size and loud voice to match. Adults typically measure between 3.5 to 6 inches in body length, and some can grow up to 8 inches. The skin of the bullfrog is generally olive-green to brown, with a smooth texture that can sometimes be mottled or speckled.

Bullfrogs are semi-aquatic. While they thrive in bodies of water, they can also make long-distance movements on land, especially when seeking new habitats or breeding sites. Bullfrogs are voracious and opportunistic predators that feed on insects, small fish, amphibians, and even small mammals and birds.

Bullfrogs are known for their aggressive territorial behavior, particularly during the

breeding season when males defend their calling sites from rivals.

Bullfrog Bellow

One of the most distinguishing features of the common bullfrog is its deep, resonant call, which can be heard during the breeding season. The call is produced by inflating a vocal sac under the chin, which amplifies the sound and can carry over considerable distances. This call is used primarily by males to attract females during the breeding season, which typically occurs in late spring to summer, and establish territory.

Not So Tiny Tadpoles

Common bullfrogs lay eggs in large masses in shallow water. The eggs hatch into tadpoles (which grow up to 6 inches) and undergo a gradual metamorphosis over several months, eventually emerging as fully developed frogs. The tadpoles are initially herbivorous, feeding on algae and plant material. As they mature, they begin to adopt a more carnivorous diet similar to that of adult bullfrogs.

Where to See Them

The common bullfrog inhabits various wetland environments around Denver, including ponds and lakes at Chatfield State Park, City Park, and Washington Park (Trips 21, 1, and 3).

Common Garter Snake

Thamnophis sirtalis

YELLOW OR WHITE STRIPES FROM HEAD TO TAIL ◆ GREEN, BROWN, OR BLACK BODY ◆ SMOOTH SCALES SLENDER

A single brood of garter snakes can consist of ten to 40 babies, depending on the size and age of the mother. Young snakes are born fully developed and are independent from birth.

Common garter snakes make their homes in yards and parks in and around Denver.

These slender, nonvenomous snakes have longitudinal stripes that run the length of their bodies that are usually yellow or white against a darker background, which can range from green to brown or black. This coloration provides effective camouflage in their natural habitats, helping them blend into the grass and leaf litter where they often hunt and hide.

They use their keen sense of smell and sharp eyesight to locate prey. Garters often feed on small invertebrates such as insects and worms but will also consume amphibians, small fish, and other small reptiles.

Garter snakes are generally shy and non-aggressive, preferring to flee from potential threats rather than confront them. They are known for their quick movements and ability to escape into dense vegetation or burrows when disturbed. During the warmer months, garter snakes are often seen basking in the sun to regulate their body temperature, as they are ectothermic and need external heat sources to stay warm.

Where to See Them

Garter snakes are well adapted to the Denver area. If a space has a food source and suitable cover for shelter, they'll set up shop there. Keep your eyes peeled for quick movement on the ground along the High Line Canal, Chatfield State Park, Roxborough State Park, Cherry Creek State Park, and Eldorado Canyon State Park (Trips 14, 21, 23, 15, and 25).

Common Watersnake

Nerodia sipedon

TAN OR REDDISH BROWN ◆ **DARK BANDS OR SPOTS** ◆ **FLAT HEAD**

Adult common watersnakes can grow to an average length of 24 to 42 inches, with some individuals reaching up to 55 inches, making them one of the larger snake species in the region.

Snakes and water might not be a connection that comes to mind when thinking about Denver, but common watersnakes do call some of our lakes home.

Their scales are patterned with dark, alternating bands or blotches against a lighter background ranging from tan to reddish brown. These markings provide effective camouflage among its habitat's submerged vegetation and muddy banks. Juvenile watersnakes are especially colorful, with more pronounced banding that fades somewhat as they age.

Like their name suggests, watersnakes are adept swimmers and spend much of their lives in or near water. Their flattened bodies and powerful tails enable them to move swiftly through water. The snake is a proficient hunter, primarily feeding on minnows, crayfish, and frogs. Sometimes they'll dive to the bottom of water bodies or strike from the surface to capture prey.

During the warmer months, the common watersnake is often seen basking on sunny rocks or logs along the edges of bodies of water. This behavior is crucial for thermoregulation, allowing the snake to maintain a healthy body temperature.

Where to See Them

The common watersnake inhabits ponds, lakes, rivers, and slow-moving streams around Denver. Look for their long bodies on top of logs and along the edges of the north end of Chatfield State Park and the Bear Creek Greenbelt Park (Trips 21 and 13).

Gopher Snake

Pituophis catenifer

BROWN OR GRAY BODY ◆ **DARK ANGULAR PATTERN** ◆ **REDDISH EYES**

Gopher snakes are sometimes referred to as bullsnakes, but bullsnakes are a subspecies of gopher snake.

Gopher snakes resemble rattlesnakes, but they lead very different lives. Recognizable by a distinctive pattern of dark, angular blotches against a lighter background, the gopher snake is nonvenomous and relies on other methods for defense and hunting.

Gopher snakes are found in habitats similar to those of their rattling relatives. Grasslands, sagebrush deserts, and open woodlands home to many small animals are their preferred places to live. Instead of relying on venom, they kill their prey by wrapping around it and squeezing until it suffocates, a method that is both efficient and effective.

Gopher snakes lay eggs rather than giving birth to live young. A female gopher snake typically lays a clutch of six to 24 eggs in a hidden, warm location, such as under a rock or in a decaying log. Once hatched, the young snakes are independent and fully capable of hunting and surviving on their own.

Hoping for Confusion

Gopher snakes sometimes intentionally look and act like rattlesnakes to scare off threats. They'll flatten their heads, puff up their bodies, and make a hissing sound that can resemble the rattle of a rattlesnake. This defensive display serves to intimidate potential predators and reduce the likelihood of an attack.

Where to See Them

People find gopher snakes along trails like Cherry Creek and High Line Canal (Trips 4 and 14), as well as in open woodland areas like Mount Falcon and North Table Mountain (Trips 20 and 17). They'll also be found in woodpiles in backyards from time to time, so be careful when moving logs.

Plains Spadefoot Toad

Spea bombifrons

BULGING EYES ◆ **BLUNT SNOUT** ◆ **GRAY OR BROWN SKIN** ◆ **SPADE ON THEIR BACK FEET**

Plains spadefoot toads can lay up to 4000 eggs at one time.

The plains spadefoot toad has a robust, squat body with a relatively short, blunt snout; prominent, bulging eyes; and as their common name suggests, a spade-like structure on the underside of their hind feet. This "spade" is an adaptation that aids in digging and burrowing, allowing the toad to create and navigate underground efficiently. Its skin color can range from gray to light brown, often with darker patterns or mottling that provide effective camouflage against the soil and vegetation of its habitat.

The plains spadefoot is well-adapted to life in arid and semi-arid environments. It is primarily nocturnal, emerging during the cooler evening and night hours to avoid the extreme temperatures of the day. After spring rains, the toads migrate to temporary ponds or shallow water bodies to breed, laying eggs that develop into tadpoles. The tadpoles undergo rapid development, metamorphosing into adult toads within a few weeks to take advantage of these short-lived aquatic habitats.

The spadefoot's diet consists mainly of insects, spiders, and worms. It uses its sticky tongue to capture prey, which it swallows whole. The toad's burrowing behavior is useful for finding food, escaping harsh environmental conditions, and avoiding predators. During dry periods, the plains spadefoot retreats to its burrow, where it can remain dormant for extended periods until favorable conditions return.

Where to See Them

Plains spadefoot toads are a little trickier to find because of how much time they spend underground. Your best bet is to look for temporary ponds or shallow water bodies at Chatfield State Park (Trip 21) during the breeding season and listen for their kazoo-sounding calls.

Pond Slider Turtle

Trachemys scripta

OLIVE-GREEN AND DARK BROWN ◆ **YELLOW OR ORANGE STRIPES ON SHELL** ◆ **ORANGE CLAWS**
RED STRIPE ON SIDE OF HEAD

Pond sliders can tolerate a range of living environments, which occasionally leads to invasive tendencies. Their adaptability and varied diet make it easy to outcompete local species quickly.

The pond slider turtle looks similar to Colorado's state reptile, the western painted turtle, but it was introduced into Colorado from the central and southern United States. Its carapace, or upper shell, is typically olive-green or dark brown with intricate patterns of yellow or orange stripes. The exact coloration depends on the turtle's age, but they all usually have a pattern of lines and blotches. The plastron, or lower shell, is usually a lighter shade, often ranging from yellow to orange with a few dark markings. The big difference between the two turtles is that sliders have a red stripe running down their head over their ear.

Pond sliders are ectothermic (cold-blooded) and rely on external heat sources to regulate their body temperatures. Basking in the sun is crucial for maintaining its metabolic processes and overall health. During these basking sessions, pond sliders will often gather on logs, rocks, or the banks of water bodies, soaking up warmth so they can survive.

Their strong jaws and sharp beaks are well adapted for slicing through vegetation and capturing prey, which is reflected in their omnivorous diets that mostly include plants, insects, and small fish.

Like sea turtles, pond sliders lay their eggs in terrestrial nests. During breeding season, typically late spring to early summer, females lay their eggs in sandy or soft soil near the water's edge. After several months, hatchlings break out of their shells and head toward water, where they begin their lives.

Where to See Them

Pond sliders are commonly found in ponds, lakes, and slow-moving creeks in the area. You'll usually see them soaking up the sun at Cherry Creek State Park and Rocky Mountain Arsenal National Wildlife Refuge (Trips 15 and 9).

Prairie Lizard

Sceloporus consobrinus

GRAY, BROWN, OR OLIVE-GREEN ◆ **DARK STRIPES AND SPOTS** ◆ **LONG TAIL** ◆ **LIGHT UNDERBELLY**

Prairie lizards sometimes shed their tails when confronted, a process known as autotomy. This allows them to escape predators while leaving the tail behind as a distraction.

Prairie lizards have a base color that ranges from grayish brown to olive-green with contrasting dark bands and spots. During mating season, a bright blue or turquoise throat patch becomes visible. The patches found on males are particularly vibrant and used for mating displays and establishing dominance. During breeding season, males will show off by doing push-ups and head-bobbing to demonstrate their fitness and attract potential mates.

The prairie lizard is a skilled hunter, feeding on ants, beetles, and other invertebrates. It's also known for its territorial nature, with males establishing and defending specific areas to attract females and deter rivals.

Prairie lizards are adept climbers often found perched on rocks or tree branches, which provide vantage points for spotting prey and potential predators. Their ability to climb is facilitated by their strong, elongated limbs and sharp claws. When threatened, prairie lizards rapidly dart into crevices or freeze, using their camouflage to blend into their surroundings and avoid confrontation altogether.

Where to See Them

Prairie lizards are commonly found in grasslands, open woodlands, and areas with scattered rocks or low vegetation. Look for them at North Table Mountain, Mount Falcon, and Waterton Canyon (Trips 17, 20, and 22).

Prairie Rattlesnake

Crotalus viridis

BROWN OR GRAY ◆ **DARK ROUNDED-DIAMOND SPOTS** ◆ **RATTLE AT TIP OF TAIL** ◆ **WIDE, FLAT HEAD**

Prairie rattlesnakes are viviparous, meaning they give birth to live young rather than laying eggs.

Chances are that you'll hear a prairie rattlesnake before you see it. If you do happen to see one, you'll recognize it immediately thanks to a distinctive rattling tail, which warns potential predators and humans alike to stay away.

Prairie rattlesnakes are well-adapted to grasslands and open woodlands that provide the snake with ample opportunities for hunting and basking. The snake's coloration, typically a blend of brown, tan, and gray with darker, irregular blotches, helps it blend seamlessly into its surroundings.

Prairie rattlesnakes are pit vipers. Heat-sensing pits between their eyes and nostrils allow the snakes to find prey even in complete darkness. The snake's venom is a complex mixture of enzymes and proteins that can immobilize prey and begin the digestion process before the snake consumes it. Rattlesnakes have a limited amount of venom, so they dry bite (without venom) about 25 percent of the time. They don't get to eat if they use venom on something that isn't prey.

What Makes a Rattle

Prairie rattlesnake rattles are made of interlocking segments of keratin, the same material found in human hair and nails. When vibrated, these segments produce a buzzing or rattling sound. The rattle's sound is an evolutionary adaptation designed to alert potential threats to the snake's presence, reducing the likelihood of an encounter escalating into a conflict.

Rattlesnake Rescue

Their venom is potent, but prairie rattlesnakes generally only strike when threatened or provoked. If a rattlesnake bites you, stay calm. When you're excited or scared, your heart pumps blood through your body faster, which spreads the venom. NEVER try to suck poison out of a wound. (That only works in movies and will only put you in danger in real life.) Instead, call 9-1-1 and carefully navigate back to your car. If your dog is bitten, call your nearest vet ahead of time to make sure they have antivenom stocked at that location.

Where to See Them

There are prairie rattlesnake dens at North Table Mountain (Trip 17), and they flock to the trails as soon as it's warm in spring and summer.

Six-lined Racerunner

Cnemidophorus sexlineatus

DARK, SLENDER BODY ◆ **LIGHT STRIPES FROM HEAD TO TAIL** ◆ **LONG, THIN TAIL**

The six-lined racerunner has been clocked running away at speeds of 18 mph.

Earning its name, the six-lined racerunner is known for its striking appearance and impressive speed. Six prominent, longitudinal stripes run down its back, alternating between light and dark colors. These stripes, usually a bright green or blue, provide excellent camouflage against the desert sands and rocky outcrops where the racerunner resides. The contrast between the stripes and the lizard's overall coloration not only aids in blending into its environment but also plays a role in communication and mating displays.

The six-lined racerunner's incredible speed is one of its primary defenses against predators. Its long, slender legs and lightweight body allow for rapid acceleration and maneuverability crucial for evading predators and capturing fast-moving prey like insects, spiders, and other small invertebrates. The lizard's keen eyesight and quick reflexes also aid in locating and capturing food, ensuring it can sustain its high metabolic rate.

Where to See Them

The six-lined racerunner prefers areas with sparse vegetation, sandy soils, and rocky outcrops that provide both basking sites and cover. Look around when you're west of the city, from the Lakewood area down to Littleton. They're all over Chatfield State Park (Trip 21), so take a pause on your hikes through their preferred ecosystems, and you'll probably spot one running past you.

Snapping Turtle

Chelydra serpentina

DARK BROWN OR OLIVE-GREEN ◆ ROUGH SCALES ◆ BEAK-LIKE JAWS ◆ THICK, POINTED TAIL

Snapping turtles are slow on land (topping out around 2 mph), but in the water, they can reach speeds of 12 mph.

Snapping turtles are one of the most well-adapted and resilient freshwater turtle species in America. They almost look like something from the prehistoric era, and for good reason; snapping turtles evolved with the dinosaurs during the late Cretaceous Period, 66 million years ago. They have a robust, heavily armored shell and powerful beak-like jaws. The carapace, or upper shell, is typically dark brown to olive in color, covered with rough, ridged scales that provide protection against predators. The plastron, or lower shell, is relatively small and less domed than other turtles', exposing more of the turtle's body. They're also huge—snapping turtles can grow up to 45 pounds.

The turtle's strong jaws and finely tuned sense of smell help in locating and capturing prey. As an omnivore, it feeds on aquatic plants, insects, fish, amphibians, and small mammals.

Oh Snap

One of the most striking characteristics of the snapping turtle is its powerful, sharp, and beak-like jaw. The snapping turtle can deliver a crushing bite strong enough to break through bone and shell, making it a formidable opponent for both predators and prey. (And an enemy to fingers and toes that find their way in front of its mouth!)

Despite its fearsome reputation, the snapping turtle is generally a solitary and reclusive creature, preferring to avoid confrontation. If avoiding said confrontation isn't possible, they won't back down and will quickly become aggressive. Snapping turtles have a distinctive defensive posture, with their long necks and powerful jaws poised to strike if approached. This aggressive behavior serves as a deterrent to potential predators and rivals.

Snapping turtles are excellent swimmers and pros at lurking motionless on the bottom of ponds, lakes, and slow-moving rivers. They use their long, flexible necks to catch prey and can remain submerged for extended periods, thanks to their slow metabolism. This ability to stay hidden and immobile helps them avoid detection by predators and conserve energy.

Where to See Them

There have been sightings of snapping turtles along Cherry Creek Trail, City Park, Chatfield State Park (Trips 4, 1, and 21), and even Confluence Park near downtown Denver.

Western Hognose Snake

Heterodon nasicus

BROWN, GRAY, AND TAN WITH PATTERNS ◆ UPTURNED, FLAT NOSE ◆ UP TO 30 INCHES

Western hognose snakes are sometimes kept as pets. It should go without saying, but never take home any wild snakes you see from the trails.

The western hognose snake is native to the Great Plains and stands out among North American snakes for one distinctive physical feature: an upturned snout. It resembles a hog's nose and serves as a useful tool for digging and foraging.

The diet of the western hognose snake primarily consists of amphibians. These snakes can even eat toxic toads and frogs thanks to their specialized jaw structure, which allows them to crush the toads' tough, poison-filled skin.

All for Show

The coloration of the western hognose snake varies greatly, from pale tan to dark brown, often with a pattern of blotches or spots that help it blend into its surroundings. This camouflage is crucial for avoiding predators, as the snake relies more on its defensive behaviors than speed or venom, like some other snakes.

When threatened, the western hognose snake bluffs before it bites. It'll flatten its neck, hiss loudly, and strike with its mouth closed to intimidate potential threats. If these measures are ineffective, the snake will roll onto its back, play dead, and even emit a foul-smelling musk from its cloacal glands to further deter predators. If you ignore these intimidating displays and do end up getting bitten, the western hognose snake is nonvenomous.

Where to See Them

The western hognose snake inhabits prairies and open woodlands. Near Denver, it is commonly found in sandy soils and grasslands where it can easily forage for its amphibian prey and seek shelter. Eldorado Canyon State Park (Trip 25) has a special exhibit featuring their resident hognose snake.

Western Painted Turtle

Chrysemys picta bellii

DARK GREEN OR BLACK • RED AND YELLOW STRIPES • LEG AND HEAD STRIPES

The top part of a turtle's shell is known as the carapace, and the underside is the plastron.

Colorado's state reptile, the western painted turtle, is a familiar sight in ponds, lakes, and slow-moving rivers in and around Denver. Their shells are typically dark green or black with bright red and yellow stripes running along the edges and duller, olive-colored undersides. The bright hues of the shell are especially prominent when the turtle basks in the sun, a behavior essential for keeping their body temperatures in check.

Western painted turtles are omnivorous, feeding on aquatic plants, insects, small fish, and even carrion. This dietary flexibility helps them thrive in diverse environments where food sources fluctuate.

Western painted turtles are well adapted to the seasonal changes in Denver. During colder months, they enter a state of brumation, a form of hibernation that allows them to survive periods of low temperature. They bury themselves in the mud at the bottom of their aquatic habitats, where cooler temperatures slow their metabolism and reduce their need for food.

Turtles are ectothermic, meaning they rely on external heat sources to regulate their body temperature. Basking on logs, rocks, or the banks of water bodies allows them to absorb sunlight, which is crucial for their metabolic processes and overall health. During these basking periods, the turtles often arrange themselves in groups, providing warmth and a social structure within their habitat.

Where to See Them

Western painted turtles prefer aquatic environments with ample basking sites and vegetation that provide both food and shelter. See if you can spot them basking at Crown Hill Park, Washington Park, Sloan's Lake, and Denver Botanic Gardens (Trips 11, 3, 6, and 2).

Western Tiger Salamander

Ambystoma tigrinum mavortium

FLATTENED HEAD ◆ SMOOTH, MOIST SKIN ◆ YELLOW OR GREEN STRIPES AND SPOTS ◆ EXTERNAL GILLS

The western tiger salamander became the official amphibian of Colorado in 2012, when a schoolteacher and students discovered that it lived in all of Colorado's counties and that fossil evidence showed it has lived in this area for more than 150,000 years.

The western tiger salamander is a member of the mole salamander family, distinguished by their preference for burrowing in moist environments and their black to dark brown bodies adorned with yellow or greenish yellow spots or bars. These markings give the salamander its "tiger" common name. Adult salamanders reach lengths of 6 to 8 inches.

The diet of the western tiger salamander is primarily carnivorous, consisting of various invertebrates such as insects, worms, and spiders. Its powerful jaws and sticky tongue enable it to capture and consume a wide range of prey.

A Change for the Tiger

During the western tiger salamander's larval stage, which occurs in aquatic environments before the salamander undergoes metamorphosis, the larvae, or tadpoles, are aquatic and have external gills they use to extract oxygen from the water. They are dark colored with lighter spots and have streamlined bodies adapted for swimming. As they mature, tadpoles undergo a dramatic transformation, losing their gills and developing lungs, which allows them to transition to a terrestrial lifestyle.

Adult western tiger salamanders spend much of their time underground in burrows that they dig or occupy from other animals. These burrows provide essential shelter from predators and harsh environmental conditions like extreme temperatures and dryness. During the breeding season, which generally occurs in spring, the salamander migrates to temporary ponds or vernal pools where it engages in breeding activities. These aquatic habitats are crucial for reproduction, as the eggs are laid in the water and hatch into larvae.

Where to See Them

Western tiger salamanders in the Denver area inhabit open grasslands and near temporary water sources. Look closely at the ponds and vernal pools in spring at Barr Lake and Chatfield State Parks (Trips 10 and 21).

Woodhouse's Toad

Anaxyrus woodhousii

WARTY SKIN ◆ **GRAY, BROWN, OR OLIVE IN COLOR** ◆ **DARK SPOTS**

This toad is named after Samuel Washington Woodhouse, a 19th-century surgeon and naturalist who explored the southwestern United States.

Woodhouse's toads are highly adaptable and can thrive in grasslands, scrublands, and urban areas. In the Denver area, these toads are commonly found in open spaces and parks where temporary water sources are available. They are known to use burrows or depressions in the soil to escape the heat and dryness of summer, often digging down several inches to reach cooler, moist conditions.

The breeding call of the male Woodhouse's toad is a distinctive, low-pitched trill that can be heard from a considerable distance. This call is used to attract females and establish breeding territories. Females lay eggs in shallow water, and the eggs quickly hatch into tadpoles that develop over several weeks. The tadpoles undergo a complete metamorphosis, transforming into adult toads.

Nighttime Toads

The Woodhouse's toad is active during evening hours, when it emerges from its burrow to forage for insects, spiders, and other small invertebrates. During the breeding season in spring and early summer, Woodhouse's toads migrate to temporary ponds or shallow water bodies where they engage in vocalizations and mating rituals.

Gland Defenses

Woodhouse's toads have large parotoid glands, which are located behind the eyes. These glands secrete a milky, toxic substance that can deter predators from consuming the toad. While the toxin is not lethal to humans, it irritates the skin and eyes.

Where to See Them

Woodhouse's toads are one of the most frequently sighted amphibians in Denver's open spaces, parks, and grasslands. Visit any lake or wetland area and wait quietly for a bit. You'll probably hear their calls.

American Kestrel

Falco sparverius

SPOTTED CHEST ◆ **BLUE-GRAY CAP** ◆ **VERTICAL BARS ON HEAD**

Kestrels don't build nests. Instead, they find nesting spots in tree cavities, old woodpecker holes, nest boxes, and abandoned buildings.

Small but colorful, the American kestrel is both more difficult and easier to spot than other falcons in the Denver area. It's a challenge because the bird is only around the size of a dove. These fierce hunters prey on insects like grasshoppers and beetles, small mammals, and other birds. They utilize a unique hunting method known as "hovering"—they can stay in one place in the air by flapping their wings rapidly while scanning the ground for prey.

ID'ing them is easy because of their coloring. Male kestrels have blue-gray wings with irregular black spots, blue-gray caps, and rust-colored back feathers with black tips. Females do a better job of blending in with their cream-colored chests and black-and-brown-striped back feathers, but they do have a small blue-gray area on their faces. If you see that blue hue, it's a kestrel.

Downsides of Development

While kestrels live all around the city, habitat loss due to urban development and expansion, as well as the use of herbicides and pesticides, are big threats. Since their diet consists primarily of insects, chemicals to treat pests can have accidental negative impacts on the birds who rely on them for food. Loss of natural spaces to build nests or deterrents like spikes

on artificial structures also pose a threat to future generations of kestrels.

Where to See Them

You can spot kestrels all over the city, but they tend to hang around areas where they have access to green space so that they can easily find food. Look at the tops of light posts as you drive around or on fence posts during a hike, especially in the state and county parks and wildlife refuges. Look for the flashes of blue-gray at Rocky Mountain Arsenal National Wildlife Refuge, Cherry Creek State Park, Belmar Park, and Crown Hill Park (Trips 9, 15, 12, and 11).

American White Pelican

Pelecanus erythrorhynchos

WHITE BODY ◆ **BLACK BARS UNDERNEATH WINGS** ◆ **BIG ORANGE-YELLOW BEAK WITH NECK FLAP GROWTHS ON TOP OF BEAK**

It's a common misconception that pelicans carry food in their bill pouches. They do use them to scoop up food, but they swallow its contents before taking off.

If you're hiking by a body of water and see groups of big white blobs hanging out on the shoreline, you're looking at American white pelicans. During spring and fall, you'll spot them flying high above the outskirts of the city as they make their way to and from their waterfront homes for summer.

One of the largest birds in the United States, the American white pelican can easily be spotted as it soars with incredible steadiness on broad, white wings with black edges. On the water, they're often seen dipping their huge yellow pouched bills under the surface to scoop up fish.

On their wintering grounds, American white pelicans forage almost exclusively during the day, but during the breeding season, they'll forage at night, often finding bigger and better fish.

Stay Cool

To regulate their body temperature in the harsh Colorado heat, pelicans face away from the sun and rapidly flutter their bill pouches. These pouches are rich in blood vessels, and moving them this way effectively dissipates excess heat.

Buddy Birds

American white pelicans and double-crested cormorants are often found nesting and foraging together. Though they mainly hunt different fish at different depths, sometimes large groups will work together to corral fish at the shallow edges where pelicans can then easily scoop them up in their pouches. As highly social creatures, pelicans form large colonies during breeding season. This communal lifestyle, however, has a competitive edge. Pelicans are notorious for stealing food from each other, often targeting those struggling to swallow large fish.

Where to See Them

American white pelicans are found at lakes and marshes, primarily nesting on isolated islands like the one at Duck Lake in City Park (Trip 1) and foraging in shallow lakes and near shores at Chatfield State Park and Sloan's Lake (Trips 21 and 6).

Bald Eagle

Haliaeetus leucocephalus

WHITE TAIL ◆ BRIGHT YELLOW BEAK

Benjamin Franklin wasn't a fan of the bald eagle being our national bird, preferring the turkey instead. In 1784, Franklin wrote, "For my own part, I wish the Bald Eagle had not been chosen the Representative of our Country. He is a Bird of bad moral Character." He continued, "Besides he is a rank Coward: The little King Bird not bigger than a Sparrow attacks him boldly and drives him out of the District."

The bald eagle, an iconic emblem of the United States, is a common sight in Colorado. Despite its name, these birds boast striking white feathered heads that contrast dramatically against their dark brown bodies. Bald eagles are often seen soaring on thermal currents at open green spaces, particularly those with a large body of water. They can be spotted snatching fish right out of the water, but they are also opportunistic feeders, often relying on the skill of other predators. A common tactic is to harass other fish-eating birds, forcing them to relinquish their catch. Fish make up the majority of the bald eagle diet, but these birds eat a wide variety of foods depending on what's available, including other birds, reptiles, amphibians, and mammals.

Bald eagles nest in trees near the trunk, high up in the tree but below the crown. Their nests are some of the largest of all bird nests—typically 2 to 4 feet tall and 5 to 6 feet in diameter. You'll often spot the nest before you see the birds.

Protected Status

Once on the brink of extinction due to pesticide use and habitat loss, the bald eagle is no longer endangered thanks to nationwide conservation efforts. Eagles are directly protected under two federal laws: the Bald and Golden Eagle Protection Act and the Migratory

Bird Treaty Act. Under these laws, it is illegal to possess, use, or sell any living eagles, their eggs, body parts, or nests—with one exception. The National Eagle Repository in Denver is operated and managed by the U.S. Fish and Wildlife Service office of law enforcement. They receive, evaluate, store, and distribute deceased golden and bald eagles, parts, and feathers for cultural purposes to Indigenous Americans who are enrolled members of federally recognized tribes throughout the United States.

Where to See Them

Bald eagles are easiest to find in winter, hunting or perching near lakes and reservoirs at Rocky Mountain Arsenal National Wildlife Refuge, Cherry Creek State Park, and Chatfield State Park (Trips 9, 15, and 21).

Black-billed Magpie

Pica hudsonia

BLUE IRIDESCENT WINGS • WHITE BLOCK ON BODY • 2 WHITE STRIPES ON WINGS • BLACK HEAD

There's a common superstition that it's bad luck to see a magpie alone. As one old rhyme goes: "One for sorrow, two for joy, three for a girl, four for a boy, five for silver, six for gold, seven for secrets to never be told."

With green-and-blue glossy feathers, long tails, and striking white wing patches, black-billed magpies stand out in Denver. You'll see them at almost any park with trees or places for them to perch. If you don't see them, you'll hear them. They're very vocal and keep up a regular stream of raucous calls.

True Opportunists

Black-billed magpie diets are pretty varied, and they've even been known to farm insects for future meals (scientists aren't sure if it's intentionally or accidentally). They pick ticks from the backs of elks, moose, and deer, sometimes

keeping them alive and saving them for later. If they don't eat them, the ticks will mate, which increases their food supply.

Magpies eat insects like grasshoppers, caterpillars, flies, and beetles, plus rodents, eggs, and young of other birds, small snakes, and carrion. In winter, they switch to a more plant-based diet that includes berries, seeds, and nuts. Magpies will steal food from other birds and follow predators like foxes and coyotes to pick up scraps they leave.

A Reputation to Remember

Historical records show that black-billed magpies have lived in community with people for a long time. They frequently followed hunting parties of Indigenous Plains tribes and fed on leftovers from bison kills. Lewis and Clark even recorded instances of magpies entering their tents to steal food.

One of the most notable magpie behaviors is how they mourn. When one magpie discovers a dead magpie, it calls loudly to attract others. The gatherings (up to 40 birds have been observed) sometimes last up to 15 minutes before the birds fly away silently.

Where to See Them

Black-billed magpies are found in forests, parks, yards, and spaces with good vantage points like fence posts and treetops. Try to spot their flashy feathers at Crown Hill Park, Berkeley Lake Park, Sloan's Lake, and Washington Park (Trips 11, 7, 6, and 3).

Black-capped Chickadee

Poecile atricapillus

BLACK CAP AND BIB ◆ **LIGHT BEIGE BODY** ◆ **TINY BODY**

Chickadee calls are complex and serve as a way to communicate about other flocks, predators, and other important information. The more "dee" notes in their "chickadee-dee-dee" call, the higher the threat level.

Black-capped chickadees are curious, and their habit of investigating people, bird feeders, and everything else in their territories make them one of the first birds people learn by name.

While the feeder is one of their favorite spots, more than half of their diet consists of insects, spiders, caterpillars, and larvae. They'll occasionally chow down on dead deer, skunks, fish, and berries.

Black-capped chickadees are loud little birds. Adults can make as many as sixteen calls, each one with a distinctly different meaning. They sing more in spring than in any other time of year.

Memory Makers

Black-capped chickadees can remember thousands of hiding places, storing up to 1000 seeds a day or 80,000 seeds a season each fall. To keep track of all these seeds, they replace neurons in their brains, overwriting old locations with new ones. Each bird's hippocampus—the part of the brain responsible for spatial memory—shrinks in spring when food is easily found and grows again when it's time to start stashing for winter.

Where to See Them

Chickadees thrive in backyards, but they can also be spotted in forests and thickets in parks like Bluff Lake Nature Center, Mount Galbraith, Roxborough State Park, and Mount Falcon (Trips 8, 18, 23, and 20).

Broad-tailed Hummingbird

Selasphorus platycercus

NARROW BEAK ◆ **SPECKLED THROAT ON FEMALES** ◆ **IRIDESCENT RUBY THROAT ON ADULT MALES**
SHIMMERY GREEN FEATHERS

The oldest broad-tailed hummingbird on record lived to be 12 years and 2 months old. She was first banded in Colorado in 1976 and was captured again and released in 1987.

The trill of the broad-tailed hummingbird can be heard in the city, at neighborhood parks, in the suburbs, and from trails in the mountains near Denver. These tiny birds will often flit and dart around high above you, occasionally diving to get nectar deep from within flowers and feeders found in yards and mountain meadows and forests. Hummingbirds also eat small insects, often grabbing them mid-air or hovering over plants to pluck them from the foliage. They've even been seen picking spiders or trapped insects from spiderwebs.

Like most hummers, broad-tailed humming-birds have a slender body, a big head, and a long pointy bill. Males have green feathers on their backs, white feathers on their chests, and stomachs with an iridescent, rosy red gorget (a patch under their throat). Females are also green and white but have rust-colored sides and bases of their tails, a white eye-ring, and long rectrices (large tail feathers used in flight) that make their tails look longer and broader when fanned, hence their name.

Sounds of Summer

You'll often hear broad-tailed hummingbirds before you spot them (they can be heard from 100 yards away), but their distinctive sound isn't a chirp or call made with their mouth; it's made by quickly moving flight feathers at the tips of male hummingbirds' wings slicing through the air. By fall, the feathers have worn down, making the birds much harder to hear until the next breeding season when they regrow.

Small but Mighty

Hummingbirds might be tiny, but they're well known for diving and being aggressive toward other hummingbirds, curious animals, and occasionally people who come too close to their feeder or natural food source. Males will also defend their territories by perching in high spots with good vantage points and chasing any intruders that come too close to their boundaries.

Where to See Them

Broad-tailed hummingbirds typically arrive in the Denver area in May and hang around until August, following the wildflowers as they bloom. See them and several other hummingbird species at the Eldorado Canyon State Park visitor-center bird feeder and at Denver Botanic Gardens, Mount Falcon, Golden Gate Canyon State Park (Trips 25, 2, 20, and 24).

Common Grackle

Quiscalus quiscula

LONG TAIL • IRIDESCENT TEAL AND PURPLE HEAD • GLOSSY BLACK BODY • YELLOW EYES

The common grackle is a member of the Icteridae family. Birds in this family use the Earth's geomagnetic fields to navigate.

The common grackle's glossy black plumage, long tail, and sharp bill make it a distinctive figure in city and natural landscapes, often perceived as a pest due to its aggressive behavior and opportunistic feeding habits.

Grackles are omnivorous and take advantage of almost any food source available, including insects, fish, frogs, eggs, berries, seeds, and even trash. These birds are adept at exploiting human-altered environments,

thriving in suburban and urban areas where they find abundant food resources. Their ability to adapt to changing conditions has allowed them to expand their range and increase their population numbers.

Stronger in Numbers

Grackles are highly social birds and form large flocks that can number in the hundreds or even thousands. These flocks provide safety, with individuals taking turns scanning for predators while others forage. They migrate, winter, and roost in these flocks, often mixed with other species, including European starlings and red-winged blackbirds.

Anting and Other Defenses

Common grackles are big fans of "anting." They lie on the ground near an ant nest, and as the ants crawl over them, they secrete formic acid on the bird's feathers, which repels lice and other parasites that commonly infest bird plumage. They've also been seen utilizing things like pieces of lemons, chokecherry juice, and marigold flowers for their insect-repellent qualities.

Where to See Them

Grackles are found in urban parks, prairies, and mountains, so look for big flocks of dark birds at Berkeley Lake Park, Belmar Park, and Crown Hill Park (Trips 7, 12, and 11).

Crow

Corvus brachyrhynchos

GLOSSY BLACK FEATHERS ♦ BLACK EYES ♦ STOUT, BLACK BILL

Don't mess with crows or make them angry. Not only will they remember your face, but they'll also pass along the grudge to their friends and children.

Crows are one of the most enigmatic and intelligent birds in the avian world. Their problem-solving abilities and utilization of tools, like using sticks to extract insects from

tree bark, have made them highly adaptable to human environments.

Crows are opportunistic and omnivorous, feeding on a wide range of food items, including insects, small animals, fruits, seeds, carrion, and garbage. Their scavenging behavior is particularly notable in urban areas, where they often forage for discarded food in parks and streets.

Raven Relatives

Crows are different from ravens (*Corvus corax*). Though they share many similarities and are often confused for one another, these members of the Corvidae family have distinct characteristics that set them apart. One of the most noticeable differences is their size and physical appearance. Ravens are generally larger than crows—adult ravens have wingspans of up to 4 feet, while crows have a wingspan of about 2.5 feet. Ravens also have a more robust and thicker bill than the slender, pointed bill of crows.

The plumage of both birds is black, but ravens have shaggy throat feathers and a more distinct wedge-shaped tail when in flight. Crows, on the other hand, have a more fan-shaped tail and less pronounced throat feathers. Additionally, ravens produce a deeper, more resonant call, often described as a croak, while crows have the familiar high-pitched "*caw*" call.

Where to See Them

American crows are highly adaptable and can be found everywhere in and around Denver, including urban parks, suburban neighborhoods, and open forests and grasslands.

Double-crested Cormorant

Nannopterum auritum

LONG NECK ◆ TURQUOISE EYES ◆ BLACK BODY

A flock of cormorants is called a gulp.

The double-crested cormorant is a distinctive waterbird, easily recognizable by its dark plumage, long neck, and hooked bill. While often seen perched on pilings or rocky outcrops with wings outstretched, these birds are truly in their element when submerged beneath the water's surface.

Cormorants are social creatures, often forming large colonies. Their nests, constructed from sticks and debris, are typically located in trees near large lakes around the city, and their nesting habits can have unintended consequences. The accumulation of droppings can damage or kill the supporting trees, forcing the colony to relocate.

A cormorant's diet is made up of almost all fish (they eat more than 250 different species). They're great at catching them—they dive and

chase fish using their webbed feet for speed and accuracy, and then they use the tip of their upper bill, which is shaped like a hook, to catch their prey.

Deep Dive

Unlike most birds, cormorant feathers are permeable to water, allowing them to become quickly waterlogged. By increasing their buoyancy, waterlogged feathers help propel the cormorant through the water more efficiently. Coupled with their dense, heavy bones, cormorants are streamlined underwater predators.

The price for this aquatic specialization is the challenge of flight takeoff. Cormorants often have to run along the water's surface to build up sufficient momentum before they can become airborne.

Where to See Them

Look near lakes and coastlines at Bear Creek Greenbelt Park, City Park, Sloan's Lake, and Waterton Canyon (Trips 13, 1, 6, and 22).

Downy Woodpecker

Dryobates pubescens

RED SPOT ON BACK OF HEAD OF MALES • POLKA DOTS IN STRIPES ON WINGS

STRIPED BLACK- AND-WHITE HEAD

The downy woodpecker is the smallest woodpecker in North America.

Downy woodpeckers are familiar faces in backyards, parks, and forests in the foothills, where they frequently join flocks of chickadees, nuthatches, and other small birds. They exhibit remarkable agility, effortlessly scaling tree trunks, clinging to slender branches, and even hanging upside down in pursuit of insects. This resourceful little woodpecker has also been known to follow nuthatches to their seed storage to swipe food.

Downy woodpeckers have soft, white feathers that contrast sharply with black plumage. Males have a red spot on their napes (back of neck). This striking pattern and its small size make it readily distinguishable from other woodpecker species commonly spotted around the city.

Just the Right Size

While primarily insectivorous, the downy woodpecker also consumes berries, acorns, and seeds, often eating food that larger woodpeckers can't reach. An acrobatic forager, this black-and-white woodpecker can balance on slender twigs to access plant galls, backyard feeders, and sycamore seed balls.

By excavating bark and drilling into trees, they prey on insects like beetle larvae, ants, and caterpillars. Their preference for drilling into dead or dying trees contributes to forest health by creating cavities that can be used by other wildlife.

Where to See Them

Downy woodpeckers are found in various habitats, including parks, yards, and forested areas from fall through early spring. They generally favor deciduous trees, so keep your eyes peeled at Fairmount Cemetery, Belmar Park, Washington Park, Lookout Mountain, and Golden Gate Canyon State Park (Trips 5, 12, 3, 16, and 24).

BIRDS

Great Horned Owl

Bubo virginianus

EAR TUFTS ◆ HORIZONTAL STRIPES ON BELLY ◆ WHITE PATCH ON THROAT

Great horned owls are the largest of the "tufted" owls in North America. Their ear tufts are feather arrangements called plumicorns that don't help with hearing but can be flattened or extended depending on the mood of the owl.

Great horned owls are one of the most commonly seen types of owl in the country, found in grasslands, deserts, forests, backyards, and the urban environment of Denver. With jarring yellow eyes and tall tufts, the great horned owl is a sight to behold. It's fearless and will hunt birds and mammals larger than itself like falcons, hawks, eagles, and other owls. It also dines on smaller prey like insects, mice, and frogs.

Eye See (and Hear) You

The eyes of great horned owls have pupils that open widely in the dark and retinas with numerous rod cells for excellent night vision. There aren't muscle attachments in the eyes, so they can't move around in their sockets. Instead, these massive birds can swivel their heads up to 270 degrees to look in any direction. Great horned owls have the largest eyes of all owl species, and their vision is ten times better than that of humans in daylight and 100 times better at night. Their hearing is also impeccable because of special facial feathers that direct sound waves to their ears.

Birds Built for Hunting

Great horned owl feathers are great for insulation and keep them warm in winter while they pursue prey. Their short, broad wings allow them to easily maneuver between branches among the forest's trees.

They are primarily nocturnal and hunt mostly at night, occasionally striking out at dusk. If they're raising young, they've been known to hunt during the day. These owls will find a perch to watch from, look and listen for any movement in the underbrush below, and swoop down to capture any prey they spot.

Terrifying fact: when great horned owl talons are clenched, they require 28 pounds of pressure to open. They use this intense grip strength to sever the spines of the larger animals they take down.

Protected Birds

Great horned owls are protected through the federal Migratory Bird Treaty Act of 1918. This Act states that it is illegal to pursue, hunt, take, capture, or kill; attempt to take, capture, or kill; or possess any migratory bird or part of a migratory bird. Violators face hefty fines and jail time.

Where to See Them

Look up when passing eastern cottonwood stands at Rocky Mountain Arsenal National Wildlife Refuge, Chatfield State Park, Belmar Park, Bluff Lake Nature Center, and the High Line Canal (Trips 9, 21, 12, 8, and 14).

House Wren

Troglodytes aedon

LONG NARROW BEAK ◆ BROWN-AND-WHITE BODY ◆ STRIPED WINGS

Wrens add spider egg sacs to their nests. The spiders that hatch help control mites and other nest parasites in a great symbiotic relationship.

This small songbird is often seen darting around in brush close to the ground with its tail held upright. Blending in with its surroundings, house wrens are brown with light-sided underbellies. They have dark bars on their tails, wings, and side bodies, and their thin, slightly curved bills and flattened heads help them reach insects deep in the bark, twigs, and fallen leaves found low or at ground level. While their diet is primarily insects that reside in the underbrush—including beetles, grasshoppers, crickets, caterpillars, moths, and flies—they also consume spiders, millipedes, and snails.

House wrens have chaotic calls. It can be hard to identify them at first because the notes are all over the place, and because it's so loud and insistent, it can be hard to believe such a small bird is making it.

A Wren for Every House

The house wren has one of the largest ranges of any songbird in the United States. A familiar backyard bird, it got its name because it can often be found nesting around homes. Wrens build their nests in crevices in buildings, nest boxes, or tree openings, sometimes taking over the nests of other cavity nesters in their area.

Where to See Them

Wrens are commonly found in yards, parks, forests, and thickets throughout the city and on some nearby hikes. Look (or better yet, listen) for these birds at Fairmount Cemetery, Cherry Creek Trail, Mount Galbraith, and Denver Botanic Gardens (Trips 5, 4, 18, and 2).

Lark Bunting

Calamospiza melanocorys

MALE: BLACK BODY WITH WHITE WING PATCH ON MALES IN SUMMER • BIG TRIANGULAR BILL
FEMALE: BROWN-AND-WHITE SPECKLED FEATHERS ON FEMALES • PALE WING PATCH • SHORT BROAD BEAK

The lark bunting is one of only six passerines (four-toed perching birds) endemic to the Great Plains of North America. Endemic species are plants and animals that are native to a specific geographical area and not found anywhere else in the world.

If you go on a prairie hike in early summer, the adult male lark bunting will stand out immediately. Between its striking coloring and impressive flight song and dance, it's a hard bird to miss. Even in winter, when the males' colors become more muted to match females and immature birds, the massive size of the flocks will still be noticeable. (The flock probably has other seed-eating birds in the group, though, like quail and other sparrows.)

Summer Suits

In winter, all lark buntings blend in with their habitat—brown, cream, and white feathers flashing as they dart between patches of grass. Adult males are unmistakable during summer. Their breeding plumage gives them velvety black bodies with contrasting white wing patches. Their aerial shows are one of the first signs of summer.

This Is My Flight Song

Lark buntings sing from a perch or in a flight display, and unlike many other birds, they have two distinctly different flight songs. In courtship, males will quickly fly up to 30 feet above the ground before gently gliding back down with outstretched wings while singing for potential partners. The other flight song, with its sharp, low notes and whistles, is meant to send a clear message to rival males to back off.

Despite the name, lark buntings are not actually related to lark species of birds. Their flight song is similar to Eurasian lark species, which is where they got their common name.

Male

Staying Power

These birds are extremely resilient and have survived incredibly tough periods of drought throughout history. In fact, during the Dust Bowl era, their populations increased. The secret lies in their diets. Lark buntings can survive periods of time without drinking water, instead getting water from beetles, bees, ants, and grasshoppers—their primary food source during summer. During winter, their diet shifts to seeds, particularly those of native grasses and drought-tolerant plants.

Where to See Them

Lark buntings are the easiest to spot in large expanses of grassland habitats during summer months. Take a visit to Rocky Mountain Arsenal Wildlife Refuge, Cherry Creek State Park, and Chatfield State Park (Trips 9, 15, and 21) and keep an eye open for males searching for their mates.

Northern Flicker

Colaptes auratus

RED WHISKER PATCH ◆ POLKA-DOT CHEST ◆ BLACK TAIL FEATHERS

The bird has a unique coloration that can make them eye-catching for humans while providing camouflage for them from other animals.

Northern flickers don't seem like woodpeckers at first glance. They hop around on the ground, and their coloration is unusual. Flickers flash bright red spots with black and white polka dots and bars on their wings when they fly.

Their primary food is ants, and they'll hammer at the soil the way other woodpeckers drill into wood. They use their long, barbed tongues to lap up the ants, along with any beetles, termites, caterpillars, and other insects they disturb. They'll also munch on berries and seeds in winter.

Flickers nest in cavities and excavate their own holes in dead or dying trees, but they won't turn down an empty existing cavity. While most woodpeckers choose new nesting cavities each year, flickers often don't. If you've seen flickers in a place in previous years, they'll probably be back.

Where to See Them

Northern flickers are frequently found in residential yards, but they do like to get away from the city to nest in quieter forests and their edges. Look at the ground at Rocky Mountain Arsenal Wildlife Refuge, Cherry Creek Trail, and Waterton Canyon (Trips 9, 4, and 22).

Red-tailed Hawk

Buteo jamaicensis

SPECKLED REDDISH AND WHITE FEATHERS

BROAD WINGS • BROWN HEADS

REDDISH BROWN TAIL WITH WHITE UNDERSIDE

Whenever a bald eagle appears onscreen in television or movies, the shrill screech you hear is almost always a red-tailed hawk.

Often spotted perched on roadside poles in Denver suburbs or gliding over green spaces and forests before swooping down to snag their prey, red-tailed hawks are the most common large hawk in the country. The birds are widespread in habitat but also physicality—their wingspans can reach up to 5 feet. The coloring of their feathers can vary slightly, but they have a distinctive reddish brown tail with a white underside that is visible in flight. Their bodies can be pale gray to dark brown, but they'll all have a contrasting white chest and a dark belly band. ID tip: look for the buteo shape (broad, rounded wings; short tail) and check for dark bars on the edge of the wing.

Adventurous Eaters

Red-tailed hawks are adaptable birds found in a variety of habitats, from open grassland to dense forest. They are skilled hunters and use their incredible eyesight to spot the movement of prey from high perches. The main things on their menus are small mammals like mice, rabbits, and squirrels. They also eat other birds, snakes, and frogs, and in a pinch, they'll eat insects and carrion.

Teamwork Makes the Dream Work

Red-tailed hawks are monogamous birds, forming pairs that mate for life. They build large nests in trees using sticks and other materials. Females lay two to four eggs at a time, which both parents incubate. They've even been seen hunting as pairs, guarding opposite sides of trees, trapping unlucky squirrels as they try to flee.

Where to See Them

If you've got sharp eyes, you'll probably spot them on your way to any of the Field Trips in this guide. In the wild, they're found in open grasslands, woodlands, and mountains.

Red-winged Blackbird

Agelaius phoeniceus

RED-AND-YELLOW PATCH ON WINGS • SHARP BEAK • BLACK BODY

The red-winged blackbird is a polygynous species—males often have many mates.

Named after the red epaulets (patches) on the males' shoulders, which are visible when they're resting, red-winged blackbirds are found in marshes, meadows, prairies, and fields near ponds. Seeds make up 75 percent of their diet, but they'll also eat small fruits, grains, insects, spiders, and carrion during the breeding season.

Seeing Red

Male red-winged blackbirds are very territorial and can be aggressive. Get too close to their boundaries and be prepared to be chased away. While small in stature, this brazen bird has been known to attack anyone it feels is an intruder, even much larger animals such as great blue herons, raptors, crows, and humans. To defend their territories and attract a mate, males will perch on high stalks with their feathers fluffed out, tails partly spread, and red shoulder patches prominent, belting it out for all to hear.

Marsh Mavens

Where there's standing water and vegetation, there will be red-winged blackbirds. Listen for the male's distinctive *"conk-la-lee!"*

song. Though a bit harder to identify, female red-winged blackbirds resemble large sparrows, with various shades of brown-streaked feathers that are also creamy white throughout the body. They primarily nest in cattails, bulrushes, bushes, or saplings close to the water's edge.

Community Focused

Despite being so aggressive, red-winged blackbirds roost in large flocks year-round. In summer, smaller groups can be found in the marshy habitats where the birds breed. During winter, flocks can be congregations of several thousand birds and include other blackbird species, grackles, cowbirds, and starlings.

Where to See Them

Red-winged blackbirds can always be found in marshy areas and wetlands. You'll see them sitting at the tops of cattails at Crown Hill Park, Bear Creek Greenbelt Park, City Park, and Chatfield State Park (Trips 11, 13, 1, and 21).

Robin

Turdus migratorius

RUST-COLORED CHEST ◆ BLACK HEADS ◆ WHITE PATCH

A common myth is that robins can hear worms moving underground, but that isn't true. They locate them by sight.

The robin's rousing call is one of the first heard in spring and summer. They might be considered harbingers of spring, but many robins spend their winters in their breeding range or only a few miles away. They spend more time roosting in trees and less time in yards, making it less likely to see them, adding to the misconception that they arrive in spring.

Not Just the Worm

Robins eat different types of food depending on the time of day: earthworms, insects, spiders, and other invertebrates in the morning and berries later in the day. They tend to eat more insects in early summer but feed heavily on fruit in winter. (Fruit makes up 60 percent of their diet year-round.) Because robins get their worms from manicured lawns and parks, they're vulnerable to pesticide poisoning. The lack of robins in a place where they were once commonly found can be an important indicator of chemical pollution.

Robin's Egg Blue

Robins raise two to three broods per season, with each clutch containing three to five light blue eggs. The enchanting robin's egg blue color is caused by a pigment called biliverdin. This compound, a byproduct of the breakdown of red blood cells, is responsible for the bluish tint. While there isn't a total consensus about why the eggs are blue, a few popular guesses from scientists are that the blue color helps to protect the developing embryo from harmful ultraviolet rays while allowing enough light for vitamin D production, or that the color blue provides a balance between absorbing and reflecting heat, helping to maintain a suitable temperature for the eggs.

Where to See Them

American robins are familiar sights on Denver lawns, often spotted tugging earthworms out of the ground, but they call wilder areas home, too. During winter, look at the top branches of berry-bearing trees at Bear Creek Greenbelt Park, Denver Botanic Gardens, High Line Canal, and Fairmount Cemetery (Trips 13, 2, 14, and 5).

Spotted Towhee

Pipilo maculatus

RED EYES ◆ RUST-COLORED PATCH UNDER WING

STRIPED BLACK-AND-WHITE WING ◆ BLACK HEAD

When disturbed, the female spotted towhee runs from her nest instead of flying away, which makes these birds easy targets for outdoor cats.

If you hear a mysterious scratching coming from the underbrush in your yard or on a hike in the foothills, fret not. It's probably just a spotted towhee. This captivating bird is renowned for its distinctive appearance and foraging behavior. Its preference for ground dwelling, its striking combination of black, white, and reddish plumage, and its telltale red eyes make it a relatively easy species to identify for even novice birdwatchers.

Hop, Skip, and a Jump

A ground-oriented species, the spotted towhee spends much of its time scratching through leaf litter in search of insects, seeds, and other invertebrates. Its unique foraging technique, involving a distinctive backward hop and a raking motion with both feet, is a hallmark of the species. This behavior, combined with its preference for dense cover, can make the spotted towhee challenging to observe directly but easy to be alerted to.

While the spotted towhee is primarily a ground-dweller, it can also climb through shrubs and low trees, allowing it to access a wider range of food resources. During the breeding season, insects form a significant portion of their diet, while seeds and berries become increasingly important when winter arrives.

Where to See Them

Spotted towhees can be found in forests, thickets, overgrown fields, and backyards. Listen for their rustling at North Table Mountain, Washington Park, Red Rocks Park, and Roxborough State Park (Trips 17, 3, 19, and 23).

Steller's Jay

Cyanocitta stelleri

GRAY-AND-BLUE OMBRE HEAD ◆ PEAK OF FEATHERS ATOP HEAD ◆ BLUE-GRAY BODY ◆ WHITE EYEBROWS

Steller's and blue jays are the only North American jays with crests. The two occasionally interbreed and produce hybrid birds.

A large, dark jay usually seen in evergreen forests at elevations up to 10,000 feet, Steller's jay can also be found in mountain backyards with bird feeders. The Steller's jay's dark colors blend well in the shadows and they tend to stay hidden, but you'll hear their brash calls if they're nearby.

These birds are opportunists and forage high in trees and low or on the ground. During summer, they'll eat berries and wild fruits, beetles, wasps, bees, spiders, bird eggs, small rodents, lizards, and sometimes table scraps. In winter, they feed heavily on pine seeds, acorns, and other nuts and seeds, using their bills as mallets to crack open any particularly tough ones.

Copycats

Steller's jays are excellent mimics. They can imitate cats, dogs, birds, squirrels, and even mechanical objects. Jays have been known to imitate hawk calls during the early breeding season when other jays crossed into their territories while their mates were present.

What's in a Name

While they are sometimes referred to as "stellar jays," this is incorrect. Steller's jays were first recorded on an Alaskan island in 1741 by naturalist Georg Steller. When scientists officially recognized the species, they named the bird after him.

Where to See Them

Steller's jays are frequently found in higher-elevation evergreen forests. Look at the branches of the pines at high-elevation trips east of the city like Eldorado Canyon State Park, Red Rocks Park, Mount Falcon, and Lookout Mountain (Trips 25, 19, 20, and 16).

Turkey Vulture

Cathartes aura

RED BALD HEAD ◆ BIG BROWN BODY

Buzzard is a colloquial term for vulture in the United States.

Distinguished by a shallow V-shaped wing posture, black wing linings contrasting against gray flight feathers, and a wobbly flight pattern as it soars in circles, the turkey vulture is a familiar sight in Colorado skies, especially when death is nearby.

Turkey vultures ride thermals in the sky, using their finely tuned sense of smell to find fresh carcasses to consume. The bald, red heads of adults (juveniles have gray heads) might look like the opposite of what you'd expect a bird to sport, but the lack of feathers helps keep cleanup to a minimum when they're chowing down on roadkill and other animals that have met their ends. The vulture's heightened sense of smell combined with the ability to digest diseased carcasses makes it a crucial element of our ecosystem. By consuming decaying matter quickly, turkey vultures prevent the spread of disease and help maintain a delicate ecological balance.

Smell Ya Immediately

Vultures are solely scavengers—their talons are too weak to catch and hold live prey. Instead, they rely on their keen sense of smell to hone in on the scent of carrion (the decaying flesh of dead animals). Their odor detection is so skilled that they can pinpoint carrion under tree canopies without seeing it. Once they find what they've been smelling, they use their sharply hooked bills to rip apart the flesh and their bald heads to get deep into what they're eating.

Flying Garbage Disposals

The stomach of turkey vultures is highly acidic, making it easy for them to digest almost anything (even anthrax, tuberculosis, and rabies) without getting sick. While it might seem gross to survive on the rotting corpses of other animals, by doing so the turkey vulture indirectly protects other creatures in our ecosystem.

Important, But Still Gross

Rotting flesh aside, turkey vultures do have some pretty nasty habits. As a defense mechanism, they may vomit on a bird, animal, or human that gets too close for comfort. Considering their decomp-heavy diets and proportionately strong stomach acid, it's an effective deterrent.

They also maintain their body temperatures in a uniquely vulture way. When it's hot outside, they defecate on their feet to cool off.

Where to See Them

Turkey vultures can be found along the sides of highways or soaring in wobbly circles above forests and grasslands. It's possible to spot them at any Field Trip in this book, but keep your eyes on the sky at Mount Falcon, Roxborough State Park, and North Table Mountain (Trips 20, 23, and 17).

American Bison

Bison bison

CURVED HORNS • STOCKY HEAD • BROWN FUR • LARGE HUMP ON BACK

Though "bison" and "buffalo" are often used interchangeably, they are two different species. Bison are native to North America and Europe, while buffalo are native to Africa and Asia. The two have many differences, including fur thickness, overall size, and head shape and size. Bison also have humps, while buffalo do not.

The American bison, sometimes referred to as buffalo, is a well-known symbol of the American West. Once numbering in the tens of millions, these majestic creatures roamed the country in vast, nomadic herds. Indigenous peoples of the Great Plains, where bison were most abundant, have deep, cultural connections with them.

During the 19th century, European settlers pushed into the Great Plains, and bison were systematically driven to the brink of extinction. By 1889, only a few hundred wild bison remained. Today, they can be found in managed and maintained populations.

Great for Grasslands

The way that bison live is highly beneficial to healthy grassland habitats. As they walk, their hooves stir up the soil to help bury seeds, while their weight pushes nutrients deep down in the soil. (Males can weigh up to 2000 pounds, females 1000 pounds.) As they walk, their hoofprints create mini microclimates for new plants to grow. When they roll around in the dirt

for their baths, the wallows they create become larger watering holes after rains that help support both plant and animal life. Their fur is soft, and when they shed, grassland-nesting birds quickly snag it for nesting material.

Happy Hump Day

The bison's massive shoulder humps have an interesting use. In winter, they swing their heads from side to side and the humps help to clear snow, which allows them to keep foraging even when everything is covered in powder.

Where to See Them

There are two publicly accessible places to see bison up close near Denver. The first is off US-70 at exit 254. This herd is managed by the City of Denver and has members that are direct descendants from the last wild herd in the country. The other is at Rocky Mountain Arsenal National Wildlife Refuge (Trip 9). You can drive through their 10,300-acre enclosure for a chance to see them from your vehicle on the 11-mile Wildlife Drive. During the drive, DO NOT get out of your car, roll down your window, or attempt to interact with bison in any way. It's dangerous for both you and the very wild animal.

Beaver

Castor canadensis

TINY EARS ◆ PRONOUNCED FRONT TEETH ◆ BROWN OR REDDISH BROWN FUR ◆ FLAT TAIL

When a predator is near, beavers slap their tails against the water, creating a loud splash that warns other members of their colony.

Beavers are the largest rodents in North America, and they can be found at some select spots in the Denver area. Not to be confused with muskrats (which appear later in this guide), adult beavers typically weigh between 40 to 60 pounds and measure up to 4 feet in length. They have a dense, waterproof layer of brown or reddish brown fur; strong, sharp teeth designed for gnawing on wood; and flat, scaly tails, which are used for balance and as a signaling tool.

These intelligent rodents are highly social and live in family groups. A single breeding pair and their offspring work together to maintain their lodge and dam structures. Beavers are

renowned for their engineering skills. They build dams across streams and rivers using branches, mud, and stones to create ponds that serve as their homes and protect them from predators. These ponds also provide a stable water level for accessing food during winter and enhance the surrounding habitat for other species. If left unchecked, the ponds created by their dams can extend over several acres.

Key Players

Beavers are considered a keystone species due to their significant environmental impact. Their dam-building activities create wetlands that support a diverse range of plant and animal life, including fish, amphibians, and birds. By modifying their habitats, beavers enhance biodiversity and contribute to the overall health of aquatic ecosystems.

Where to See Them

Beavers thrive in riparian zones along rivers and streams, as well as in wetlands, ponds, and lakes. Look for them at Waterton Canyon, Cherry Creek Trail, and Bluff Lake Nature Center (Trips 22, 4, and 8).

Big Brown Bat

Eptesicus fuscus

ROUNDED FACE • BIG NOSE • FURRY BROWN BODY

Eighteen species of bats call Colorado home.

Big brown bats are nocturnal and primarily use echolocation—high-frequency sounds that bounce off objects—to hunt for insects during the night, especially in areas with streetlights that attract small flying insects, such as moths, beetles, and flies, which make up the majority of their diet.

Big brown bats enter torpor, a state of reduced metabolic rate, during colder months to conserve energy when food is scarce. During winter, they hibernate in secluded locations such as caves, mines, and sometimes attics, where temperatures remain relatively stable. This hibernation helps them survive periods of low insect availability and cold weather.

Safe and Stable

Big brown bats are often found roosting in buildings, man-made bat boxes, and natural sites like caves and hollow trees. They stick to areas where they can easily find food, which includes near bodies of water, open fields, and in urban and suburban areas where insects are attracted to the light.

Beneficial Bats

Big brown bats are generally nonaggressive and beneficial to humans, as they play a significant role in controlling insect populations. By consuming large quantities of insects (they can eat hundreds or even thousands in a single night), they help reduce the need for pesticides and contribute to healthier ecosystems.

Where to See Them

The big brown bat inhabits various environments in Denver, including neighborhoods near downtown, all of the city parks, and the larger parks and wildlife areas outside the city limits. Look up at dusk at City Park, Fairmount Cemetery, Denver Botanic Gardens, and Bear Creek Greenbelt Park (Trips 1, 5, 2, and 13).

Bighorn Sheep

Ovis canadensis

LARGE, CURVED HORNS ◆ BROWN OR GRAY FUR ◆ WHITE RUMP

Bighorn sheep are exceptional climbers, capable of scaling nearly vertical rock faces with ease. This remarkable ability is thanks to their specialized hooves, which have a rough texture and a unique split that provides excellent grip on steep surfaces.

The bighorn sheep, the state mammal of Colorado, has large, curved horns that are particularly pronounced in males, known as rams. These horns can weigh up to 30 pounds and are used in dramatic head-butting contests during the mating season to establish dominance and attract mates. The females, or ewes, have smaller, more slender horns but are equally adept at navigating the steep, rocky terrain that is their home. Their coats are typically a mix of brown and gray, providing excellent camouflage against the rocky slopes and sagebrush of their habitat.

Bighorn sheep live in groups called herds, which can vary in size from a few individuals to several dozen. Herds are generally composed of females and their young, while adult males tend to form separate groups or live solitary lives, especially outside the mating season. This social organization helps them to manage resources and reduce the risk of predation, as the collective vigilance of the herd provides increased protection against threats.

While they are not as vocal as some other wildlife, bighorn sheep communicate through grunts, bleats, and snorts. These sounds are used to maintain contact within the herd, alert others to potential dangers, and express distress or excitement.

Where to See Them

Bighorn sheep can be found traversing rocky cliffs and steep slopes and grazing in alpine meadows. Eagle-eyed visitors to Waterton Canyon (Trip 22) will spot them on the hillsides, and if you go early in the morning, you might even share the trail with them. Keep your distance! Bighorn sheep can be fast and dangerous when provoked or if they feel threatened.

Black Bear

Ursus americanus

BLACK OR DARK BROWN FUR ♦ **STOCKY BUILD** ♦ **LONG SNOUT** ♦ **ROUNDED EARS**

Despite its name, black bear fur can vary in hue. Sometimes they look dark brown or even have a reddish tint.

In spring and summer, black bears are found primarily in lower elevations, and as the seasons shift, they move to higher elevations to take advantage of increased availability of food. During the winter months, they enter a state of hibernation in dens, which are usually located in tree hollows, caves, or dug into the earth.

Black bears are omnivorous. In spring and summer, they mainly eat a mix of plants, berries, and insects. In fall, their diets shift to include more high-calorie foods like acorns and nuts to build fat reserves for hibernation. Black bears are known for their excellent climbing skills, which they use to escape from predators and forage for food.

These bears are solitary animals, except during mating season or when a mother is rearing her cubs. Black bears typically prefer to make their homes in forested or heavily vegetated areas that offer ample cover and food sources.

Handling Bear Confrontations

Black bears have been known to wander into suburban areas, particularly where human food sources like garbage bins or bird feeders are accessible. While they generally avoid human contact, bears that become accustomed to human food can lose their natural wariness, leading to dangerous encounters, potential property damage, and the death of the bear.

Remain calm if you spot a black bear. If they don't see you, slowly back away. If they do spot you and start to approach, make yourself as big as possible. Yell, and wave your

bags and jackets around, anything to try to convince the bear you aren't worth the trouble. NEVER try to run; bears can reach speeds of up to 35 mph and will chase you. If attacked, fight back. Carry bear spray if you're hiking in a place with active bears and use it if necessary.

The best thing you can do to prevent a hostile encounter is to make noise while you're on a trail in active bear areas. Dangerous conflicts typically result from bears being surprised and feeling like retreat isn't an option.

Where to See Them

Black bears are active during certain times of the year at places like Golden Gate Canyon State Park, Eldorado Canyon State Park, Waterton Canyon, and Roxborough State Park (Trips 24, 25, 22, and 23).

Black-footed Ferret

Mustela nigripes

PALE YELLOW AND LIGHT BROWN FUR ◆ **BLACK MASK AROUND EYES AND LEGS** ◆ **BLACK-TIPPED TAIL TINY ROUNDED EARS**

Rocky Mountain Arsenal National Wildlife Refuge played a crucial role in saving black-footed ferrets from going extinct.

The black-footed ferret is a conservation success story. These critters were once widespread across the Great Plains of North America, including the grasslands of Colorado, but their populations plummeted in the 20th century due to habitat loss, disease, and the widespread extermination of prairie dogs, their primary food source. By the 1980s, black-footed ferrets were believed to be extinct in the wild, but one remaining population was discovered in Wyoming in 1981. Reintroduction programs boosted their numbers. Ferrets were bred in captivity and released into carefully managed habitats, and their populations eventually began to grow.

Prairie Dog Predators

Black-footed ferrets are nocturnal hunters. Their slender bodies are adapted for digging and maneuvering through the underground

burrows of prairie dogs. As a top predator in their habitat, black-footed ferrets control prairie dog populations and maintain ecological balance. By preying on prairie dogs, they help regulate these colonies, which in turn influences plant communities and the overall health of the prairie ecosystem.

While the ferrets are a remarkable symbol of the power of conservation, they're also a demonstration of the fragility of ecosystems. Their hunting and foraging activities are highly specialized, making them particularly vulnerable to environmental changes, especially the decline of prairie dog populations.

Where to See Them

The only place you're guaranteed to see one in the Denver area is at Rocky Mountain Arsenal Wildlife Refuge (Trip 9). You can try to spot one on the Wildlife Drive, or you can visit their enclosure behind the visitor center for an up-close look at a few of the curious creatures.

Black-tailed Prairie Dog

Cynomys ludovicianus

SANDY BROWN FUR ◆ **ROUND FACE** ◆ **MEDIUM-LENGTH TAIL**

During winter, black-tailed prairie dogs enter a state of torpor, a light hibernation-like state that conserves energy until spring.

Black-tailed prairie dogs will pop their little heads up from their burrows and chirp at you as you walk by vacant residential lots or open grassland trails around the Denver area. They're highly social animals that live in large colonies, known as towns, which can cover extensive areas up to several hundred acres. Their social structure is organized into family groups called coteries, each consisting of a breeding pair and their offspring. Communication within these

colonies is sophisticated, with prairie dogs using a series of chirps, barks, and other vocalizations to relay information about predators and other threats.

Black-tailed prairie dogs are native to the Great Plains region of North America, with significant populations in Colorado's expansive grasslands.

Dig Deeper

Prairie dogs prefer open, flat terrains with sandy soils that support their extensive digging. Their complex burrow systems, with multiple chambers and entrances, offer protection from predators and harsh Colorado weather.

These tunnels also provide shelter for other species, including insects, reptiles, and small mammals. While they can sometimes be seen as a nuisance, prairie dog burrows help aerate the soil and decrease soil compaction.

Where to See Them

Black-tailed prairie dogs inhabit a range of environments, from vacant lots in the city to expansive grasslands like the ones found at Rocky Mountain Arsenal National Wildlife Refuge, Chatfield State Park, Bear Creek Greenbelt Park, High Line Canal, and Cherry Creek Trail (Trips 9, 21, 13, 14, and 4).

Bobcat

Lynx rufus

TAWNY OR GRAY-BROWN FUR ◆ **BLACK SPOTS AND STRIPES** ◆ **TUFTED EARS**

Bobcats are often confused for lynx, but they are different species. Lynx have grayish pelts, while bobcats have reddish brown pelts with more spots and streaks.

The bobcat is one of Denver's two wild felines. About twice the size of an average housecat, it's a solitary and territorial creature, known for stealthy and efficient hunting techniques. It's often spotted during dawn and dusk, which allows it to hunt and avoid other competing predators. Its diet is varied, consisting of small to medium-sized mammals such as rabbits, hares, rodents, birds, and occasionally insects. Bobcats use a combination of stealth and speed to ambush their prey, often employing a crouching stance and silent approach before launching a quick, powerful attack.

Sightings on the Rise

Although bobcats are generally shy and elusive, they do occasionally wander to where people live. Overall, bobcat populations in the state have been on the rise, but development is too. This can cause problems when bobcats venture into residential areas looking for food. Bobcats are typically wary of people and avoid human contact whenever possible, but they may occasionally prey on domestic animals.

Top of the Food Chain

Bobcats are apex predators, meaning nothing else in this area eats them. As such, they play a critical role in regulating the populations of their prey species. By controlling the number of small mammals and birds, they help maintain the balance of their ecosystems and prevent vegetation from being overgrazed.

Where to See Them

The bobcat is highly adaptable and can be found in various habitats ranging from dense forests to open plains, but it's especially prevalent in areas with a mix of vegetation and cover that provide both shelter and hunting grounds. In the foothills, it seeks out areas with dense underbrush and rocky outcrops that offer ideal hiding spots and vantage points for stalking

prey. You probably (and hopefully) won't spot one within the city limits, but it's possible at Waterton Canyon, Eldorado Canyon State Park, Golden Gate Canyon State Park, and Mount Falcon (Trips 22, 25, 24, and 20).

Colorado Chipmunk

Tamias quadrivittatus

STRIPES RUNNING FROM HEAD TO TAIL • LONG TAIL • BROWN-AND-GRAY FUR

Colorado chipmunks are mostly diurnal, meaning they are most active during daylight hours, often seen darting across the forest floor or climbing up trees.

Chipmunks are curious creatures, and you'll definitely see them at any trailheads where they've been fed before or on boulders along the trails. Their diet consists mainly of seeds, nuts, fruits, and insects, which they gather and store in their cheek pouches to hoard for winter. This behavior is crucial for their survival, as they rely on stored food during the colder months when resources are scarce.

They live in coniferous forests, mixed woodlands, and alpine meadows, preferring rocky outcroppings with dense undergrowth and scattered vegetation, which provides both food and cover.

Don't Let Beggars Be Choosers

While chipmunks are not known to cause significant problems for humans, their presence is often noted in recreational areas such as hiking trails and campgrounds. They are sometimes bold, especially when food is involved, and can easily become too reliant on humans. Do not give a chipmunk any of your trail snacks, no matter how cute it may be.

Circle of Life

Chipmunks play a crucial role in their ecosystems as seed dispersers and prey for larger predators. By storing and forgetting their seeds and nuts, they help with forest regeneration and plant diversity. As a food source for birds of prey, snakes, and larger mammals, they help with the circle of life.

Where to See Them

Colorado chipmunks are commonly seen at pretty much every major trailhead or outcropping. You won't have to look hard to see them at Eldorado Canyon State Park, Mount Galbraith, Golden Gate Canyon State Park (Trips 25, 18, and 24).

Coyote

Canis latrans

GRAY OR BROWN FUR ◆ **BUSHY TAIL** ◆ **ERECT EARS** ◆ **SLENDER BODY**

Coyote scat (poop) is a good way to tell if you're in their territory. They like to "go" right in the middle of the trail, and you can tell it's not regular dog poop because it probably has some berries in it and is always pinched off at the end.

Often heard howling in the night, the coyote is a fixture of Colorado's natural soundscape. Their distinctive vocalizations include a series of yips, barks, and howls and are used to communicate within their packs.

Coyotes can sometimes be mistaken for loose dogs, but their slender builds, bushy tails, and reluctance to come near people are often giveaways that these are not pets. (And, in fact, they're the perfect reason to make sure yours are always on a leash.)

This wild canine is highly adaptable and while its peak activity is during dawn and dusk, you may see a coyote during the day, especially during mating season.

Coyotes often take advantage of the natural cover provided by dense shrubs and rocky outcrops of the foothills to hunt and evade larger predators. In plains and grasslands, they hunt small mammals while navigating vast, open terrain. Their diet is omnivorous and opportunistic, consisting of small mammals, birds, insects, fruits, and occasionally carrion. Their ability to thrive in both the wilderness and suburban areas illustrates their remarkable adaptability and resourcefulness.

Coyote Conflicts

Coyotes can be found in nearly every environment in the state, from high-alpine meadows to the fringes of the city, so it's no surprise they often encounter humans, especially where development meets their natural habitat. While they are generally wary of people, they have been known to scavenge from garbage bins and prey on small pets. During mating season, there are occasional conflicts with off-leash dogs they see as competition.

Where to See Them

A few resident coyotes call Crown Hill Park (Trip 11) home. You can often spot them wandering near the seasonally open wildlife refuge at the west end of the park, near the stand of cottonwood trees at the north side of the park, and sometimes even near the parking lot areas, depending on the time of year. You can also try to spot their camouflaged coats at Rocky Mountain Arsenal National Wildlife Refuge, North Table Mountain, and Cherry Creek State Park (Trips 9, 17, and 15).

Desert Cottontail

Sylvilagus audubonii

BROWN, GRAY, AND REDDISH FUR ◆ LONG, STRAIGHT EARS ◆ ROUND EYES

Desert cottontails are crepuscular, meaning they are most active at dawn and dusk, which helps them avoid the peak heat of the day.

The desert cottontail's name is misleading—these rabbits can be found all over Denver. They favor areas with sufficient shrub and grass cover that hide them from predators and provide potential nesting sites. Desert cottontails also inhabit residential areas, where they can take advantage of gardens for additional food sources.

A skilled digger, the desert cottontail creates shallow burrows or uses existing natural crevices for shelter. Its diet primarily consists of grasses, herbs, and some woody plants, which it can survive on even when food is scarce. To survive periods of drought, it will eat plants with high moisture content and can survive long periods without direct water sources.

Desert cottontails play a significant role in their ecosystems as prey and herbivores. Their ravenous feeding habits influence plant community structure by controlling the growth of various plant species.

Where to See Them

Look in the grass at any park or yard in the suburbs, and you'll probably spot at least one (if not more) cottontails.

Fox Squirrel

Sciurus niger

BUSHY TAIL ◆ REDDISH BROWN FUR ON BACK ◆ SHARP CLAWS

Fox squirrels communicate with a range of sounds, from high-pitched warning calls to chattering noises when they feel threatened. This vocal repertoire alerts other squirrels to danger or asserts dominance when something (or someone) enters their territory.

Fox squirrels live anywhere there are trees. While their appearances can vary, their reddish brown backs and white underbellies provide excellent camouflage, and their large eyes, which are well adapted to detecting movement, allow them to spot potential predators and food sources from a distance.

These squirrels are highly active and dart from trees to rooftops, foraging on hellstrips and in home gardens. Their agile movements and impressive climbing skills come from their strong limbs and sharp claws, enabling them to leap from branches to brick walls and fences easily.

Tree Planting

During the fall and winter months, squirrels engage in a behavior known as caching, where they bury nuts and seeds in the ground to store food for the colder months. This habit not only helps them survive winter but also aids in forest

regeneration, as undiscovered cached nuts germinate and grow into new trees.

Where to See Them

City squirrels take charge in parks, green spaces, and residential backyards with space for foraging and nesting. You'll only have to look for a second to see them at City Park, Washington Park, and Sloan's Lake (Trips 1, 3, and 6).

Meadow Vole

Microtus pennsylvanicus

ROUNDED EARS ◆ ROUND BLACK EYES ◆ SOFT BROWN OR GRAY-BROWN FUR

Voles have high reproductive rates—a single female can have multiple litters each year. This prolific breeding helps to cancel out their high predation rates and ensures a sustainable population.

The meadow vole is great at chewing. Their sharp teeth are designed for gnawing on various plant materials, including grasses, seeds, and roots. Most people interact with voles as nuisance animals in their yards, as they create extensive networks of tunnels and nests beneath the soil surface. While these tunnels can destroy lawns and gardens, they also provide shelter from predators and offer easy access to food sources.

Meadow voles are found throughout grasslands, meadows, and residential areas like parks and yards. These environments offer ideal conditions for their burrowing activities and provide ample resources for their herbivorous diet. Meadow voles are important prey for many predators, including hawks, eagles, snakes, and larger mammals.

People Problems

Meadow voles can come into conflict with human activities, particularly in agricultural areas where they may damage crops and in residential areas where they damage irrigation systems and landscaping plant roots. Because of this, they aren't common sights in well-maintained parks (for long, at least).

Where to See Them

To catch a glimpse of a vole, head to Cherry Creek State Park, Chatfield State Park, and Rocky Mountain Arsenal National Wildlife Refuge (Trips 15, 21, and 9).

Mountain Lion

Puma concolor

BEIGE COAT ◆ **LONG, SLENDER, BLACK-TIPPED TAIL** ◆ **ROUNDED EARS**

Mountain lion, puma, and cougar . . . three names to describe the same elusive large feline roaming the natural areas in the outskirts of the city.

The mountain lion is solitary and highly territorial, but with a range that stretches from Canada to the southern tip of South America, it's one of the most widespread large mammals in the Americas.

Unlike large predators confined to specific habitats, the mountain lion can thrive in a variety of environments, from dense forests and rocky canyons to open grasslands and arid deserts. Its adaptability is mainly due to its diet, which includes a wide range of prey, from small mammals and birds to larger mammals like deer and elk.

A Different Kind of Roar

While mountain lions are generally silent and stealthy predators, they use their voices when needed. These include a range of growls, hisses, and screams, the most notable being the eerie, high-pitched scream that can be mistaken for a human in distress. This vocalization is often used during mating season or to establish territory.

Conflicts on the Rise

While known for their adaptability, there are some changes that mountain lions can't adjust to. Habitat loss due to urban expansion and human activity poses a significant threat to their populations. As Colorado's cities and towns expand into formerly wild areas, the mountain lion's natural habitat has become increasingly fragmented, leading to potential conflicts with humans and reduced access to prey.

Where to See Them

Mountain lions prefer areas with ample cover and access to prey, including dense forests, rocky outcrops, and open meadows. While the general consensus is that your day is about to get worse if you lay eyes on a mountain lion, there's a chance they could be watching you on the trails at Eldorado Canyon State Park and Roxborough State Park (Trips 25 and 23).

MAMMALS

Mule Deer

Odocoileus hemionus

LARGE, MULE-LIKE EARS ◆ BROWN, SCRAGGLY FUR ◆ LONG SNOUT

Mule deer can cover up to 30 feet in a single jump.

Mule deer are named for their large, mule-like ears that help them detect predators and navigate their surroundings. Adults typically weigh between 150 and 300 pounds, with males, or bucks, being significantly larger than females, or does. Bucks have impressive antlers, which they shed and regrow annually, with their size and branching reflecting their age and health.

Most of the year, mule deer are solitary or stick to small groups, but they form larger herds during the winter months for better protection and resource utilization.

On the Move

Mule deer are highly adaptable and occupy a broad range of habitats in Colorado, from arid sagebrush plains of Rocky Mountain Arsenal National Wildlife Refuge to forested areas of the foothills to high mountain meadows. In spring and summer, mule deer are often found in higher elevations, where they graze on fresh vegetation and browse on shrubs and young trees. During fall and winter, they migrate to lower elevations where food is easier to find and snow cover is less severe.

Mule Deer vs. White-tailed Deer

We have both mule and white-tailed deer in the Denver area, but mule deer are more common on the trails. The mule deer is typically the larger of the two, identifiable by its ears, while the agile white-tailed deer has its distinctive white tail it raises when alarmed. Mule deer also tend to look more worse for wear than their white-tailed relatives.

Where to See Them

You won't see a mule deer downtown, but you'll probably catch a glimpse of them in the early morning or at dusk at Cherry Creek State Park, Chatfield State Park, Bluff Lake Nature Center, and Crown Hill Park (Trips 15, 21, 8, and 11).

Muskrat

Ondatra zibethicus

LONG, RAT-LIKE TAIL • BROWN FUR • ROUNDED EARS

Muskrats have angled back ankles, which makes their back legs great for paddling but not ideal for walking.

Often mistaken for a small beaver or otter, the muskrat is another resident in our marshes. You can tell if you're looking at a beaver or a muskrat in the water based on whether its

head is out of the water—muskrats like to keep everything at the water's surface, while beavers swim with just their heads above water. Their tails are also a good giveaway. Muskrats have long tails, while beavers have flat, paddle-like tails.

The most distinctive features of muskrats are their large, partially webbed hind feet, which are well-adapted for swimming, and those rat-like tails, which act as rudders in the water.

Muskrats build complex structures known as lodges using reeds, cattails, and mud. They're usually built in shallow water and serve as both homes and protection from predators. They create extensive tunnels to get to and from the lodge, which can provide a quick escape if a predator ever threatens it.

Their diet primarily consists of aquatic plants like cattails and waterlilies, but they also eat small animals or insects from time to time.

Making Microhabitats

Muskrat lodges and burrows create microhabitats for various aquatic and semi-aquatic species, including insects, amphibians, and birds. Additionally, by feeding on aquatic plants, muskrats greatly influence the vegetation in an area.

Where to See Them

Muskrats are commonly found in wetland areas, including marshes, slow-moving rivers, and ponds with plenty of vegetation. You might catch a glimpse of them at Sloan's Lake, Washington Park, Belmar Park, and Bear Creek Greenbelt Park (Trips 6, 3, 12, and 13).

Red Fox

Vulpes vulpes

REDDISH ORANGE FUR ◆ WHITE UNDERBELLY ◆ BLACK "STOCKINGS"

Red fox fur was highly prized for its softness and warmth, leading to a long tradition of fur trapping and hunting. There were several successful fox farms west of the city back in the 1930s.

Whether darting through forests, meadows, or even suburban areas, the red fox is a master of survival. This fox sports a reddish orange coat, white underbelly, and a distinctive black set of "stockings" on its legs. Its tail, bushy and tipped with white, is one of the fox's most notable features, used for balance and communication. The red fox is an omnivore with a diet that includes fruits, insects, and even garbage in the city's outskirts, where they live mostly undetected.

While many people are familiar with the fox's characteristic bark, the species can produce a variety of sounds. From high-pitched screams to a series of sharp yipping noises, these vocalizations serve various purposes, including marking territory and communicating with mates. The sounds can be startling if heard at night.

Red foxes are also known for their resourceful denning behaviors. They dig elaborate burrow systems, often utilizing abandoned burrows of other animals. These dens are carefully constructed to provide a safe and comfortable environment for raising their young. In winter, the fox may rely on its den to shelter from harsh weather conditions and store food.

Where to See Them

Red foxes can make a home in nearly any environment that offers food and shelter. Watch for flashes of red at Rocky Mountain Arsenal National Wildlife Refuge, Roxborough State Park, Lookout Mountain, and Sloan's Lake (Trips 9, 23, 16, and 6).

MAMMALS

Rocky Mountain Elk

Cervus canadensis nelsoni

**LARGE ANTLERS • REDDISH BROWN COAT IN SUMMER • DARK BROWN OR GRAY IN WINTER
STOCKY SNOUT**

With more than 280,000 animals, Colorado's elk population is the largest in the world.

Elk were once a thriving species in North America, but overhunting and habitat destruction led to the decimation of their population. By the 1900s, there were only 40,000 left. Relocation and joint conservation efforts helped to bring them back, and now the Rocky Mountain elk, a subspecies of the North American elk, is abundant in Colorado.

The most striking features of the Rocky Mountain elk are its size and antlers. Males, or bulls, have the biggest antlers of all North American elk species. They can span up to 4 feet and are shed and regrown annually. These antlers are not only used for mating displays but also for establishing dominance among rivals. During the rut, or mating season, which peaks in September and October, the forest comes alive with the haunting, resonant bugles of bull elk hoping to attract a mate and ward off any nearby males.

Elks' diet varies depending on the season. They prefer grasses and herbaceous plants in summer and shrubs and tree bark in winter. This seasonal dietary shift is crucial for surviving Colorado's harsh winters when food sources become scarce.

Where to See Them

You won't see elk in the city, but you don't have to travel far to catch a glimpse of them. They're a common sight in Golden during fall and can be spotted at Golden Gate Canyon State Park (Trip 24), Chatfield State Park (Trip 21), and when you're driving on US-6 in Golden, where the resident herd has its own crossing lights between Heritage Road and 19th Street.

Shiras Moose

Alces alces shirasi

BROAD ANTLERS ◆ **DARK BROWN FUR** ◆ **LONG NOSE** ◆ **LONG LEGS**

The moose is the most dangerous animal in Colorado. There are more moose attacks in the state than the number of attacks by bears and mountain lions combined.

It's hard to believe, but the Shiras moose, named after the naturalist Charles Shiras, who first identified it, is the smallest subspecies of North American moose. Males, or bulls, typically weigh 600 to 800 pounds and stand about 5 to 6 feet tall at the shoulder. They have broad, palmate antlers that are covered in velvet during the growing season and used to attract mates during the rut (breeding season) and to establish dominance among other males.

Their long legs and large hooves are well adapted for traversing snowy and marshy terrain, while their broad, shovel-shaped snouts are perfect for nabbing vegetation.

Rollin' Solo

Shiras moose are solitary animals, except during the breeding season or when a mother is accompanied by her young. Moose are generally shy and will try to avoid human contact, making their appearances in Colorado's backcountry even more special. When moose and human conflicts do occur, it's often because people assume moose are gentle and approach them or have pets who run up to the animals quickly and then back to their humans for help once the moose begins to charge. Moose are fast and can be very destructive if provoked. Always keep your distance and keep your dog on a leash (or consider leaving them at home) if you're hiking in moose territory.

Where to See Them

The Shiras moose lives in mountainous and forested areas. In summer, they stay near lakes, rivers, and marshes to feed on aquatic plants and cool off. As winter sets in, they move to lower elevations, where they browse shrubs and tree bark. Look for them on your leaf-peeping visits to Golden Gate Canyon State Park and Eldorado Canyon State Park (Trips 24 and 25).

FIELD TRIPS

FIELD TRIPS

With dozens of urban parks, networks of paved trails that traverse the city, hundreds of miles of hiking trails in Denver Mountain Parks and Jeffco Open Space, and massive mountains directly to the west, it's no surprise that Denver is a popular city for outdoor enthusiasts. Whether you're looking for a casual stroll in the city, a more adventurous mountain adventure, or something in between, the following 25 trips will give you the chance to see Denver's outdoor offerings for yourself.

Here's how to make the most of your time outside in the Mile High City.

STEP 1. Pick a place.

The field trips in this book range from flat, paved sidewalks to multi-mile treks with elevation gain. Choose one within your physical limits and with what you're looking for, whether it's plants, animals, scenery, or all of the above.

STEP 2. Decide on the best time to visit.

Most locations will be busier on weekends, so if you want to get a parking spot or are looking for peace and quiet on the trail, get to the trailhead early in the morning or go during the week. All the trips in this guide are available year-round, but keep in mind that different hikes will have different appeal depending on when you visit.

WINTER
Snow and freezing temperatures often keep crowds away, so go when it's cold out if you want the trails to yourself. Because it's winter, you won't be able to see as much plant and active animal life as you will in warmer seasons.

SPRING
If you're in the woods, be aware that many larger animals are waking up from a long hibernation and might be focused on looking for a tasty post-nap snack. Make your presence known, as not to startle them, and always keep your distance from wildlife. With spring comes the mud (thanks to ice and snowmelt), so follow the posted mud rules and stay on the trail to avoid doing long-term damage to park ecosystems.

SUMMER
Summer is a popular time to hike, so go early before it gets hot and before storms come. It's also an active time for rattlesnakes, moose, and other potentially dangerous animals, so brush up on your wildlife safety skills before you hit the trails.

FALL

Fall brings cooler temperatures and chances to go leaf peeping. It's also a time to be wary of bears trying to pack on as much weight as they can before winter. Always be aware of what's around you and keep your distance.

STEP 3. Get prepared.

You'll need different supplies depending on the length and difficulty of your hike, but make sure you bring enough water no matter which trail you travel on. A general rule of thumb is to hit halfway with your water at the halfway point in your trek.

Apply sunscreen before any hike. We're a mile closer to the sun here, so you'll burn faster.

Always check the weather before you head out. Denver's weather can change on a dime, so bring layers. It's always better to have more than you need than to need something you chose not to pack. Never go out when a storm is coming. At higher elevations, always turn back if a storm is coming in to prevent lightning strikes. The trail will be there next time. Don't risk it.

If you choose a trip outside of the city or one that's longer than a mile, bring along the ten essentials: a map, first-aid kit, sun protection, extra layers, headlamp, emergency shelter, a fire starter, a multi-tool or knife, extra food, and plenty of water.

STEP 4. Enjoy your hike and leave no trace.

Be respectful of nature and other trailgoers. Don't leave anything behind—pack it in, pack it out. That includes orange peels, pet waste, or toilet paper. (It's not going to degrade any time soon.) Bring an extra bag to hold any trash and help keep these places beautiful for generations to come.

KEY TO THE TRIP MAPS:

 ROADS

RECOMMENDED ROUTE

OTHER TRAILS

 BODY OF WATER

BUILDING

 PARKING

City Park

See the city skyline against the backdrop of the mountains at Denver's largest park and a popular stopover spot in the Central Flyway.

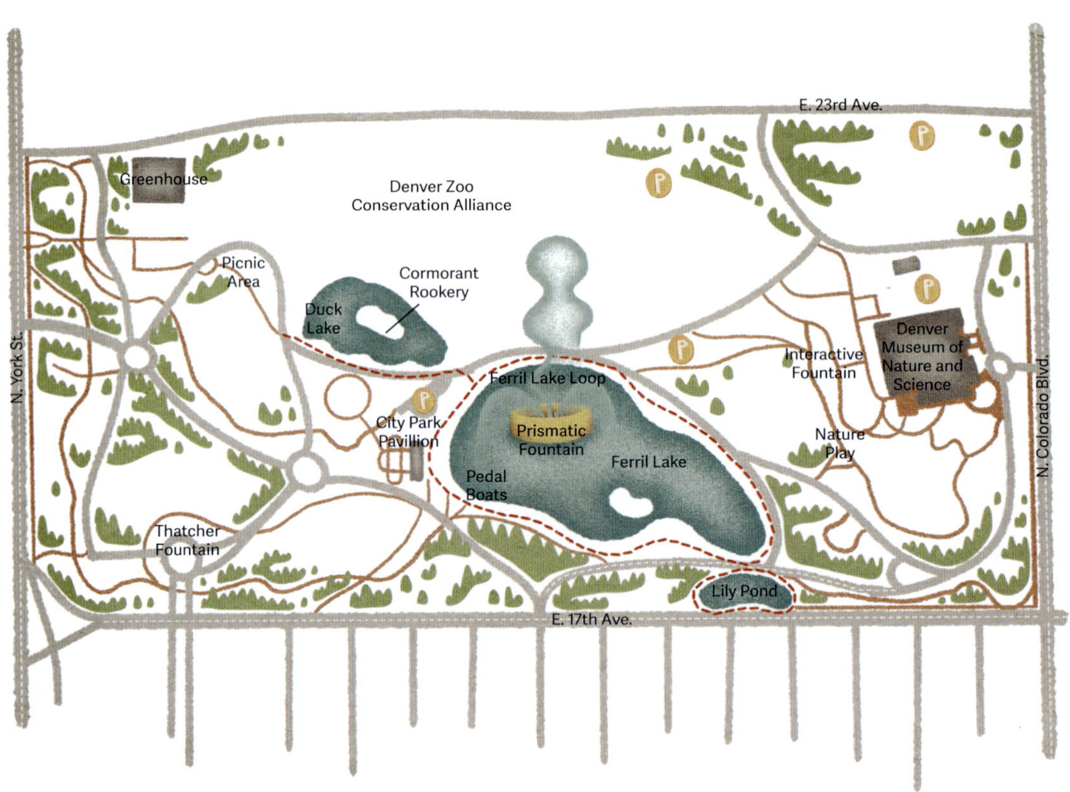

▲ City Park is a natural oasis in the middle of the city

At 330 acres, City Park is Denver's largest park and one of the oldest in the city. The Denver Zoo Conservation Alliance and the Denver Museum of Nature and Science lie within its boundaries. Back in the late 1800s, there was a lack of green space in the city, and landscape architect Henry Merryweather set out to change that. He modeled City Park after New York's renowned Central Park in an attempt to bring the same romantic traditional park style to the West.

During the early years of City Park, there weren't intentional tree plantings, so the park was a wide-open grassland with a few low shrubs. To help create some shady spaces, Denver schoolchildren planted trees every Arbor Day, and by 1890, there were about 600 shade trees around the park. City Park eventually grew to include gorgeous gardens, two lakes, playgrounds, a greenhouse, picnic areas, and thousands of trees for visitors to enjoy.

WHERE: 2001 Steele St., Denver, CO 80205
PARKING: Ample free parking.
DIFFICULTY: Easy, with paved and crushed gravel trails. Flat, paved Ferril Lake loop is popular.
FACILITIES: Restrooms and picnic areas scattered throughout.

Prismatic Fountain, the massive fountain in the middle of Ferril Lake, was erected in 1908.

There are several ways to get in, but if you head to the City Park Pavilion and park at that lot, you can easily access the Ferril Lake Loop. It's a 1.3-mile

paved trail with lots of benches to rest and take in the view of the city with the backdrop of the mountains. If the swan boats are out, you can rent one and see the park from the lake.

When you've finished the Ferril Lake Loop, head north of the parking lot to pick up the trail to Duck Lake. See if you can spot cormorants, eagles, or pelicans nesting on the shore of the little island—a haven for these massive birds.

Lake Life in a Landlocked State

City Park has two bodies of water that birds and other marine life frequent: Ferril Lake and Duck Lake.

Ferril Lake, the largest, is a popular spot for all types of wildlife, especially Canada geese. During certain times of the year, the geese enjoy the park a little too much, and the overrun leads to conflicts and population control efforts by the city. While Canada geese can be aggressive if provoked, the real problem is a byproduct of a large population of any animal in one spot:

▲ Closer to the ground, plants like butterfly weed help attract and feed migrating monarch butterflies

too much poop. Not only does it make walking on the sidewalks a nightmare, but the waste from the birds can quickly degrade the ecosystem and cause long-lasting shifts and problems in the future.

Technically, there's a third body of water at City Park. Originally known as Little Lake, the now-named Lily Pond was created to transform a sediment pond into a vibrant, beautiful little lake full of pond lilies (hence the name). It's been mostly dry since the 1970s, but there are restoration efforts in progress.

Extend Your Visit

Since you're already in the park, pay a visit to the Denver Museum of Nature and Science. As one of the city's oldest museums (and originally just known as the Denver Natural History Museum), you'll get a deeper look not just at Denver, but Colorado's ecology and history.

Don't have time? The museum's Nature Play, a 4-acre immersive experience designed for young visitors, shares the history of Denver's ecosystems, from the alpine tundra to prairie grasslands, giving you a chance to dive deeper into the natural history of the city without having to make a separate trip to the museum.

Denver Botanic Gardens at York Street

See more than 36,000 plants from around the world at this natural sanctuary in the middle of the city.

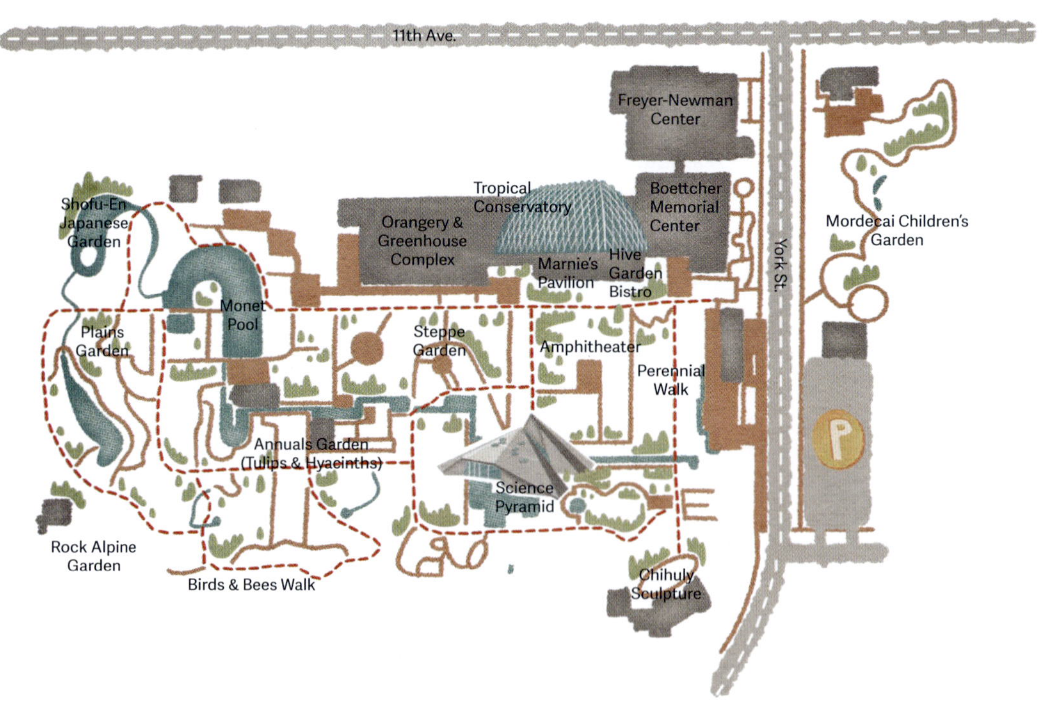

▲ The plants growing in the Rock Alpine Garden can thrive without much water

Denver Botanic Gardens is a 24-acre oasis in the Congress Park neighborhood. From the serene Shofu-En Japanese Garden, where koi fish glide through tranquil ponds and turtles sun themselves on logs and rocks, to the Mordecai Children's Garden, where young explorers can discover the wonders of nature, there's something to captivate every visitor. The Tropical Conservatory, with its lush rainforest environment and exotic blooms, offers warmth and color no matter the season. (Visit on a snowy day if you want to feel worlds away.) The Rock Alpine Garden features hardy plants that thrive in challenging conditions. There's even a sunken, in-ground amphitheater for summer concerts and events.

Visit in spring to see thousands of tulips in bloom at the Annuals Garden and Pavilion, or stop by Marnie's Pavilion to watch the stinky corpse flower bloom (that timing is a little harder to predict).

WHERE: 1007 York St., Denver, CO 80206
PARKING: Free surface parking lot and garage across the street from the entrance. Street parking nearby; check for permit requirements.
DIFFICULTY: Easy and accessible. Main trails paved with crushed gravel offshoots.
FACILITIES: Bathrooms in the Freyer-Newman Center, Boettcher Memorial Center, Marnie's Pavilion, and Hive Garden Bistro.
SPECIAL NOTES: No pets allowed.

NATIVE PLANTS AND FIRE

The Denver Botanic Gardens defines native flora as "plants that are known to occur naturally (pre-European settlement) in Colorado and the West," and they've got more than 700 species throughout the gardens.

As drought conditions worsen and water restrictions increase, incorporating native plants into home landscapes is gaining traction, and being able to see how they grow (and that many of them are just as beautiful as common high-water flowers) is a good way to inspire more people to incorporate them into their spaces.

The Plains Garden features a natural assortment of the native plants, as opposed to the more manicured look of some of the other sections in the gardens. Some of the native plant areas haven't been watered in twenty years! Maintaining a healthy native plant environment means mimicking the conditions found in the wild, which is why Denver Botanic Gardens also simulates one of the most important ecological processes in nature: fire. They stage controlled burns with experts watching the fire closely, and within four months, many colorful flowers and grasses reappear. Blanket flower, golden aster, leadplant, and even Indian paintbrush (a notoriously difficult native to cultivate) appear in the field, adding pops of color to an area with shadows of char if you look closely enough.

LONG LIVE THE LILY PADS

One of the most eye-catching features at the gardens is the Monet Pool. Visit between June and September to see aquatic plants like tropical and Victoria waterlilies in peak bloom. (The annual Water Blossom Festival is usually held in early August.)

▼ More than 16,000 tulips are planted each year

▲ Ducklings can be found exploring and sometimes resting adorably on the giant pads in the pool

► Koichi Kawana designed the Shofu-En Garden, which means "Garden of the Pine Winds"

Steppe It Up

A biome is a large geographical region characterized by specific climate, vegetation, and animal life. Colorado is in what's known as a steppe biome—a semi-arid region with cold winters and extremely hot summers. They're well known for swaths of grasslands and shrublands, but they are also home to colorful wildflowers and a wide range of foliage. At the Steppe Garden, you can see plants from the following regions.

- **Central Asian Steppe:** This is the largest steppe on Earth and the origin of the wild forms of plants such as apples, tulips, and irises.

- **North American Steppe:** The Intermountain North American Steppe (west of the Rocky Mountains) and the Great Plains (east of the Rockies) make up this biome.

- **South African Steppe:** Known for having the highest concentration of bulb and succulent species globally, this steppe has so many wildflowers that some areas are thought to be the inspiration for cultivated gardens.

- **South American Steppe:** Predominantly found in the Patagonia region of Argentina, this steppe is characterized by its dominance of shrubs and cushion plants.

Joseph Bory Latour-Marliac, considered the father of hardy waterlily hybridizing, wanted to expand beyond the white-flowering waterlily most Europeans were familiar with, so he created over 100 hybrids in a rainbow of colors using species from around the world. He showcased them at the World's Fair in Paris, where they caught the attention of Claude Monet, who added them to his garden in Giverny and eventually to his art.

Though many of Latour-Marliac's hybrids were lost to time, twenty varieties (including popular 'Albatros', 'Gloriosa', and 'Virginalis') can be found at the Monet Pool.

• •

The water in the Monet Pool looks black because it is! Nontoxic, food-grade black dye is added to block out sunlight and prevent the growth of single-celled and string algae.

• •

TRIP 3
Washington Park

Designed to replicate the grand and elaborate Victorian parks of the 1800s, this two-lake park was once the fanciest in the city.

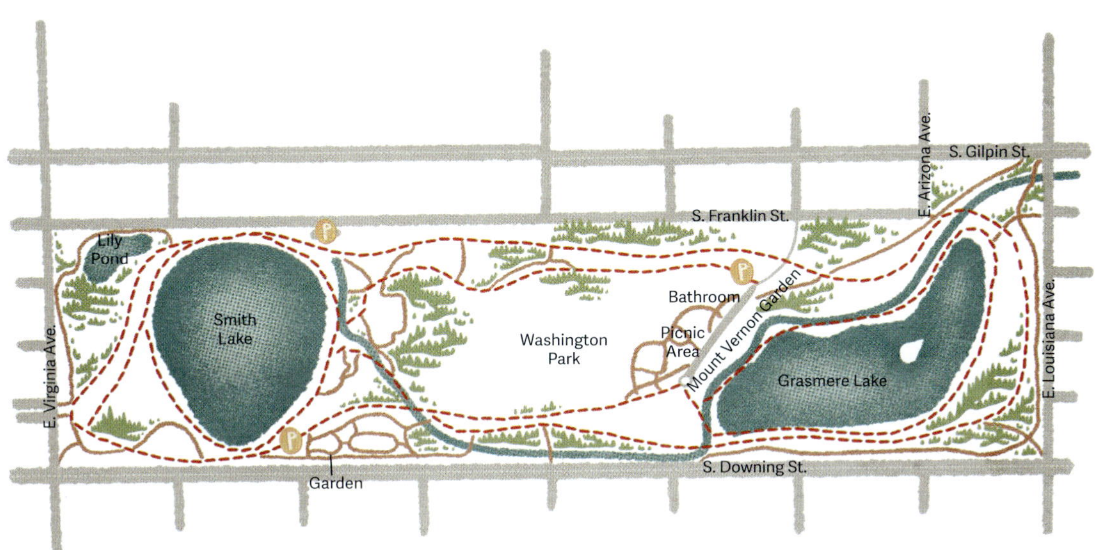

WHERE: 701 S Franklin St., Denver, CO 80209
PARKING: Free parking lots and street parking available.
DIFFICULTY: Easy. Paved and crushed gravel trails crisscross park.
FACILITIES: Bathrooms and picnic areas near parking lots.

◄ Grackles can mimic other birds and even human-made sounds

▲ Rocky Mountain bee plant attracts more than just bees; hummingbird moths also frequent the tubular blooms

When it was first designed, Washington Park stood out in Denver. In a landscape of vast, open prairies, this park had two beautiful lakes—Smith Lake and Grasmere Lake—a huge meadow, city ditch access, a forested hill, deciduous trees, and the largest flower garden in Denver: a Victorian-style perennial garden with an elliptical lawn and symmetrical flowerbeds containing 15,000 varieties.

Today, many of those features still exist, but there are efforts to convert some beds around the park into low-water gardens with plants like Rocky Mountain bee plant, yarrow, evening primrose, coneflower, and milkweed. These plants are native to the region and require far less water for equally beautiful blooms. The park's meadows are also being naturalized with native flowers and grasses to help reduce water consumption and lakeshore restoration is prioritizing aquatic health.

• •

Before freezers had icemakers, people had to find natural sources to keep things cool. Smith Lake was used in the 1890s for ice production. There were once three icehouses near the lake.

• •

Dr. Bergtold's Bird Book

Grasmere Lake has attracted birds since it was first built. Dr. William Bergtold, a Denver physician and avian enthusiast, documented Denver bird sightings at Washington Park in his 1918 book *Birds of Denver*. Many of those birds are still seen today. Look on the lakes for American white pelican, double-crested cormorant, mallard, Canada goose, and swan. Look in the

► Walk carefully during breeding seasons for robins, as fledglings like to rest in the grass

►►Yarrow comes in an array of colors, from classic white to vibrant pink, red, and yellow

Find a Living Fossil

Ginkgo trees are unique because they're gymnosperms—plants with seeds that are "naked" and not inside of fruit or flowers. They are the oldest known tree species, dating back millions of years. Despite their longevity, they haven't gone through much change, so they're known as "living fossils." Female trees can be smelly, but their nuts are edible, and they have gorgeous golden leaves in fall.

trees for cooper's hawk, grackle, swallow, black-capped chickadee, sparrow, and other small songbirds. Look on the ground for northern flicker, robin, and nesting red-winged blackbird. But be careful of the latter—the males will swoop at you if you get too close.

Green Spaces in Big Cities

Denver has seen massive growth, and places like Washington Park help ensure that animals that still call the city home have a place to exist safely. Migrating birds can use the lakes or green space as a rest stop for their long journeys. Coyote, raccoon, and other urban wildlife can find spots to hide out where they won't disturb others and won't be disturbed.

Old-growth Trees

Washington Park is packed with trees—nearly 2000 of them. There are dozens of different species, some of which date back decades. Some of the cotton-woods along the path near Ohio Avenue and Downing Street are 100 feet tall. While their origin dates are unknown, many have grown in the park for quite a while. There are American elms, Kentucky coffee trees, lindens, and oaks with trunks too big to wrap your arms around.

Creekside Park to Lollipop Lake, Cherry Creek Trail

Walk or bike this segment of the trail that follows the historic Cherry Creek to get a glimpse into the past and at some of the city's more popular wild residents.

WHERE: Creekside Park, S Cherry St., Glendale, CO 80246
Lollipop Lake, S. Holly St., Denver, CO 80246
PARKING: Small parking lots and street parking areas at both locations.
DIFFICULTY: Easy. Cherry Creek Trail paved and mostly flat.
FACILITIES: Porta-potties at Creekside Park.
SPECIAL NOTES: A fishing license is required if you want to catch anything at Lollipop Lake.

Starting at Confluence Park in downtown Denver and running through Douglas County down to Castlewood Canyon, Cherry Creek Trail is a popular regional trail system for hiking and biking through the city. The trail was built as part of Denver's bikeway plan, and it was the first of its kind for a major city in the United States.

This trail follows Cherry Creek—one of Denver's first major waterways and the site of a massive flood that wiped out the original Cherry Creek borders back in 1864. Days of rain led to Denver's first big flood, and overflowing banks wiped out homes and took the lives of a few residents caught in its path. These days, the areas around the creek and the trail have mostly been redeveloped, but you'll notice flood warning signs posted along the trail. Don't ignore them. Every few years, Denver is hit with flooding that completely overtakes the trail.

Taking a trip down Cherry Creek Trail is a good way to see the gradual change from Denver's metropolitan atmosphere to a rural environment. In the city and along this stretch of the trail, you'll see common urban wildlife, including squirrel, raccoon, Canada goose, black-capped chickadee, and grasshopper. As you go farther south, you'll begin to see species like bullsnake, prairie dog, rabbit, and raptors like red-tailed hawk.

Green Corridor

Most animals don't stay in one space their entire lives, so even if you have parks and green spaces in a city, there have to be safe ways to travel between them. Setting aside areas that connect the bigger green spaces, or at least get closer to them, is crucial for maintaining biodiversity. By connecting fragmented ecosystems, green corridors provide essential habitats for plant and animal species, filter pollutants, and regulate water flow. These benefits

▲ Gadwalls actually prefer open lakes and ponds that don't have a lot of vegetation

▲ Egrets mainly eat fish, but occasionally opt for crustaceans, aquatic insects, and small mammals

improve air and water quality and help slow down the negative impacts of urban development on the ecosystem.

This field trip ends (or begins, depending on which way you choose to do it—both are great) at Lollipop Lake. There isn't much shade around this urban pond, so it's not as active as ponds that have shady spots and support different plant life. As far as animals go, the pond is a stopover for birds, and it's stocked with rainbow trout, brown trout, and cutthroat trout. (Make sure you have a license if you decide to fish.)

Share the Trail

While it's sometimes marketed as a bike trail, the Cherry Creek Trail is officially multi-use, which means you'll encounter people going at different speeds using different methods, whether on foot, wheels, or some other way to get around. Take it slow if you aren't sure what's coming, announce your presence, and treat everyone and everything in your path with respect.

Extend Your Visit

Along this segment, you'll pass Four Mile Historic Park. This gateway to Denver's Western heritage is a 12-acre working farm and home to Denver's oldest standing structure, the Four Mile House museum.

▲ Four Mile Historic Park lets visitors get a glimpse of what Denver used to be like

TRIP 5
Fairmount Cemetery

See Champion Trees and heritage roses dating back to the settlers at the city's second-oldest cemetery.

WHERE: 430 S Quebec St., Denver, CO 80247
PARKING: Free parking lot near welcome center, or park throughout the grounds.
DIFFICULTY: Easy. Paved roads with gravel paths between them.
FACILITIES: Bathrooms at welcome center.
SPECIAL NOTES: This is an active cemetery. Show respect and be considerate of others, living and deceased.

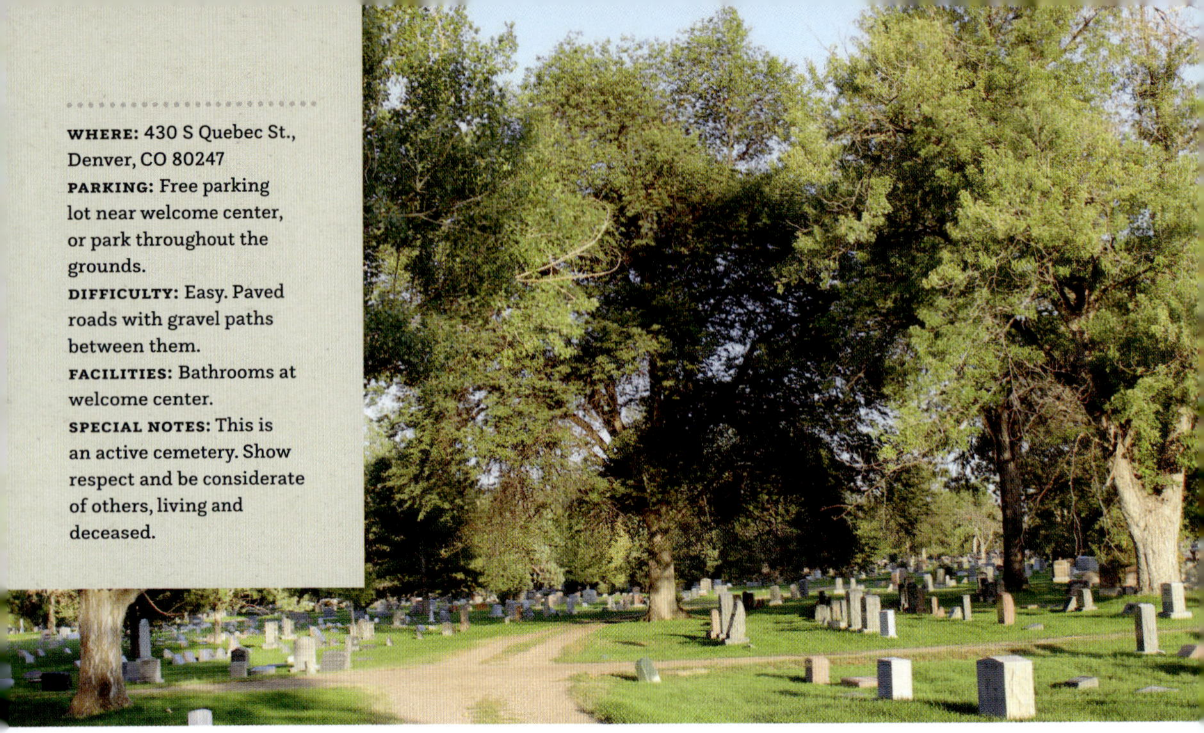

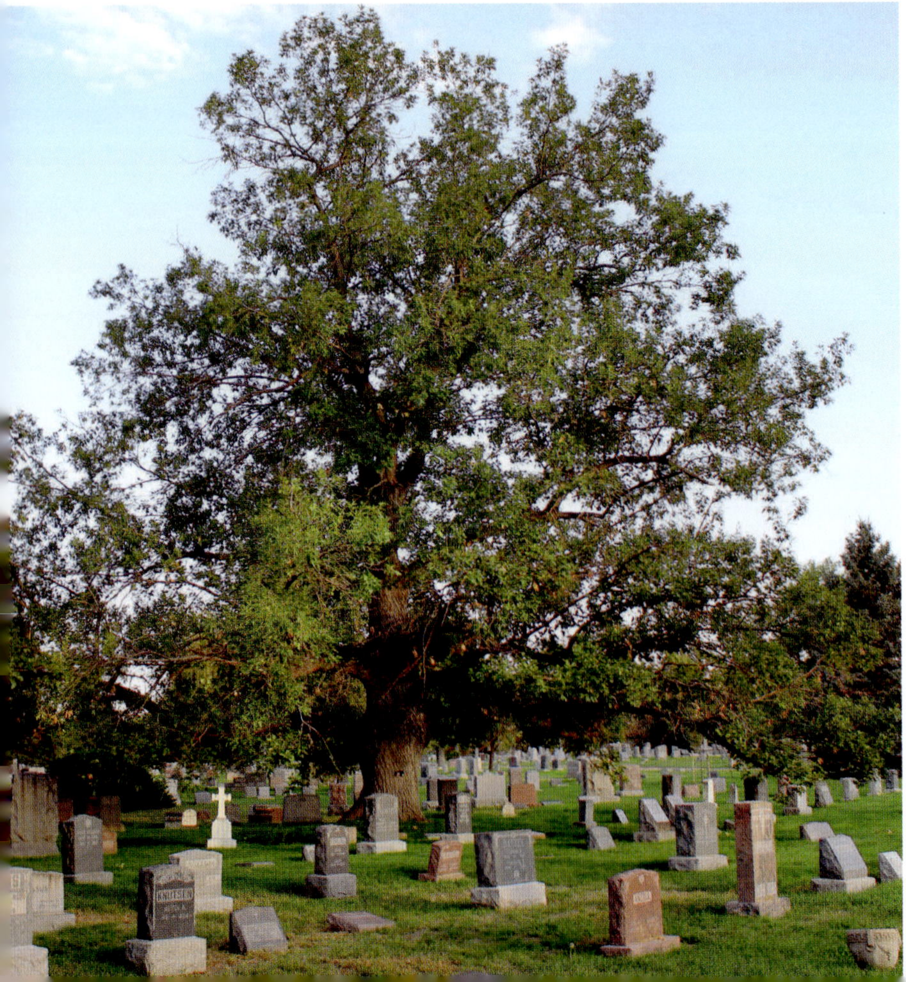

▲ Fairmount is a resting place for many of Denver's early residents

◄ This massive scarlet oak is one of the Champion Trees on the grounds

It might feel odd to visit a cemetery to connect with nature, but as one of the most extensive arboreta in Colorado, a designated wildlife observation site, and home to some of the oldest heirloom roses in the country, Fairmount Cemetery is definitely the place to go. It's Denver's second-oldest operating cemetery, the first being Riverside Cemetery, located north of Denver at the bottom tip of Commerce City.

Back in 1890, the cemetery began as a 280-acre parcel, the largest developed plot of land west of the Mississippi at the time. Reinhard Schuetze, who would later go on to help design City Park, Congress Park, and Washington Park, created this space with the future in mind. He wanted it to be a lush park where people could find peace in visiting the final resting places of family and friends.

Heritage of Trees

The first year of the cemetery, Schuetze established almost 7500 plantings: more than 4000 saplings, 220 evergreens, 100 large trees, nearly 2000 shrubs, 200 vines and creepers, 380 roses, and 585 herbaceous plants. It's no surprise that Fairmount is home to numerous Champion Trees—trees judged to be the largest of their species. The formula to determine which trees earn the title is a point system based on trunk circumference, height, and crown spread. To be eligible, trees must be native or naturalized to the United States.

▼ Head to block 62 and see if you can count all the rings on this massive stump to figure out how old the tree was when it was cut down

MURLEY
ROMIG
WILLIS
NETTIE
JOHN EMERY
1878 — 1937
LOWE
MARGARET M.
1888 — 1966

As you wander around, you'll find more than 100 ash and juniper trees, more than 200 maples and spruce trees, and fruit trees like apple, cherry, and pear alongside ash, hackberry, and oak. Fairmount's trail of trees brochure will take you on a self-guided walk past some of their more notable trees. Several of these date back hundreds of years, while some have been planted more recently to replace those lost to time.

The Gall of It All

Have you ever noticed trees with warty-looking leaves? Those bumps are called galls—abnormal growths found on leaves. These growths are often caused by feeding or egg-laying by insects such as aphids, lice, and mites. Galls might look gross, but they're usually harmless to plants.

Roses to Remember

Fairmount Cemetery is home to one of the largest collections of "old garden roses" in the country. The rose garden at block 85 has heritage roses from when the pioneers first arrived in Denver, often bringing cuttings of their favorites from homes they left behind. Schuetze planted 380 roses from a nursery back in 1891, but many settlers brought rose cuttings to the cemetery to plant at the graves of their loved ones. Varieties found in the garden today include 'Alba semiplena', 'Fairmount Red', 'Banshee', 'Fairmount Proserpine', and the native woods rose. A number of the roses once found at Fairmount have been lost over the years, so there are efforts to preserve those that remain.

History Lesson

Several of Denver's famed landscape architects and other people who helped to create the city parks and destinations in this guide are buried at Fairmount. Look for the graves of Robert W. Speer, a Denver mayor who oversaw significant park development during his tenure; Reinhard Schuetze, the landscape architect who designed Fairmount and many of Denver's parks; David Moffat, a railroad magnate and philanthropist who donated land for parks; and Marjorie Perry, who owned land that was preserved and donated to create a portion of the High Line Canal and Marjorie Perry Nature Preserve featured in this guide.

There are more than 130 years of Denver history here, so take a stroll, read the tombstones, and see if you can spot anything living in the land of the dead.

Sloan's Lake

No matter what you call it, this park is the perfect place to see migratory birds and a lake teeming with life.

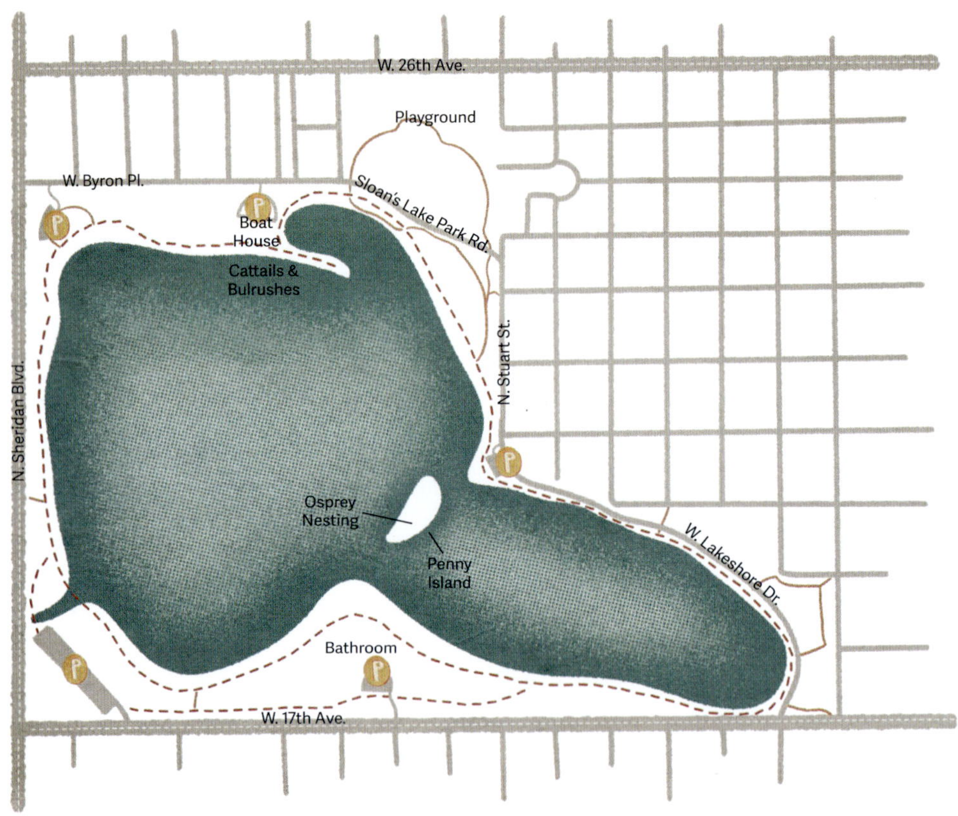

▲ The sunsets at Sloan's Lake offer great views of the city skyline

Sloan's Lake, Sloans Lake, Sloan Lake . . . you'll probably see all three names referring to the second-largest park in Denver. The lake, park, and neighborhood are all named after Thomas M. Sloan, a farmer who, as the story goes, hit an aquifer on his property in 1861. Sloan tried to dig a well on some land he was farming on the west side of the city, and the next morning, he discovered that water had been spilling out of the well all night, forming a lake. Eventually, it stopped filling and became known as Sloan's Lake (or some variation of that). Ever so clever, some townsfolk also called it "Sloan's Leak."

WHERE: 1700 N Sheridan Blvd., Denver, CO 80214
PARKING: Free parking lots and street parking nearby.
DIFFICULTY: Easy and accessible 2.6-mile lake loop. Paved and packed gravel trails around park perimeter.
FACILITIES: Bathrooms and picnic areas near parking lots.

Before Denver was even a city, the area was used as a bison wallow, and because of that, it depressed naturally to hold rainwater.

Urban Lake Life

At 177 acres, Sloan's is Denver's largest lake, and with lakes come fish. Sloan's is stocked with brown, cutthroat, and rainbow trout, as well as bluegill, catfish, carp, minnow, and northern pike. The shallow shores provide a habitat for wading birds and muskrats, and the cottonwoods are good nesting spots

for owls and eagles. As you can imagine, such a large lake is appealing to birds, especially migratory ones. Every year, thousands of ducks, geese, pelicans, and seagulls swarm the lake. Listen for red-winged blackbirds as they sing their songs among the cattails and bulrushes at the lake's edge.

One thing to keep in mind with city lakes is that runoff and imbalances created by pollution from the urban environment and waste from waterfowl (looking at you, Canada geese) often lead to algal blooms and avian diseases. In the last few years alone, there has been an increase in toxic blue algae in the water. Make sure that you and any furry friends you bring to the park stick to the shores and don't consume the water.

The 2.6-mile loop around the lake can take 45 minutes to an hour to complete, and you'll pass several different habitats along the way. If you do want to see the park from the water (remember, surface only), you can take a kayak or canoe out. You'll get a better view of the aquatic life and can even head over to Penny Island. Found in the center of the lake, Penny Island is a mostly barren nesting island covering more than 67,000 square feet.

Keep Your Eyes on the Damselflies (and Dragonflies)

When you walk by the lake, you'll spot damselflies called bluets, close cousins to dragonflies, flitting around on the shore. Male bluets are a cerulean blue with black markings; females have more variation in their coloring, which sometimes makes them harder to ID. Some andromorphic (having male characteristics) females are also cerulean blue, but with more black patterning on their bodies than their male counterparts. Other females have more of a brown or green-brown coloring. Scientists believe that different morphs help limit the amount of attention females receive when near the water. Pick a spot by the shore and watch for a while. You might spot dragonfly species like black saddlebags, blue dashers, widow skimmers, and eastern or western pondhawks.

▲ Penny Island is home to a man-made osprey nesting structure constructed in 2014

◄ Red-winged blackbirds can always be found in the marshes at Sloan's Lake

► You can tell a muskrat (pictured here) from a beaver by its rat-like tail

Berkeley Lake Park

From mature historic trees to newer native plants, this neighborhood park right off US-70 has a bit of everything.

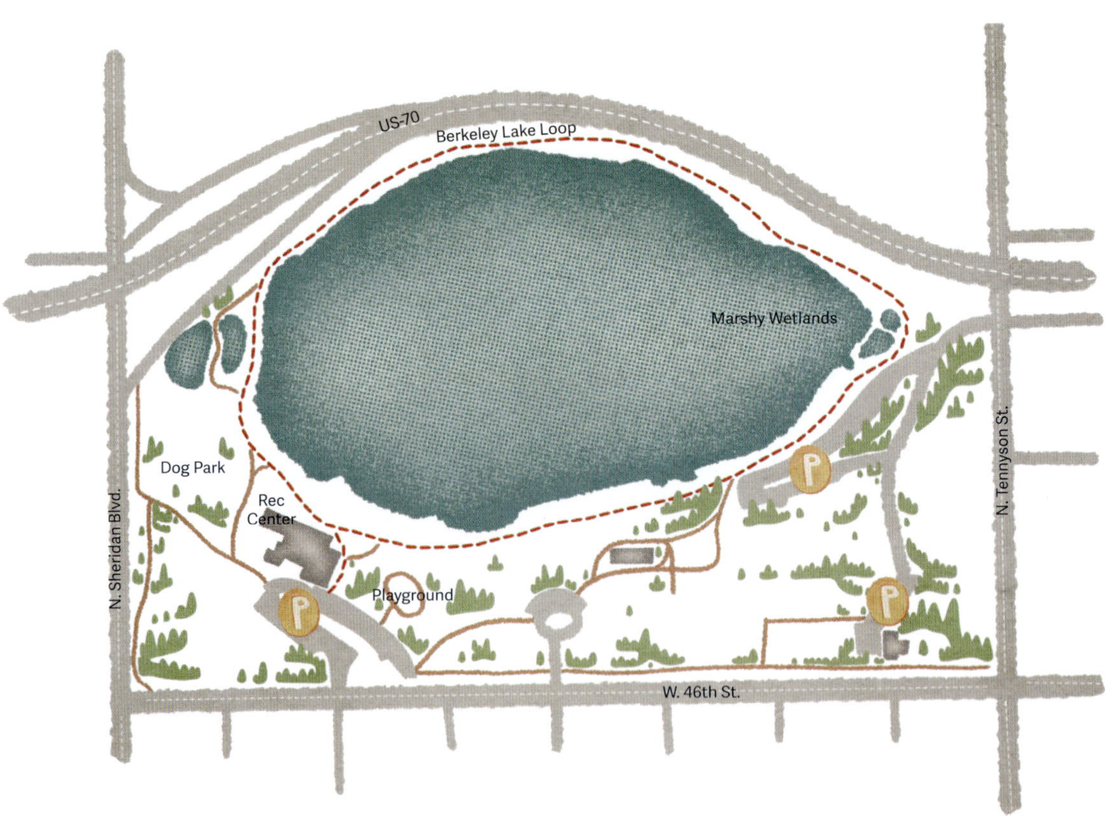

▲ Berkeley Lake Park was cut in half in the 1960s when developers ran US-70 through the land

Berkeley Lake Park is an 83-acre park home to some of the most mature trees in the Denver area. Because of its proximity to US-70, it's not as peaceful a walk as other trails can be, but if you go in the middle of the day, you can avoid crowds and might get lucky with less highway noise.

Once used to irrigate alfalfa fields, Berkeley Lake eventually became the centerpiece of a small horse racetrack and resort. The city purchased the site in 1906 and included it in the plan for the Denver Park and Parkway System. Denver's first public golf course was built to the north of the lake in 1910, and a boat dock, manicured lawns, a pavilion, and trees were installed on the south shore. The park continued to shift in small ways, but a big change came in 1927, when S.R. DeBoer redesigned the roads through the park to discourage vehicle traffic and make it pedestrian friendly.

When the park was first designed, it consisted of open lawns and meadow areas with cedar, oak, and pine dotted throughout. A row of elm trees lined the south edge of the park, and cottonwoods were planted to provide shade along the path around the lake. The trees provided shelter for animals, and if you look closely while you're walking around the lake, you'll see red-tailed hawks on the prowl for mice and other small mammals, squirrels using the tree cavities for nesting and the tree itself as a food source, the occasional raccoon, and possibly even an opossum.

WHERE: 4601 W 46th Ave., Denver, CO 80212
PARKING: Free parking lot.
DIFFICULTY: Easy, accessible 1.1-mile paved loop around lake.
FACILITIES: Bathrooms and picnic area near parking lots.

What Trees Are These?

Berkeley Lake Park is home to a lot of old-growth trees. Here's how to identify a few:

- ELM: serrated, asymmetrical leaves and a vase-shaped canopy

- ASH: compound leaves with five to nine leaflets and distinct diamond-shaped ridges on the bark

- OAK: lobed leaves, acorns, and rugged bark

- COTTONWOOD: triangular, serrated leaves and thick, furrowed bark

- MAPLE: palmate leaves with three to five lobes and distinctive winged seed pods (samaras)

◄ Cottonwood trees can be identified by their triangle-shaped leaves with serrated edges

◄ Samaras, the winged seeds of trees like maples and ashes, spin as they fall, which helps disperse the seeds over a wider area

Bugs and Birds

Healthy trees make good habitats for bugs. Birds like woodpeckers, nut-hatches, and chickadees know how to check healthy trees for insects and seeds in the branches and bark. Water also attracts insects, so stay near the shore to see blue dasher and widow skimmer dragonflies, gnats, and mosquitoes (eaten by the dragonflies, thankfully). Bugs attract birds on the water too, so you'll also get to see the likes of black-crowned night heron, wood duck, great egret, red-winged blackbird, American coot, pelican, and double-crested cormorant nesting and hunting nearby.

Plants in the Park

Native plants are scattered throughout the landscape at Berkeley Lake Park. Look for the whimsical blooms of Apache plume, the slender blue-green and bronze blades of little bluestem, tall, familiar blossoms of Maximilian sun-flowers, and the bright petals of white prairie aster. Shrubs like rabbitbrush and woods rose are also easy to spot, with their greenish gray foliage and

► American coots look a lot like chickens or ducks but are actually members of the rail family

► Look for the white flowers and whimsical seeds of Apache plume, a low-water native plant

telltale rose blooms and hips, respectively. Goldenrod plants will be busy with bug traffic in fall as their yellow blooms burst at the tips of green stalks.

Aquatic plants provide habitat for wildlife, filter pollutants from the water, and offer shelter for birds, small mammals, and amphibians. Common water-loving plants found in the park include cattails, bulrushes, broadleaf arrowhead, and duckweed.

▲ You can see the difference between the cattails (top) with cigar tops and bulrushes (bottom) with their clusters

People often blame goldenrod for allergies late in the season, but they aren't the culprit. They just happen to bloom at the same time as ragweed, which is notorious for setting off allergies.

While they do grow in the same place, cattails are different from bulrushes. Cattails have the trademark cigar at the end of their tall stalks, while bulrushes have clusters of flowers. All of these plants play a part in balancing the wetland ecosystem, from filtering water to providing shade to reduce algae blooms.

TRIP 8

Bluff Lake Nature Center

Located next to Sand Creek on the eastern edge of the former Stapleton airport, this nature center is a popular spot for birders.

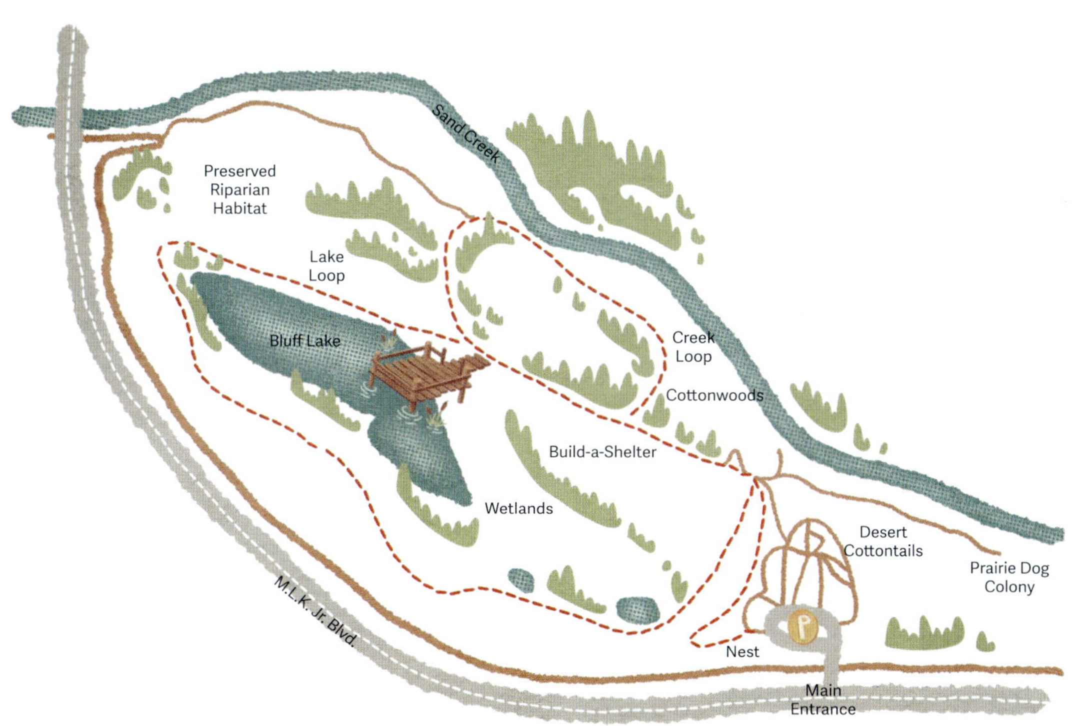

▲ A walk through Bluff Lake Nature Center takes visitors through different eco-systems

Bluff Lake's history is a storied one. Before serving as a resource to Indigenous tribes who lived in this area, the 9-acre lake, adjoining land, and Sand Creek were the perfect example of a native shortgrass prairie with bluffs that were carved from the streams flowing from the mountains, bringing sediment and soil into the eastern plains. Bison and deer roamed the land. Cheyenne and Arapaho people who lived here hunted them, and when the pioneers arrived in the area, they also used them as a food source. As time marched on and Denver became more developed, Bluff Lake was tapped as an irrigation reservoir that provided a reliable source of water for nearby residents.

When plans for the Stapleton International Airport were completed in the 1930s, the 123 acres set aside for Bluff Lake became the airport's crash zone. The lake itself was fenced off, and an independently functioning ecosystem was created over the next 50 years, but the influence of planes flying overhead had negative effects on many of the animal residents. The prairie dogs were rumored to be easier prey because they had lost their hearing and ability to detect predators from the deafening roar of the engines as planes took off and landed.

The property saw further problems when deicing fluid-retention ponds were inadequately maintained and damaging pollution led to a lawsuit. One positive from the experience was that all this led to the creation of Friends of Bluff Lake, which later became Bluff Lake Nature Center. The property was deeded to the organization, and they have made it their mission to protect it to the fullest, providing vital habitat for all the plants, insects, and animals who call it home.

From Bunnies to Beavers to Bullsnakes

When you arrive at Bluff Lake parking lot, take a stroll through a garden packed with rabbitbrush and desert cottontails. Rabbitbrush is a low-water plant that thrives and spreads readily in disturbed or open areas. Desert cottontails have a grayish brown coat that blends in with the grassland land-scape of the garden and powerful hind legs that help them to jump quickly to evade predators (or people walking through the garden). Desert cottontails are more active when temperatures are cooler, so if you come early in the morning or closer to evening, you'll see them hopping all around.

As you head deeper into the park, you'll have the option of stairs or a long trail that takes you past a giant nest that gives you a chance to see the park through the eyes of a red-tailed hawk. This fake nest is one of several hands-on exhibits that both children and adults are encouraged to experience.

► Desert cotton-tails are right at home in the rubber rabbitbrush near the main entrance

► In this human-sized replica nest, you can see what it's like to be a baby hawk.

Back when pioneers were exploring the area, they often looked for cottonwood trees because they meant water was nearby. These trees are easy to spot in summer thanks to their fluffy white seeds that float through the air or their bright golden leaves in fall. American beavers also love using cottonwoods for their dams, and both can be found at the creek. In fact, a busy beaver has built several dams in at Sand Creek over the years.

Bullsnakes are one of the most common snakes in Colorado, and in summer they can often be found sunbathing on trails or cooling off in brush, but don't worry—these snakes are virtually harmless. Unlike rattlesnakes, which they are occasionally confused for, bullsnakes are nonvenomous (though they will try to bite if provoked, so keep your distance!).

Scat, Tracks, and Other Things Left Behind

Even if you don't see any animals during your visit to Bluff Lake Nature Center, you'll know they've been there if you pay close attention to the hints they leave behind. Tracks in mud are always a great example, and after a good rain or along the creek bed, you might be able to see coyote, fox, turkey, duck, goose, and even bobcat tracks.

Scat, or excrement (or poop, if you want to keep it really simple), is a great way to not only identify what was around, but how long ago they were there. Dry scat indicates that some time may have passed between the animal's visit, but fresh scat is a good reminder to keep your eyes peeled as you walk along the trails.

Sometimes animals won't leave anything physical behind, but you can still tell they've been there by the destruction that they've caused. Chewed branches and bark damage are the biggest giveaways. Beavers gnawing on tree trunks, deer rubbing as they wander through the woods, and bark beetles burrowing into layers can all be telltale signs.

Marsh Madness

As you continue along the trail, you'll come across a boardwalk that leads to a marsh—a shallow body of water surrounded by wetland plants such as cattails, reeds, and bulrushes.

The marsh at Bluff Lake Nature Center is home to a variety of birds including ducks, geese, herons, egrets, and belted kingfishers. Belted kingfishers aren't as common in Denver, but they stand out at the Bluff Lake marsh. Their bright blue upperparts, white underparts, sharp black beaks, and distinctive blue breastbands are easy to see as they perch near water, scanning for fish and insects. The marsh is also a popular spot for amphibians, such as frogs and toads, which can be heard calling at dusk.

▲ Herons put on a show in Sand Creek

TRIP 9

Rocky Mountain Arsenal National Wildlife Refuge

See a wildlife-rehabilitation success story or watch bison roam the plains from your car at this wildlife refuge east of the city.

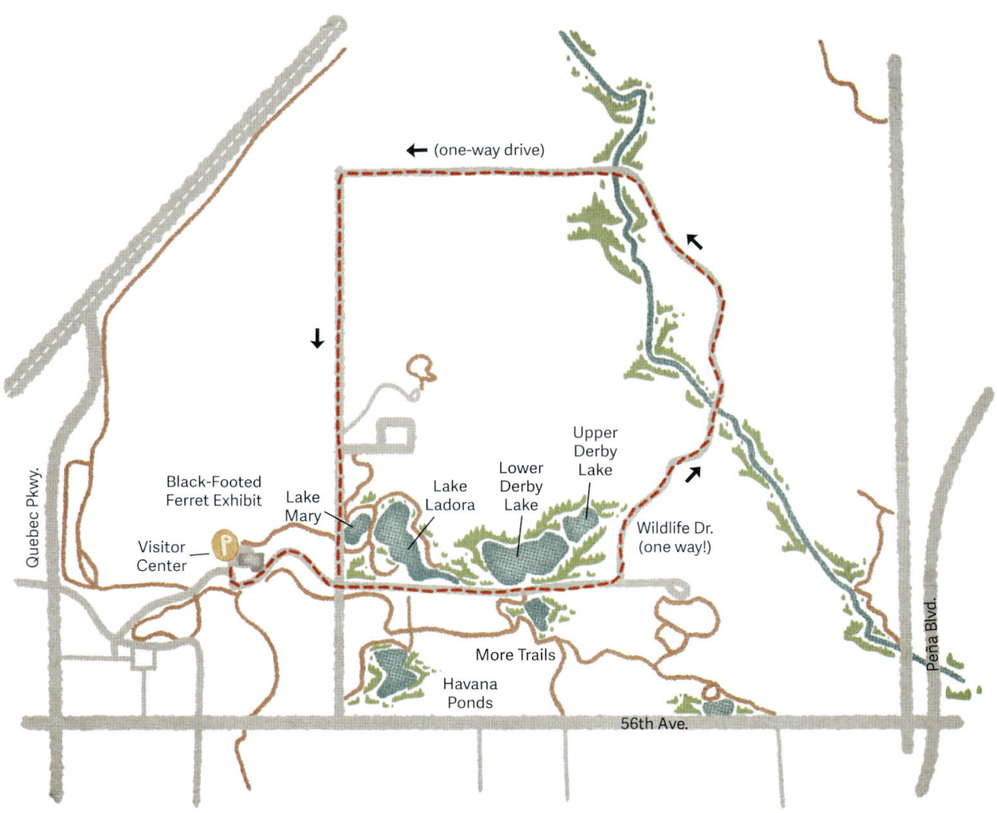

▲ Mule deer have thousands of acres to roam freely

Rocky Mountain Arsenal National Wildlife Refuge is ten miles northeast of the city. It's a great place to stretch your legs after flying into Denver International Airport or if you want to kill some time before a Colorado Rapids soccer match at Dick's Sporting Goods Park next door. It's one of the largest urban refuges in the country—a nearly 16,000-acre prairie home to more than 330 species of wildlife.

Arsenal Origins

After the attack on Pearl Harbor, the U.S. Army transformed the area that is now the refuge into a chemical-weapons manufacturing facility called the Rocky Mountain Arsenal. As production declined at the end of World War II, some facilities were leased to Shell Chemical Company to make agricultural chemicals, and the arsenal was used for Cold War-weapons production. In the 1980s, after the threat of war had passed, the site was evaluated for other uses. The Army and Shell conducted a massive environmental cleanup to meet federal and state regulatory requirements so the land could be transferred to the U.S. Fish and Wildlife Service. The refuge was officially established in 2004, and the cleanup was finally finished in 2010, which allowed its final size to be expanded to 15,988 acres.

▲ You can see bald eagles actively nesting at the refuge during the winter months

► Birds and bison coexist in the refuge

New Place for Nature

Today, the refuge is home to a wide variety of wildlife. Bison were introduced in 2007 to help sustain prairie grasses. They now roam freely on more than 10,000 acres, and you can see them up close (a minimum of 75 feet, please!) on the 11-mile Wildlife Drive that takes you directly through their habitat. Depending on the time of day, you might encounter them crossing the road. Give them plenty of space and stay in your vehicle—they can run up to 36 mph and do considerable damage to vehicles or people.

Since its formation, more than 280 species of birds have been recorded at the refuge. There are many viewing blinds along the trails if you want to try and see some of the harder-to-find species that excel at hiding.

Staff at the refuge have been working to restore 11,000 acres of native grasslands and remove nonnative invasive species from the area using methods like bison grazing, prescribed burns, mowing, and collecting and planting native seed.

A Black-footed Ferret Win

One critically endangered species happily calls the refuge home: the black-footed ferret. See one up close at the enclosure behind the visitor center or try to spot them in the open grassland on Wildlife Drive. In 2015, it was America's most endangered mammal. It was reintroduced to the refuge, and thanks to the site's ever-growing black-tailed prairie dog population (the ferret's main food source), it was able to survive and reproduce.

Twice a year, the refuge conducts surveys to determine how well the ferrets are surviving and reproducing in the wild. The best time to catch them is when they're hunting for prairie dogs at night.

The Refuge Through the Seasons

No matter what time of year you visit, you'll see wildlife at the refuge. In spring, the woodlands come alive as orioles, warblers, finches, and other migrating songbirds arrive. The grasslands are filled with prairie-loving western meadowlarks and kingbirds; cinnamon-colored bison calves play near their mothers; and American avocets and great blue herons wade in the shallows of Lake Ladora. Prairie dog pups peek out of their burrows, and black-footed ferrets emerge ready to find their dinner on the plains.

Summer brings the blooms of wildflowers and prairie grasses. White pelicans fish alongside cormorants, and burrowing owls nest in abandoned prairie dog burrows. Coyotes blend into the golden grasses, hunting near prairie dog towns, while mule deer find cooler temps in the shade of the shrubs.

In fall, the refuge lakes provide sanctuary for migrating waterfowl like northern pintail and redhead. Cottonwood leaves make Wildlife Drive look spectacular, and cooler temperatures make it easier to spot wildlife active during the day.

In winter, great horned owls remain perched silently in the trees, and the tracks of deer and other wildlife can be seen in the snow, marking their presence in the quiet refuge. Dark spots dot the landscape as bison roam their enclosure. Bald eagles nest in the trees along the shores of Lake Ladora and in the bison preserve. The landscape takes on a serene stillness, with snow occasionally blanketing the ground.

Barr Lake State Park

Located northeast of Denver, this state park is one of the most renowned birdwatching destinations in the country.

▲ Pelicans and double-crested cormorants are frequently spotted at Barr Lake

In the middle of this 2715-acre state park is an expansive 1950-acre reservoir bordered by stands of cottonwoods and marshes. The park is a prime habitat for birds and other wildlife, particularly in the southern half, which has been designated a wildlife refuge.

The park features a variety of ecosystems, including wetlands, grasslands, forests, and open water. Visitors can expect to see a wide array of waterfowl, such as American black duck, northern pintail, and Canada goose, particularly during spring and fall migrations. Shorebirds like sandpiper and plover can often be spotted along the water's edge, while red-tailed hawk, bald eagle, and great horned owl hunt over the lake or perch on nearby trees looking for their next meal.

The park has well-placed observation platforms along its trails, providing excellent opportunities for observing birds in their natural habitats, even for the novice birdwatcher. More than 370 species of birds have been spotted here. Educational programs and guided birdwatching tours are available for those interested in learning more about all the awesome avians that visit the park.

Birds for Beginners

If you're new to birdwatching, there are a few things you can do to make your visit a more enjoyable experience. Go in the early morning and late afternoon,

WHERE: 13401 Picadilly Rd., Brighton, CO 80603
PARKING: Parking lots at visitor center.
DIFFICULTY: Easy to moderate. Mostly flat, but an 8-mile loop.
FACILITIES: Bathrooms and picnic areas at nature center.
SPECIAL NOTES: Daily park fee or state parks pass required for entrance.

219

American white pelicans and double-crested cormorants often mingle while nesting

▶ Bald eagle nests are massive, and they're even easier to spot in winter around Barr Lake

◀ Some walking trails take you through groves of trees

especially if you're trying to see migratory species. You can also research specific birds and time your visits to migration seasons (spring and fall are usually peak periods). Sometimes it's easier to hear a bird before you see it, so learn some common bird calls. Guess by sound and confirm by sight.

The wetlands around Barr Lake are good places to spot waterfowl, shorebirds, and wading birds, while the forest edges and open areas attract a variety of songbirds. Take advantage of the observation platforms located around the loop. These make it easier for you to lessen your presence so that birds feel comfortable coming out of their hiding spots. Finally, be patient. Birds can be shy or sensitive to movement or noise, so it's important to be patient and observe quietly.

To be the best possible birder you can be, always follow good birding practices. Do not approach nests or disturb birds in any way, respect the environment by following Leave No Trace principles. If you aren't sure where

to start, joining a local birding group can be a great way to learn more about birds and connect with other budding enthusiasts.

More Than Just Birds

While Barr Lake State Park is known for its birds, there are some cool aquatic insects and amphibians to look for. You can also go out on a boat or kayak in specific areas and see fish up close. Largemouth bass are a popular game fish in Barr Lake, along with crappie, bluegill, and catfish.

Dragonflies and damselflies can be found flying around the lake, hunting for smaller insects. Mayflies are often seen emerging from the water in large swarms, and water beetles can be spotted swimming in the lake, feeding on aquatic plants and insects.

▲ Adult largemouth bass are the top predators in aquatic ecosystems

Crown Hill Park

This 242-acre park has 10 miles of trails and a seasonal wildlife sanctuary smack-dab in the middle of the suburbs.

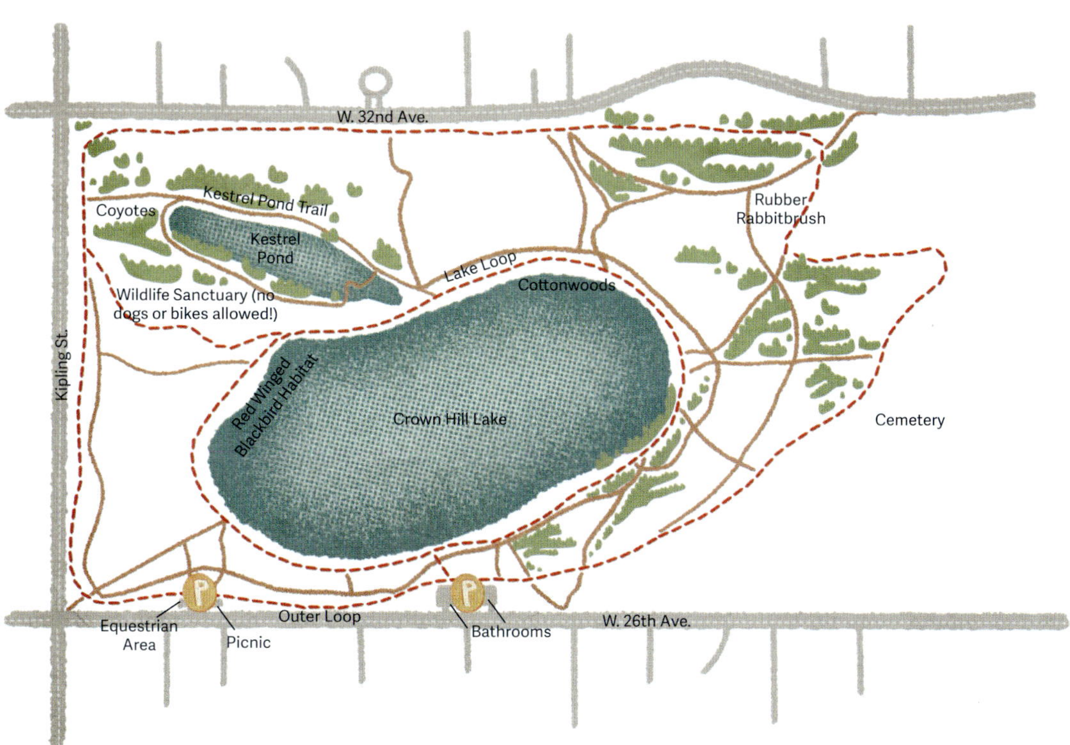

WHERE: 9357 W 26th Ave.,
Wheat Ridge, CO 80033
PARKING: Two free
parking lots.
DIFFICULTY: Easy.
Accessible paved loops and
crushed gravel trails.
FACILITIES: Bathrooms
and picnic area near main
trailhead.
SPECIAL NOTES: Wildlife
sanctuary has seasonal
closures.

Located right at the Wheat Ridge and Lakewood border, Crown Hill Park offers a peaceful retreat where visitors can appreciate diverse birdlife and enjoy lakeside recreation. At the northwest corner you'll find Kestrel Pond, a designated wildlife sanctuary that attracts birds, coyotes, and deer.

Crown Hill Park's history dates back to 1860 when Henry and William Lee homesteaded the land, initially cultivating produce for nearby mining camps and planting the area's first apple orchard. In 1907, the Lees sold the land to the Crown Hill Association, which later opened the cemetery on the eastern portion of the property. In 1972, plans for a high-rise development raised community concerns about preserving the lake and open space, prompting Jefferson County Open Space to work with the cities of Lakewood and Wheat Ridge to acquire the land, creating the Crown Hill Park and Kestrel Pond National Urban Wildlife Refuge.

It's important to note that while Jefferson County Open Space manages the park, it does not own the water rights to Crown Hill Lake. The water is managed by the Crown Hill Cemetery for irrigation purposes, which leads to annual fluctuations in the lake's water level as the pump house on the east side draws water for the cemetery's plots.

Coyote Central

At night, you might hear the haunting call of coyotes echoing through the park. These adaptable creatures have made Crown Hill their home, finding a protected environment amid the city at the west end of the park. Coyotes make their dens in shrubs and cottonwood stands and can often be spotted roaming throughout the day. Because of coyote activity and behavior, it's important to keep dogs on a leash while visiting the park.

Coyotes are opportunistic feeders, preying on small mammals like mice, rabbits, and squirrels, as well as consuming fruits, vegetables, insects, birds, and occasionally scavenging for garbage. While they are generally curious and tend to wander, it's crucial not to encourage any interaction, as this can lead to conflicts with humans and pets.

Most active at dawn and dusk, coyotes can be seen throughout the day, especially during breeding season in February and March when they are more likely to be out hunting for mates. Keep an eye out for newborns in spring and early summer. You might also come across coyote scat on the trails, which can be identified by its contents and shape—berries and small bones, pinched at the end, often left in the middle of the trail to mark their territory.

Wildlife Sanctuary

Crown Hill Park has a fenced-in wildlife sanctuary at the western edge of the park. A .25-mile gravel trail with a boardwalk lets visitors make a loop through the area with spots to pause and take in the sights and sounds of this protected part of the park. The sanctuary is closed every spring through early summer to protect nesting and brooding waterfowl. This closure also ensures a vital refuge for various wildlife—including deer, coyote, and other bird species—during a crucial period in their seasonal life cycle.

Birds Abound

Crown Hill Park is a popular birding destination, attracting both migratory and local species throughout the year. Some birds can be spotted year-round, including Canada goose, gadwall, mallard, red-tailed hawk, ring-billed gull, mourning dove, northern flicker, black-billed magpie, song sparrow, European starling, American robin, hooded merganser, American coot, and red-winged blackbird.

In winter, you might encounter dark-eyed junco, northern harrier, great horned owl, belted kingfisher, and downy woodpecker. As spring arrives, keep an eye out for common grackle, American goldfinch, mountain bluebird, yellow warbler, and blue-winged teal, along with various species of grebe. You'll also spot double-crested cormorant and American white pelican, as well as great blue heron, turkey vulture, Cooper's hawk, and Swainson's hawk, not to mention American avocet and both spotted and solitary sandpipers. Summer is particularly active, with snowy egret, black-crowned night heron, Virginia rail, and killdeer guarding their nests, alongside western meadowlark and Bullock's oriole. As temperatures begin to drop in fall, listen for the rustling of spotted towhee, the trills of Say's phoebe, and sightings of bufflehead, northern shoveler, and Wilson's snipe.

▲ The wildlife refuge is typically open July through February

▲ Broadleaf arrowhead and other aquatic plants help filter the wetland water

► Say's phoebes will nest in almost any structure and occasionally in old nests of other birds

Belmar Park

Acres of natural grasslands surround a 17-acre lake at an authentic history park and museum in Lakewood.

▲ The 17-acre lake at Belmar Park is a resting spot for migrating birds passing through the area

Belmar Park offers excellent birding, particularly during the spring and fall migration seasons. Kountze Lake attracts waterfowl, including ducks, geese, and swans, while the rest of the park is home to a variety of songbirds such as warblers, sparrows, and orioles. Look up to spot raptors soaring overhead, and stroll along the shoreline to observe species like plover, sandpiper, and heron. Spend some time on the platform to get a good look at the waterfowl and turtles up close.

WHERE: 801 S Wadsworth Blvd., Lakewood, CO 80226
PARKING: Parking available at Belmar Library or Heritage Lakewood center.
DIFFICULTY: Easy. Paved and crushed gravel trails.
FACILITIES: Bathrooms at Heritage Lakewood center.

Rewilding the Park

Belmar Park was once a working ranch, and there have been efforts to return it to its native prairie roots. Belmar Park's restoration efforts focused on reintroducing a variety of native plants that thrive in the local environment, enhancing its ecological diversity. Among these are blue grama grass and buffalo grass, drought-tolerant species that serve as staples of the plains and provide essential habitat for wildlife. Purple coneflower, goldenrod, and western salsify add beauty to the landscape and support various pollinators with their beautiful blooms, while leadplant, a small shrub, benefits pollinators and stabilizes soil. By reintroducing these native species, Belmar Park not only enhances its natural beauty but also fosters a sustainable environment that supports local wildlife and reflects the region's ecological heritage.

▲ A snowy egret
hunts for fish at the
shore of the lake

◄ View the birds
on the island in the
middle of Kountze
Lake

▲ Turtles bask on branches to regulate their core temperatures and keep warm

► Heritage Lakewood Belmar Park has more than a dozen restored buildings from the town's past

Riparian Habitat

Riparian habitats are those found along rivers, streams, and lakes. These areas support a wide variety of plant and animal species, offering food, shelter, and breeding grounds. Vegetation like native willows in riparian zones helps filter pollutants from water, improving its quality for both aquatic and terrestrial organisms. The roots of riparian plants stabilize the soil, preventing erosion, runoff, and sedimentation that can negatively affect aquatic habitats.

Extend Your Visit

If you park at the Heritage Lakewood center, check out the museum to see exhibits that highlight Lakewood's past and development, and spend some time walking through the restored and replica buildings there.

Bear Creek Greenbelt Park

Spot beavers, cormorants, and prairie dogs at this sizeable greenbelt south of the city.

▲ Bear Creek Greenbelt is a 2-mile shared-use corridor

Bear Creek Greenbelt Park is a 379-acre urban park in Lakewood that, as the name suggests, follows Bear Creek. The greenbelt crosses through various habitats including wetlands, riparian forests, and open meadows, making it an ideal place to look for wildlife.

Greenbelts are linear parks or open spaces that connect urban areas with natural landscapes. These invaluable ecological corridors protect biodiversity and provide essential food sources, shelter, and breeding grounds. By connecting fragmented habitats across the city and surrounding suburbs, greenbelts allow animals and plants to move freely.

In addition to their ecological importance, greenbelts also play a crucial role in improving air and water quality. Trees and other vegetation found in greenbelts absorb air pollutants, reducing their concentration and improving the overall health of the environment.

Different Ecosystems

Bear Creek Greenbelt Park has a diverse range of habitats, providing visitors with a unique opportunity to experience several different ecosystems in a single location. Along the creek, the riparian forest features trees such as

WHERE: 2800 S Estes St., Lakewood, CO 80227
PARKING: Free parking lot at Stone House. Street parking along greenbelt.
DIFFICULTY: Easy to moderate, depending on length. Paved and crushed gravel trails.
FACILITIES: Bathroom and covered picnic area near parking lot.

cottonwood, willow, and aspen, offering shade and stabilizing riverbanks while supporting species like mule deer, fox, and numerous birds like red-tailed hawk and downy woodpecker. The park also includes several wetlands, marshes, and ponds, which are home to aquatic plants and animals like cattail, salamander, frogs, mallard, and wood ducks.

Open meadows and grasslands are scattered throughout the park, often adorned with vibrant wildflowers like prairie coneflower and lupine attracting bees and butterflies. These meadows may also be frequented by grazing animals like rabbits and mule deer. Scrubland areas consist of low-growing shrubs, trees, and plenty of cheatgrass, creating habitats for various birds, including song sparrow and western meadowlark, and small mammals like rabbits and rodents.

Creek Creatures

As you travel the trail, you'll come across a bridge. Choose between the bench or the pull-offs on each side and look for a resident beaver (their dams have been spotted near the bridge), cormorants, and turtles. Listen for birds calling to each other in the trees above or the frogs and toads calling from below at certain times of the day.

▲ In addition to observing wildlife, you can also fish in the lakes on the greenbelt (as long as you have a fishing license!)

◄ Muskrats, double-crested cormorants, turtles, and song-birds can be spotted along the creek

► Ducks stay warm in water because their leg blood circulation stays in the legs and doesn't travel through their entire bodies

FIELD TRIP 13

Prairie Dogs

Bear Creek Greenbelt Park is home to several prairie dog colonies. Depending on the time of day, you'll hear them calling to warn each other about potential threats. They're more used to people than the average prairie dog, thanks to their proximity to the trail, so they won't be as quick to flee.

Prairie dogs are highly social animals, and their colonies are often referred to as towns. Their burrows are complex structures that can extend deep underground, providing shelter from predators and harsh weather conditions. These burrows also help aerate soil and improve drainage, which can benefit plant growth.

Prairie dogs are herbivores and primarily feed on grasses and other vegetation. Their foraging activities can help to maintain a healthy prairie ecosystem by preventing the growth of invasive plants.

▲ Prairie dogs are observant and will alert their colony to threats by loudly yipping

TRIP 14

Segment 12, High Line Canal

This trail segment takes you through a historic-farm-turned-nature-preserve, offering some of the best wildlife watching along the High Line Canal.

The High Line Canal is one of the longest continuous urban trails in the country. The original canal was built back in 1883 as a way for farms in the Front Range to get access to water for irrigation. With 71 miles of trails, this 860-acre natural corridor takes visitors on a journey from Green Valley Ranch down to Waterton Canyon in Littleton. It's a lot to do in one day, so the trail has 27 segments that highlight different aspects of the outdoors and allow you to make it more of an ongoing journey.

▼ Red-tailed hawks are the most common hawk in North America

▲ The red spot on the back of their heads is an easy way to ID downy woodpeckers on trees along the trail

See What's at Segment 12

Trail segment 12 starts at mile 30 at the East Orchard Road trailhead and finishes at East Belleview Avenue, passing through a historic farm and nature preserve. As you take in the scenery, keep an eye out for ducks, blackbirds, foxes, coyotes, red-tailed hawks, American kestrel, bats, and even the occasional deer. The red barn at mile 30, along with some chickens and a donkey, adds a quaint touch meant to remind you of Denver's farming roots.

Right before mile 32, you'll reach the Marjorie Perry Nature Preserve. Cattails and bulrushes are everywhere in the wetland area, and the aquatic plants offer habitat for hiding for night heron, blue heron, and egret. As you walk around the preserve, look out for bat boxes and the bats that have

▲ Cedar waxwings play an important role in seed spreading; seeds that pass through the bird are much more likely to germinate

taken up residence in them. The mosquitoes that water attracts might be a nuisance, but they make delicious buffets for brown bats.

When you hit mile 32, the canal trail connects with the Greenwood Gulch Trail at the east end of the preserve, toward the segment's end at mile 32.75.

Water means mosquitoes. Wear plenty of bug spray in summer to prevent bites and the spread of disease.

Waterworks

Construction of the original High Line Canal began in 1883, initiated by a group of forward-thinking farmers and engineers who aimed to harness water from the South Platte River to irrigate arid land. Known as the South Platte Ditch Company, the group was successful in creating a lifeline for local agriculture, allowing farmers to cultivate crops in what was once a dry landscape.

In the early 20th century, as Denver expanded, the ownership of the canal transitioned to the Denver Water Board. This marked a pivotal moment, as the city recognized the canal's potential not only for irrigation but also as a critical water supply for its burgeoning population.

In the 1970s, as urban development intensified, Denver Water began to recognize the need for more green spaces and began to expand the canal's

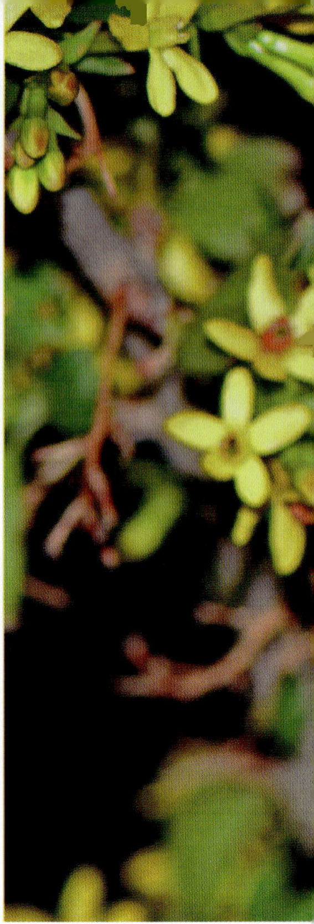

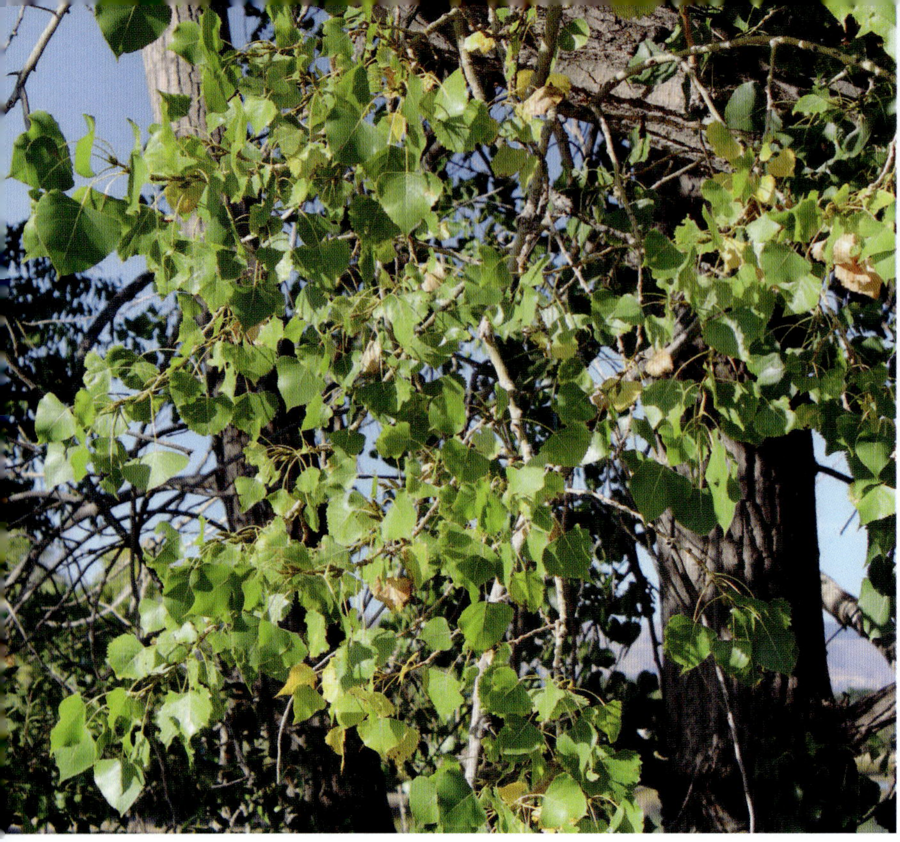

▸ Cottonwood trees turn a vibrant yellow in fall

role from solely an irrigation channel to a recreational asset. They collaborated with local communities to develop the High Line Canal Trail, which transformed its banks into a vibrant living space for plants and animals and a place for residents to recreate without having to leave the city.

In 2024, Denver Water transferred 45 acres of the land to Arapahoe County and placed the canal under a conservation easement (a legal agreement that permanently restricts land use to protect its conservation values) managed by the High Line Canal Conservancy. This ensures that it remains a public space, preserving its natural and recreational features, and protecting the land for generations to come.

Look Around

More than 23,000 trees were planted along the canal over the past century. Bur oak, catalpa, hackberry, honey locust, cottonwood, and box elder are just a few of the species you'll come across that you can easily identify by their leaf shape and seed pods.

Twenty species of cavity-nesting birds have been spotted along the canal corridor.

Habitat trees, also known as snags, are dead or dying trees that are left along the corridor instead of being removed. Keeping the dead trees has its benefits—their cavities act as places to nest and foraging sites for bugs, birds, and small mammals. Downy woodpecker, northern flicker, great horned owl, raccoon, and even wood duck can be found in these habitat trees along the canal.

The living mature trees on the banks of the High Line Canal also create a vibrant habitat for a variety of bird species, from small songbirds to raptors. Among the songbirds, you can find the brightly colored western bluebird, which often perches on fence posts, as well as American robin, known for its cheerful, melodic songs. Song sparrow, with its complex vocalizations, are also common in the area, as is black-capped chickadee, recognizable by its curious demeanor and black-and-white plumage. Additionally, the canal supports larger birds of prey, such as red-tailed hawk, often seen soaring overhead, and barn owl, with its silent flight and heart-shaped face.

Cherry Creek State Park

Spend time on the water or bring your furry friend to the off-leash dog area at Denver's closest state park.

▲ There are 35 miles of trails at Cherry Creek State Park

Cherry Creek State Park is a 4200-acre park southeast of the city with an 880-acre reservoir. It's a popular destination for recreation on the water, while the extensive trail system provides opportunities for outdoor exploration.

The establishment of Cherry Creek State Park was largely driven by the need for effective flood management in the Denver metro area. The Cherry Creek drainage basin has historically been prone to flooding, particularly during spring runoff and heavy rainstorms. To address this issue, the Army Corps of Engineers constructed the dam in 1950, creating a reservoir that helps control floodwaters. This infrastructure not only mitigates flooding but also enhances the park's recreational offerings by providing a safe area for boating, fishing, and other water activities.

WHERE: 4201 S Parker Rd., Aurora, CO 80014
PARKING: Multiple parking lots.
DIFFICULTY: Easy to moderate, depending on distance. Trails mostly flat or rolling terrain.
FACILITIES: Bathrooms available at several trailheads. First-come, first-served picnic tables located around the lake.
SPECIAL NOTES: Daily fee or state parks pass required for entry.

Water Water Everywhere

One of the most prominent ecosystems in the park is the aquatic reservoir ecosystem. More than two dozen fish species have been recorded in Cherry Creek State Park including carp, crappie, walleye, northern pike, bluegill, largemouth bass, yellow perch, and channel catfish.

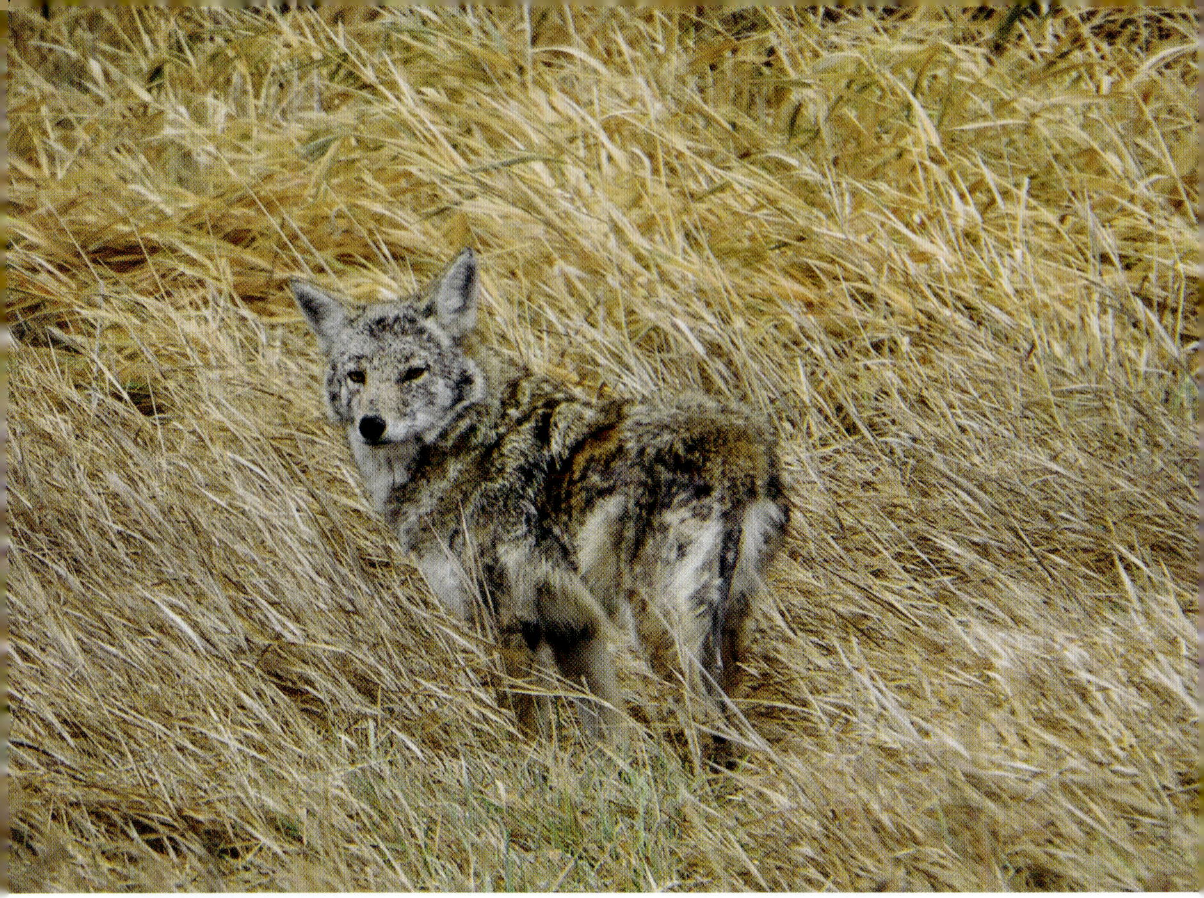

▲ Coyotes roam through the grassland areas of the park

◄ Walleye have really sharp teeth, which help them eat other fish, crayfish, frogs, snails, and insects

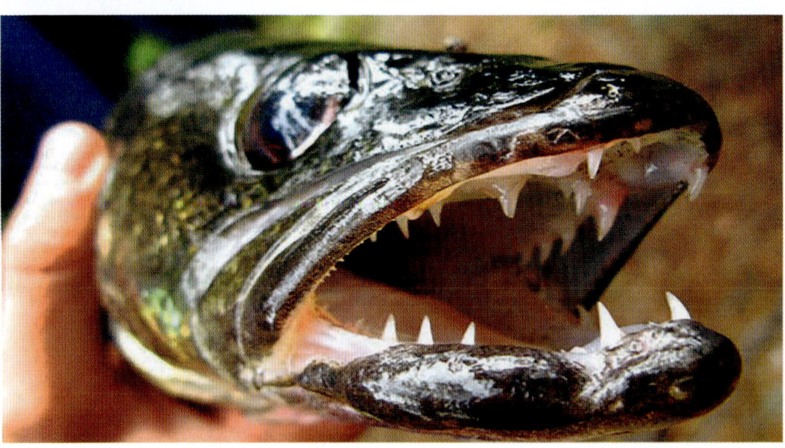

The riparian forest and wetland areas with saturated soils and a high water table help maintain water quality and provide habitat for birds, mammals, and amphibians, and support trees like cottonwood, willow, and aspen. The reservoir's shallow areas are home to emergent plants like cattail and bulrush, while deeper areas support submerged plants like pondweed. Wetlands are important for filtering pollutants from water, providing habitat for wildlife, and mitigating the impacts of floods.

Grasslands for the Greater Good

The park also has open grassland areas, which are dominated by grasses and other herbaceous plants. While it might not seem like it from the surface, thriving grasslands often have water below the surface. Their deep root systems help to absorb rainfall, reduce runoff, and maintain groundwater levels, which contributes to healthier watersheds and improved water quality. By slowing down water movement, grasslands minimize soil erosion and promote moisture retention. They also provide habitat for prairie dogs, rabbits, coyotes, and birds.

Grasslands are often more efficient than forests in terms of carbon sequestration due to their extensive root systems, which can store carbon over long periods. It's estimated that grasslands currently store up to 30 percent of the world's carbon. Unlike forests, which rely on aboveground biomass for carbon storage, grasslands store a significant amount of carbon underground, making them less susceptible to disturbances like fires or logging. Grasslands also have a higher rate of plant turnover and can recover quickly from disturbances, allowing for continual carbon uptake.

Adventures in Animal Spotting

Due to the size of the reservoir, Cherry Creek State Park is a popular destination for large flocks of birds. Canada goose and American white pelican often gather in large flocks, especially during the spring and fall migrations. Mallard, pintail, teal, and ring-billed seagull are also often seen in large flocks, especially near the shoreline.

Though dependent on season, dawn and dusk are usually the best times for viewing wildlife.

► Plains leopard frogs blend in well with their surroundings; you'll have an easier time finding them by sound

More than 40 mammal species have been documented throughout the park, including cottontail rabbit, coyote, beaver, muskrat, raccoon, weasel, and squirrel. Visitors might see white-tailed or mule deer grazing in the grasslands and hear black-tailed prairie dogs chirping loudly to alert their dens about potential threats.

Plains garter snake, western hognose snake, and bullsnake, sometimes mistaken for rattlesnakes, also call the park home. Amphibians at the park include Woodhouse's toad, striped chorus frog, bullfrog, and plains leopard frog.

▲ Adult pelicans get a "horn" every year during breeding season that falls off— similar to antlers on elk and deer

TRIP 16

Lookout Mountain Preserve and Nature Center

Known for its jaw-dropping views of the Continental Divide, Golden, and Denver, this park is also home to some of the area's most interesting wildlife.

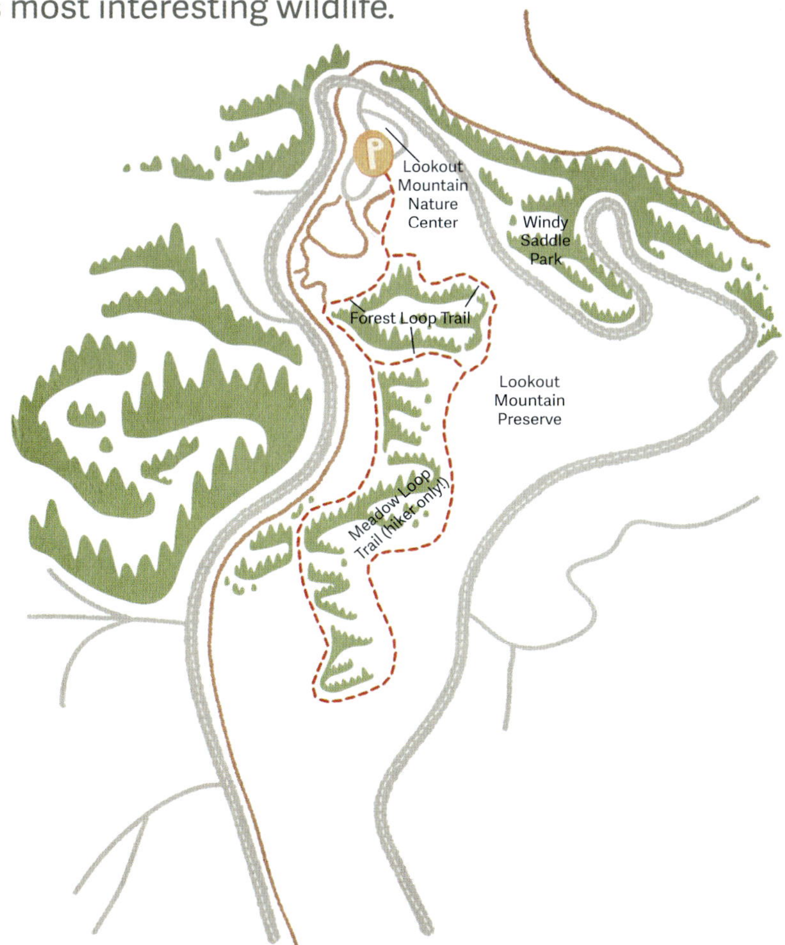

At 7377 feet, Lookout Mountain's summit provides panoramic views that stretch across Denver to the plains, and on clear days, the snow-capped peaks of the Continental Divide. It's a popular destination for visitors seeking breathtaking vistas and a chance to escape the hustle and bustle of city life without the work of a big hike.

The park has two trails, each offering its own unique experience. Colorow Mountain Forest Loop Trail is a .6-mile loop that takes you through the forest with a stop at an overlook with stunning views. The second trail is a 1.3-mile loop that starts at the nature center and goes through the Forest Loop Trail and Meadow Loop Trail.

Because the trails are shaded, they can stay muddy through spring. Be prepared and wear shoes you don't mind getting dirty. Walk through the mud to avoid eroding the soil next to the trail.

For those interested in geology, Lookout Mountain is composed of various rock types, including granite and gneiss, which date back millions of years. These formations contribute to the area's rugged terrain and offer valuable insights into the geological processes that shaped the Front Range.

Look Closely at Lookout Mountain

Lookout Mountain is a fantastic spot for wildlife enthusiasts who don't want to venture too far from the city. You can find mule deer grazing in the meadows, black bears in the forests, and colorful mountain bluebirds darting

▲ Temperature inversions can cause dense layers of low-lying fog

► Robins call Lookout Mountain home year-round

◄ Steller's jays can be seen (and heard) at high elevation

through the trees. Peregrine falcons, known for their incredible speed, soar overhead, while the howls of coyotes can often be heard at dusk. The western terrestrial garter snake is commonly seen in grasslands and forest edges, and the tiger salamander prefers damp environments near streams and ponds.

Plant life is equally diverse on Lookout Mountain. Colorado's state flower, the columbine, features striking blue-and-white blooms, and Indian paintbrush adds splashes of red and orange to the landscape. Blue grama,

a native grass, grows well in the mountain's dry conditions, forming dense clumps. Tall, colorful spikes of lupine dot the grassland areas, ponderosa pines and their scented bark stand sentry, and mountain mahogany with its twisted seeds thrives in the rocks.

Extend Your Trip

If you're up for a challenge, Beaver Brook Trail is a difficult 9-mile hiker-only trail that connects Lookout Mountain, Clear Creek Canyon Park, Denver Mountain Parks' Genesee Park, and Windy Saddle Park.

▲ The curly, feathery structure of mountain mahogany's seeds helps with their dispersal

TRIP 17

North Table Mountain

One of two of the table mesas in Golden, North Table is home to an impressive collection of lichen and a stunning view of Denver.

There are two prominent mesas in Golden: North Table Mountain and South Table Mountain. Mesas are flat-topped hills or mountains with steep sides formed through erosion and sedimentation. Layers of sedimentary rock accumulate over time, and as geological forces uplift the region, these sedimentary layers become exposed as forces such as wind and water wear away the softer rock surrounding the mesa. Harder, more resistant layers are left behind.

The history of North and South Table Mountains is also intertwined with the history of the city of Golden. The area around the mountains was once seasonally home to Cheyenne, Arapaho, and occasionally Ute people who used the mesas for shelter and hunting. Later, the mountains became a popular destination for early settlers and pioneers, who were drawn to the area's natural beauty and resources.

While you can hike either mesa, North Table Mountain is a little more accessible for parking and ability. The park's trails range from easy to moderate, with the shortest at about 1 mile and the longest coming in at more than 3 miles. Some sections on the longer trails can be steep and rocky, so be prepared before you head out. As you hike, keep an eye out for mule deer, prairie rattlesnake, bullsnake, prairie lizard, and the western widow spider. Due to its higher elevation and limited tree coverage, the park offers expansive views of the surrounding landscape, but it also means it's easier to run into heat exhaustion problems. Visit in spring, fall, or winter if you aren't accustomed to the climate.

▲ North (left) and South (right) Table Mountains were formed by lava flows

Look at the Lava

Three discernible cliff-forming lava flows can be seen on North Table Mountain: one part of the way up its northwest slope, and two that make up its cap. The Ralston Dike, a vent from which these lava flows erupted, is located about 2 miles away. The flows have been dated to about 62 to 64 million years old, which places them in the early Paleocene.

Rattlesnake Central

If you hike this trail, be prepared to encounter rattlesnakes, especially late spring through fall. Prairie rattlesnakes have a distinctive rattle on the end of their tails. This rattle is composed of interlocking segments that create a warning sound when shaken. The number of segments on the rattle does not necessarily indicate the age of the snake, as new segments can be added throughout the year.

► Prairie rattlesnakes often return to the same den year after year

▼ Four lava flows led to the current formation of the cap of North Table Mountain

There is an ongoing rattlesnake study at North Table Mountain Park, so be aware that you may notice researchers off trail, especially on sunny days. While rattlesnakes are generally shy and will avoid confrontation, it is important to be cautious and give them space. If you encounter a rattlesnake, do not attempt to approach or handle it. Instead, back away slowly and avoid making sudden movements.

While rattlesnakes try to avoid conflict, sometimes it happens. If you're bitten, remain calm and call 911 immediately with your exact location on the trail. Keep the bitten area at or below the level of the heart. Do not attempt to cut into, suck, or interfere with the bite area. If your pet is bitten, immediately head to a vet's office. Call ahead to make sure your vet stocks anti-venom. If they do not, they can advise of the closest location that does.

If you see a rattlesnake, follow the 30/30 rule: back away by 30 feet and give the snake 30 seconds to decide to leave.

Wonderful Wildflowers

Despite the arid conditions, North Table Mountain is home to a vibrant display of native wildflowers. Among the most notable blooms are the striking purple penstemon, the delicate reddish peach blossoms of the globemallow, cheerful bright yellow gumweed, stark white thistle poppy, and the pollinator-attracting Rocky Mountain bee plant.

Mount Galbraith Park

With sweeping vistas of the Denver skyline and the majestic Rocky Mountains, this hiker-only park gives you the chance to see sun-loving plants and animals up close and at your own pace.

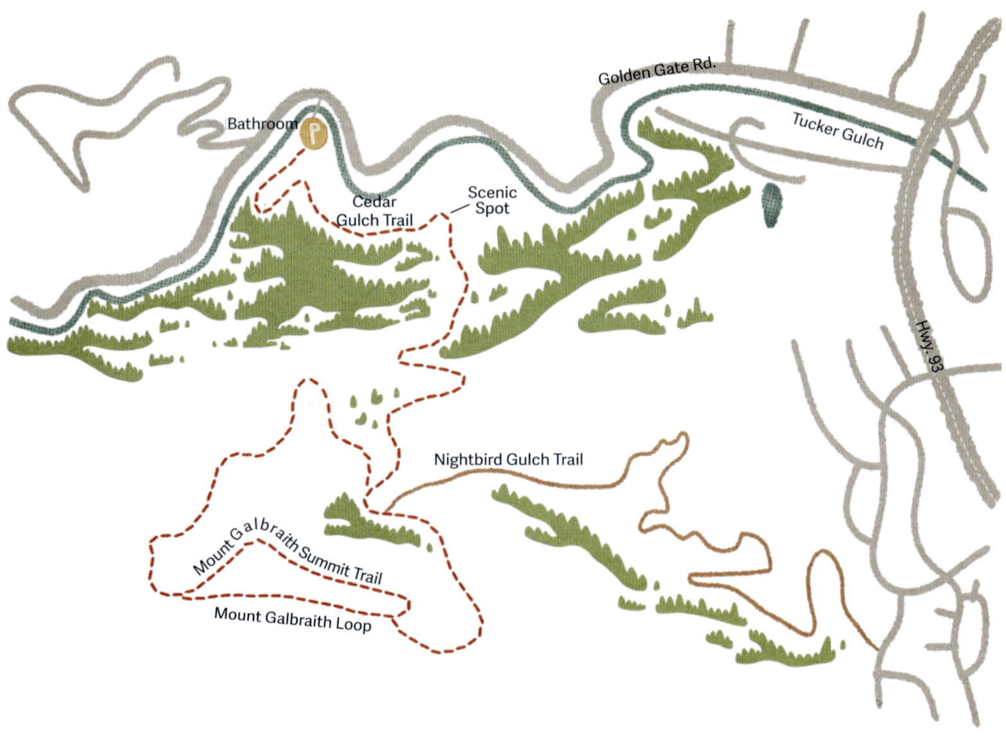

▲ Indian paintbrush is a hemiparasitic plant, meaning it can draw nutrients from the roots of neighboring plants

Mount Galbraith Park is a hiker-only park with 5.2 miles of moderately steep, rocky trails. The Mt. Galbraith Loop circles 1.6 miles around the top of the 7260-foot peak and offers views of Golden, the plains, and the Continental Divide. There isn't much shade, so be prepared to get hot if you go during summer.

WHERE: 21992 Golden Gate Canyon Rd., Golden, CO 80403
PARKING: Small parking lot at trailhead.
DIFFICULTY: Moderate to difficult. Trails range from 3.4 to 7.5 miles.
FACILITIES: Bathroom at trailhead.

Rattlesnakes, Racerunners, and Prairie Lizards

Mount Galbraith is a popular park for ectothermic reptiles, meaning they rely on external sources of heat to regulate their body temperature. Basking in the sun helps them warm up and become more active, allowing them to hunt, mate, and digest food more efficiently.

Prairie rattlesnakes are venomous snakes known for their distinctive rattle and ability to strike with great speed. They are typically found in rocky

areas or in open grasslands. While they can be dangerous, rattlesnakes generally avoid confrontation and will only bite if they feel threatened.

Six-lined racerunners are long, slender, fast lizards. Like their name suggests, they are excellent runners and can often outrun predators. They're typically found in open areas feeding on insects and small vertebrates that also love the heat.

Prairie lizards are smaller, typically brown or gray in color, and have a stocky build. These lizards are diurnal, meaning they are active during the day, and primarily insectivorous.

Sun-loving Plants

The plants at Mount Galbraith have to be able to survive the sun. Native plants do this better than most. Purple and blue asters, for example, are vibrant perennials that bloom from late summer to fall. Their eye-catching flowers attract a variety of pollinators, including bees, butterflies, and hummingbirds.

Indian paintbrush is a wildflower famed for its vivid red, orange, or yellow bracts that resemble a painter's brush dipped in color. These flowers often emerge in spring and can be found in meadows and prairies.

Gold cobblestone lichen is a crustose lichen found predominantly on rocks. It has a yellow hue and bumpy, cobblestone-like texture. This lichen plays a significant ecological role by breaking down the rocks it grows on, which aids in soil formation and nutrient release.

Creeping mahonia is a low-growing evergreen shrub that features clusters of bright yellow flowers in early spring, glossy leaves, and small blue berries in summer and fall. The berries are particularly attractive to birds.

Look for Lions

Mount Galbraith Park is home to a variety of wildlife, including the elusive mountain lion, also known as the cougar or puma. These solitary predators are an essential part of Colorado's ecosystem, playing a crucial role in maintaining the balance of prey populations, particularly deer. Mountain lions are highly adaptable and can thrive in diverse habitats, from mountainous areas to foothills and even neighborhoods. While the chance of encountering a mountain lion on a trail is relatively low, awareness and precaution are essential. Keeping dogs on a leash not only protects them, it also helps avoid drawing a mountain lion's attention, as domestic animals can trigger their hunting instincts.

If you do encounter a mountain lion, staying calm is critical. These big cats prefer to avoid humans but can lash out if they feel cornered. In such situations, back away slowly, but without turning your back, make yourself appear larger by raising your arms, and make loud noises like yelling or clapping. If the mountain lion approaches and you feel threatened, bear spray can provide an additional layer of protection. Hiking in groups or making noise while on solo hikes can significantly reduce the likelihood of an encounter, as mountain lions are less inclined to approach larger gatherings of people.

▼ They're adorable, but *never* approach mountain lion kittens, as their mother is probably nearby

TRIP 19

Red Rocks Park and Amphitheater

Home to the iconic music venue, this park also has walking trails that take you up close to the sedimentary rocks that give the area its name.

Red Rocks Amphitheater is a world-renowned music venue, but many people don't know that it's located inside a park. From the top of the amphitheater, you'll see a panoramic view of Denver and the surrounding plains, all framed by towering 300-foot sandstone formations that create a stunning natural backdrop. This iconic amphitheater, completed in 1941, is celebrated for its remarkable acoustics and has hosted legendary musicians. The park's historic trading post, built in 1931, houses a visitor center with a restaurant, gift shop, and educational exhibits that highlight the park's natural and cultural history. Scenic roads wind through the park, making it a popular route for cyclists; drive slowly throughout the park.

For a quick trip, try the 1.4-mile Trading Post Trail, which begins and ends at the trading post and takes you on an immersive journey through spectacular rock formations, valleys, and meadows.

▲ The view at Red Rocks Park from Trading Post Trail

What Makes the Rocks Red

The reddish color of the rocks here is due to the presence of iron oxide. Also known as rust, iron oxide is a common mineral found in the rocks of the Denver Basin, which includes Red Rocks Park.

Iron oxide in the rocks gives them a reddish brown hue, which is particularly noticeable when they're exposed to sunlight and weathering. Over time, the iron oxide can become more concentrated, resulting in the deep red color that characterizes the rocks at the park. Their specific shade of red can vary depending on the concentration of iron oxide and other minerals present in the sandstone. Prolonged exposure to wind, rain, and sunlight can affect their color too.

▲ Snow and wind change the colors of these rocks over time

Pause for Plants and Birds

If the rocks are the headliner, the plants and birds are the openers, and they're worth watching. Rocky Mountain juniper is a hardy evergreen tree that flourishes at high altitudes, often found in rocky soils where other trees struggle. This species not only provides essential cover for wildlife but also helps stabilize soil with its extensive root system. Sagebrush, with its distinctive aromatic scent, and rubber rabbitbrush, recognizable by bright yellow flowers that bloom in late summer, provide nectar for pollinators and shelter swallows, finches, and other small birds seeking protection from raptors that hunt in the area.

Lots of edible trees (both for people and animals) can be found at the park. Chokecherry and American plum are flowering shrubs that produce delicious fruits, and the Gambel oak, a small deciduous tree, has acorns, which are a food source for various animals.

When it comes to birds, it's easier to find them by pausing and listening for movement or song. Lesser goldfinches are small, yellow birds often seen feeding on seeds. Spotted towhees are known for their distinctive speckled plumage and habit of scratching the ground for food. Woodhouse's scrub jays are noisy, intelligent birds often seen in scrubby habitats, hence their name. Black-billed magpies are large, black-and-white birds also known for their intelligence, as well as their ability to mimic sounds.

◄ Unlike many oaks that spread by acorns, Gambel oak trees actually reproduce better through rhizomes underground

▲ Look for the bright yellow of lesser goldfinches

▼ Woodhouse's scrub jay sometimes sits on the backs of mule deer and eats ticks off them

▲ Chokecherry trees have hanging clusters of white flowers that turn into edible dark red berries

Extend Your Visit

You're already there, so stop by the amphitheater during your visit. The construction of Red Rocks Amphitheater was a remarkable feat of engineering. Due to its natural sandstone formations, traditional construction methods were not feasible. Instead, workers carefully carved and shaped the existing rock to create the stage, seating areas, and other features. This process was labor-intensive and required skilled craftsmanship.

The amphitheater's unique design takes advantage of the natural acoustics of the sandstone formations. The curved walls of the amphitheater reflect sound waves, creating a rich and powerful acoustic experience for both performers and audience members. This natural amplification has made Red Rocks a world-renowned venue for music concerts and other events.

► (next spread) Red Rocks Amphitheater typically hosts shows from April through November

FIELD TRIP 19

Mount Falcon Park

See the remnants of a castle and the location of a proposed summer White House at this mountain in Morrison.

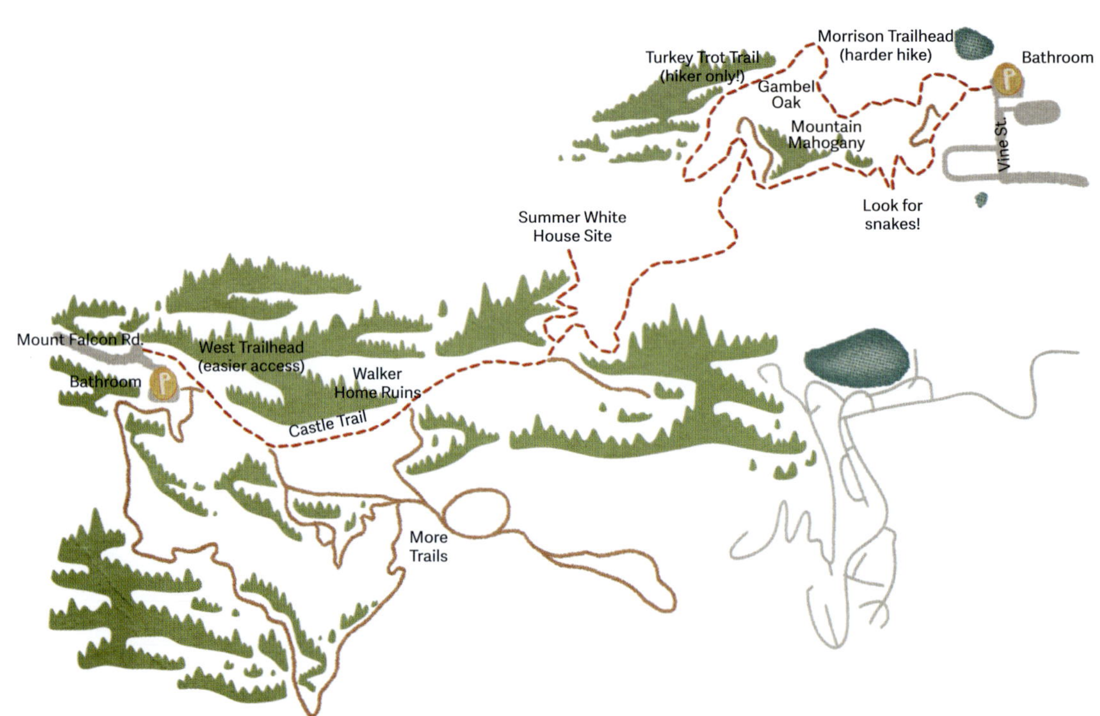

▲ Mount Falcon is popular with runners and mountain bikers—stay alert when you're on the trail

There are two ways to get to the castle at Mount Falcon. For those looking for a heart-pumping challenge, start at the east trailhead. The Turkey Trot to Castle Trail has a steep ascent and a 2000-foot elevation gain right out the gate. If you're able to make the journey, you'll be rewarded with incredible views of Denver as you wind up the mountain. At the top are two historic sites: the ruins of John Brisben Walker's castle and the cornerstone of a proposed summer White House for American presidents.

If you're in the mood for a more leisurely stroll, head to the west trailhead, where you'll find easier trails that still have great views and plenty of native plants. At lower elevations, look for sagebrush and rabbitbrush, which adds splashes of yellow during blooming season. As you ascend, piñon pines and juniper trees fill the forest. In spring and early summer, wildflowers like Indian paintbrush and Colorado's state flower, the columbine, come to life. The lush undergrowth features shrubs like serviceberry and mountain mahogany, providing food and shelter for wildlife.

WHERE: Mount Falcon West Trailhead, 21074 Mount Falcon Rd., Indian Hills, CO 80454
Mount Falcon Morrison Trailhead, 3852 Vine Street, Morrison, CO 80465
PARKING: Parking lots at trailheads.
DIFFICULTY: Easy to difficult depending on trail.
FACILITIES: Bathrooms and picnic area at Morrison Trailhead. Bathroom at west trailhead with picnic area .3 miles away.
SPECIAL NOTES: Trailheads are far apart and require a car. West trailhead has easier trails.

No matter which trailhead you start at, weekends during summer at Mount Falcon can be bustling. For nature watching during quieter times, visit during the offseason or arrive early.

Trees and Bees

The trees on Mount Falcon are hardy—they have to be to survive the open exposure, wind, and snow. The Rocky Mountain juniper stands out with its twisted branches and bluish green foliage, while the mountain mahogany has leathery leaves and corkscrew-shaped seeds. Gambel oak features a rounded crown and lobed leaves that provide essential food for wildlife. Lodgepole pine is a towering tree with long, thin needles and a remarkable ability to regenerate after forest fires. Ponderosa pine's puzzle-piece bark is a dead ID giveaway, as well as its long, drooping needles. It's one of the most commonly spotted trees in our forests. Douglas firs are also found here. Identify them by their flat, cone-shaped cones.

Identifying conifers is easy by examining their needles. Pine needles are typically thin and grow in clusters, while spruce needles are sharp. Fir needles, on the other hand, are flat and blunt-tipped.

With the blooms come the bees, and Mount Falcon has no shortage of either. The golden sweat bee is a small, metallic green bee commonly found

▲ You can walk through the ruins of the Walker Home at the top of Castle Trail

◄ Ponderosa pine trees have very unique bark, both in look and in scent; scratch it for a whiff of vanilla or butterscotch

▲ Golden sweat bees are active from spring through early fall

▼ Two-striped grasshoppers are big: females can grow up to 2.25 inches and males 1.25 inches

in our area. They're important pollinators of many flowering plants. As their name suggests, they are attracted to the sweat of humans and animals and will often land on them to lick it off to get salt. Golden sweat bees are solitary bees, meaning they do not live in colonies like honeybees. Instead, they build their own nests in the ground or in wood. Females collect pollen and nectar to feed their young. They are gentle bees that are not aggressive and rarely sting.

Another bee you'll see a lot in this park is Hunt's bumblebee. This bee is larger and a member of the Apidae family, which also includes honeybees, though it doesn't produce honey. Unlike sweat bees, Hunt's bees are social and live in colonies, with a queen, workers, and drones. Hunt's bumblebees are big and fuzzy, with a black-and-yellow-striped pattern and an orange band on their backs. They are powerful fliers and often seen foraging for nectar and pollen on flowers.

Grasshoppers

As you walk along the trail, you'll see and hear grasshoppers as they scatter to avoid you. Three common ones at Mount Falcon are two-striped, pallid-winged, and Keeler's spur-throat grasshopper. The two-striped grasshopper is medium-sized, brown or green, with two dark stripes running down its back. It is a generalist feeder, consuming a wide variety of plants. The pallid-winged grasshopper is smaller, with a pale green or yellow coloration. It's a specialist feeder, primarily consuming grasses. Keeler's spur-throat grasshopper is the largest of the three, with a brown coloration and a distinctive spur on its hind legs. It is also a generalist feeder.

◄ Albert's squirrels can reach the seeds inside of pine cones

Yes, That's a Black Squirrel

The black coloration of Albert's squirrels, also known as Rocky Mountain squirrels, is an adaptation to their environment. This coloration provides several benefits for survival in the mountainous regions of Colorado. First, it helps them absorb heat from the sun. This is particularly important during the cooler months of the year, when Albert's squirrels need to keep warm. Second, black fur can help camouflage them in the rocky terrain of the mountains. The dark color of their fur blends in with the shadows and rocks, making it more difficult for predators to spot them.

Extend Your Visit

The Morrison Natural History Museum is right next to the Morrison Trailhead (the east one). The museum features interactive exhibits that bring the prehistoric to life, allowing visitors to explore the fascinating world of dinosaurs and other ancient creatures. Kids and adults will be captivated by life-sized dinosaur replicas, touch exhibits, and hands-on activities. The museum also exhibits fossils of other prehistoric animals, plants, and insects found in the Morrison Formation. Visit to learn about the diverse ecosystem that existed millions of years ago in this region.

Chatfield State Park

Spend the day searching for herps, birds, and other animals at one of the largest publicly accessible reservoirs in the Denver area.

WHERE: 9700 S Wadsworth Blvd., Littleton, CO 80128 11500 N Roxborough Park Rd., Littleton, CO 80125
PARKING: Multiple parking lots.
DIFFICULTY: Easy to moderate. Mostly flat trails, many paved and accessible.
FACILITIES: Restrooms and picnic areas located throughout park.
SPECIAL NOTES: Daily fee or state parks pass required for entry.

▲▲ Sections of the reservoir are open to boating and other water sports

▲ Chatfield State Park has more than 32 miles of trails

Chatfield State Park is south of the city and the biggest spot for water recreation in the Denver metro area. At the heart of the park is a nearly 1500-surface-acre reservoir, open for boating, fishing, swimming, kayaking, and canoeing in designated areas. The reservoir hosts a diverse range of fish species, making it a popular spot for anglers. Visitors can rent boats, kayaks, or paddleboards to explore the waters and take in the picturesque views.

Water is important for wildlife and Chatfield State Park is home to a lot of it. Ecologically rich, the park showcases mixed prairie communities

and wetland areas, supported by features like the South Platte River and Plum Creek floodplains. Deer, coyotes, red foxes, and playful raccoons are residents, along with prairie dogs and various species of squirrels. Reptiles like painted turtle and western rattlesnake can be found basking in the sun, while amphibians such as bullfrog and tiger salamander add to the park's rich biodiversity.

The park is a haven for birdwatchers, boasting more than 212 species that visit throughout the year. Look out for bald eagle, white pelican, Caspian tern, seagull, and burrowing owl. Other avian visitors may include great blue heron, American bittern, and red-winged blackbird.

For those who prefer land-based activities, Chatfield State Park has dozens of trails that meander through the park's varied landscapes, offering opportunities for scenic vistas in addition to wildlife observation.

Reptiles and Amphibians

Reptiles and amphibians, collectively known as herpetofauna or "herps," can also be found in the park. Among reptiles, you'll find prairie rattlesnake, a native pit viper recognized for its distinctive rattle and ability to help control rodent populations. Western yellow-bellied racer is another, known for its speed, gliding gracefully through grasslands, while the western hognose snake, with its unique upturned snout, is famous for its defensive behaviors, including playing dead when threatened.

Various garter snake species, such as the western terrestrial garter, plains garter, and common garter prey on smaller mammals, amphibians, and even fish. Bullsnakes, impressive constrictors, mimic rattlesnakes when

▲ Caspian terns (the orange beak with the black cap in the center) are the largest of the tern species

◄ Western hognose snakes look similar to some venomous snakes, but their upturned snout is an ID giveaway

▲ While they might vary in color from brown to green to gray, the leopard-like spots on northern leopard frogs will always be present

▼ Despite their common name, crappie are prized catches for fishermen—the nickname comes from the French-Canadian word *crapet*

threatened but are virtually harmless. Additionally, the park is home to several turtle species including the snapping turtle, known for its powerful jaws, and the western painted turtle, easily recognizable by the brightly colored markings on its shell.

The park's amphibian population is equally diverse. Northern leopard frog, characterized by its distinct leopard-like spots, is often found in wetlands during breeding season. Western chorus frog is known for its recognizable call and thrives in both grasslands and marshy areas. Large and vocal, the deep croak of the bullfrog can be heard around smaller pond areas during certain times of the year, and Woodhouse's toad seeks out shelter in habitats near water sources, hunting insects and small invertebrates.

Fish Found at Chatfield

The lake at Chatfield is home to several different fish species, making it a popular destination for both anglers and nature enthusiasts. There are game fish, including largemouth bass, known for its size and fighting ability, and smallmouth bass thriving in rocky areas. Various species of trout also live in the lake, including rainbow and brown trout. Walleye, with its sharp vision and secretive nature, and crappie, both black and white, can be found in abundance during the warmer months, especially near submerged structures.

Extend Your Trip

Extend your trip with a visit to Denver Audubon at the south end of the park. You can either take the Waterton Link and Wetlands Connector trails from inside of the park, or go directly to the address at 11280 Waterton Road, Littleton. Denver Audubon is dedicated to inspiring actions that protect birds, other wildlife, and their habitats through education, conservation, and research.

TRIP 22

Waterton Canyon

Share the trail with bighorn sheep in a canyon that supplies the city with a big portion of its drinking water.

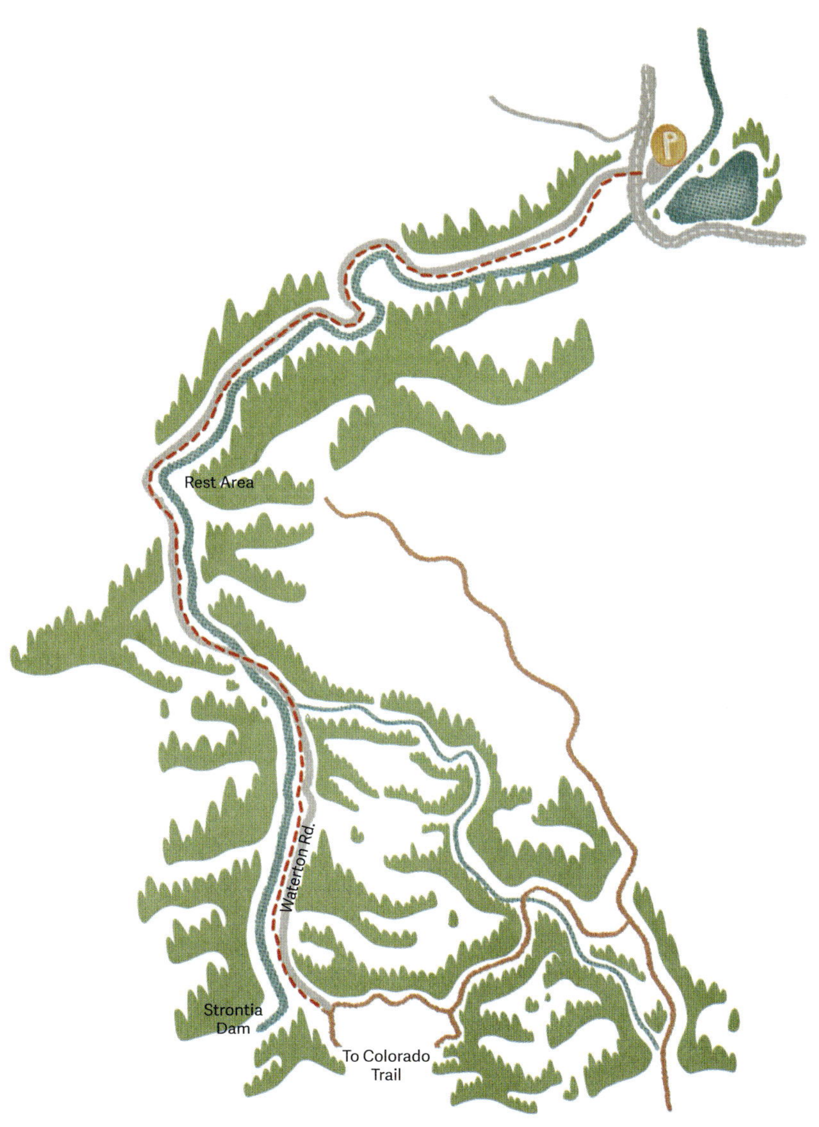

WHERE: 12437–12489 Waterton Canyon, Littleton, CO 80127

PARKING: Free parking lot across the street from the trailhead.

DIFFICULTY: Easy to moderate. Mostly flat, wide-open gravel out-and-back trail. The dam is 6.2 miles in, but you can choose your distance.

FACILITIES: Restrooms and picnic areas every few miles along the trail.

SPECIAL NOTES: No dogs or other pets allowed to protect bighorn sheep. Last point of potable water located at Last Chance water fountain at start of trail.

▲ The Waterton Canyon trail follows the South Platte River

The trail at Waterton Canyon in Littleton is on the easier side. It has a very gradual incline but is mostly a flat gravel trail. The difficulty can be deceptive, though; the trail is an out and back with very limited shade, so plan your hike accordingly—whatever distance you walk in, you'll need to hike back out.

The trail follows an old railroad track-turned–Denver Water Board road taking you through the canyon alongside the South Platte River. Enhance your experience by taking breaks at the benches and covered picnic tables along the way for some nature watching.

The canyon is teeming with wildlife, making it a prime spot for birdwatching and animal sightings. Bighorn sheep are a standout attraction, often seen grazing on the rocky slopes or on the trails. Mule deer are also common in the area. Keep an eye out for other mammals such as mountain lion and elk grazing in the brush and reptiles like prairie lizard and rattlesnake basking in the sun. Bird enthusiasts will enjoy spotting over 40 species, including American robin, western meadowlark, and common flicker flitting among the trees. The South Platte River is popular for fishing, with opportunities to catch trout in a tranquil setting.

Waterton Canyon also features unique geological formations, shaped by millions of years of erosion and sedimentation. The trail serves as the first leg of the Colorado Trail—a 486-mile-long hiking path that traverses the Rocky Mountains, connecting Denver to Durango—making it an excellent starting point for those looking to explore farther into the beautiful Colorado wilderness.

To protect bighorn sheep and their habitat, dogs and other pets are not allowed on the trails. If you do forget and bring your furry friend, head 5 miles up the road to Chatfield State Park where leashed dogs are welcome.

▲ Double-crested cormorants sunning on a boulder in the South Platte River

Strontia Springs Dam

Strontia Springs Dam is located 6.2 miles from the start of the trail, and it plays a crucial role in water management for the Denver metropolitan area. Built in 1983, this impressive structure rises 243 feet above the riverbed and diverts water from the Strontia Springs Reservoir to the Foothills and Marston water-treatment plants.

One major concern with this reservoir, as well as others in the Denver area, is sediment buildup. Sediment flows, consisting of coarse material from the foothills, threaten to reduce the reservoir's capacity and potentially clog the dam's operations. While some sediment buildup is normal and expected, the problem has been exacerbated by wildfires and intense rainfall. Engineers at Denver Water are focused on developing long-term, sustainable approaches to manage sediment buildup at Strontia Reservoir. Given that the reservoir accounts for over 80 percent of the water supply for 1.5 million residents, addressing this issue is critical.

Make Room for Bighorns

Bighorn sheep are one of the most captivating wildlife species in Waterton Canyon. They're well adapted to the rugged terrain, with powerful legs and sturdy hooves that allow them to navigate steep, rocky slopes with ease. Bighorn sheep are social creatures, often found in small herds that can range from a few individuals to over a dozen. One telltale feature of bighorn sheep are their impressive, curved horns, which can weigh up to 30 pounds in males. The canyon's varied elevations and rocky outcrops provide an ideal habitat, offering food sources like grasses and shrubs, as well as natural cover to avoid predators such as mountain lions and coyotes.

The best times to spot bighorn sheep are typically in the early morning or late afternoon when they are most active. During spring and early summer, lambs are born, making these months especially rewarding for wildlife observers. While the sheep are generally accustomed to human presence, always maintain a respectful distance. They can be surprisingly agile, able to leap over obstacles, climb steep cliffs, and charge people on the trail who get too close. Never approach or attempt to feed them, as this can disrupt their natural behaviors and induce stress. Observing from a distance with binoculars or a camera lens ensures you can appreciate their beauty without intruding on their space. Sticking to designated trails and respecting park regulations helps protect both wildlife and the natural environment of the canyon.

South Platte and the Canyon

The South Platte River begins in the Rocky Mountains, fed by several streams, including the South Fork and the North Fork, which converge near Como, Colorado. From its mountainous origins, the river flows southeast for approximately 440 miles, winding through picturesque canyons, rolling hills, and agricultural plains before finally merging with the North Platte River near North Platte, Nebraska.

▲ Every so often, the area will have an increase in snowmelt and rainfall that causes the dam to overflow—it's worth the hike to see it, but keep in mind it'll be a 12-mile day

► Bighorn sheep are fast runners—give them plenty of space on the trail

▼ Bighorn sheep coats blend in with their rocky habitat, so they can be hard to spot from far away

As the river flows through the canyon, it provides essential resources that sustain a wide variety of plants and wildlife, including fish, birds, and mammals. The river's banks are lined with riparian vegetation, including cottonwoods, willows, and various grasses, which provide habitat. Trout thrive in its cool, clear waters, while its lush riverbanks are home to birds like herons and kingfishers that rely on the river for feeding.

▼ Deer can be spotted in the shrubby brush next to the river

TRIP 23

Roxborough State Park

Roxborough State Park is home to 15 miles of trails where you can spot 145 different species of birds, distinct plant communities, and incredible red-rock formations—a miniature version of Colorado's famed Garden of the Gods without the drive!

Roxborough State Park, located south of Denver near Littleton, spans about 3400 acres and is known for its iconic red-rock formations. Roxborough features a network of well-maintained trails suitable for all skill levels, making it easy to explore its natural beauty. For wildlife observation, the Lyons Loop Trail and Willow Creek Trail are top choices. Lions Loop offers overlooks where you can spot deer and birds, while Willow Creek winds through lush areas, perfect for seeing songbirds. Common avian sightings include golden eagle, often soaring high above the park, and red-tailed hawk, frequently found perched on trees or gliding in search of prey. Mountain bluebird adds a splash of color to the landscape, while western meadowlark is known for its distinctive songs and bright yellow underparts. Song sparrows are also prevalent, often heard singing in meadows and brushy areas.

▲ Roxborough State Park has 15 miles of trails

The Rocks of Roxborough

The vibrant red and orange sandstone spires, rugged outcrops, and expansive rock formations are one of the biggest draws to Roxborough State Park. The rich colors of the rocks come from iron oxide, deposited over millions of years, while erosion, uplift, and other geological processes have shaped these sedimentary layers, resulting in the unique structures you see today.

The Fountain Valley Overlook is close to the visitor center and offers stunning views of several remarkable rock formations, including the Dakota Hogback, Fountain Formation, and Lyons Formation. Visitors are treated to a breathtaking panorama of the surrounding area, which includes views of the Cathedral Spires and the Tower of Babel, both of which showcase the striking red and orange hues characteristic of the Fountain Formation. These formations are a testament to millions of years of sedimentation, erosion, and geological activity. In addition to these impressive structures, the Fountain Valley Overlook provides a clear view of the Roxborough Pinnacles, a series of jagged, pointed rock formations that rise dramatically from the valley floor.

▼ Golden eagles can live up to 40 years in protected habitats

A Designated Park

Roxborough State Park has been designated as an Important Bird Area by the Audubon Society, underscoring its critical role as a habitat for various bird species. This designation highlights the park's significance as a breeding, feeding, and migratory stopover site. With diverse environments such as grasslands, shrublands, and ponderosa pine forests, Roxborough supports a rich avian population year-round. The park is especially noted for its nesting raptors, including aforementioned golden eagle and red-tailed hawk, majestic as they soar above its rock formations. The variety of songbirds that thrive here also reflect the health of the park's ecosystems and effectiveness of its conservation efforts.

Beyond its avian importance, Roxborough State Park is recognized for its exceptional natural and cultural significance. It's designated as a Colorado Natural Area and a National Natural Landmark. The park is also a national archeological district, emphasizing its historical and cultural heritage, and has achieved "Gold Standard" status from the organization Leave No Trace, demonstrating its commitment to environmental stewardship and sustainable recreation practices.

Winter Recreation

During the winter months, Roxborough's serene and picturesque landscape is less crowded, so if you're willing to bundle up, the trails invite peaceful winter hikes and nature walks, especially when covered with snow. Snowshoeing is particularly popular, as the park's relatively flat and gently rolling terrain is accessible for beginners and gives people a chance to try out this winter hobby without having to head deep into the mountains.

Winter is also a great time for wildlife observation, as many birds and animals remain active despite the colder temperatures. The songbirds and red-tailed hawks supported by the park's diverse habitats stand out against the stark winter backdrop. Northern flicker and American blue jay can be seen flitting among the trees in winter, while smaller birds like black-capped chickadee and nuthatch search for seeds and insects.

Mammals like mule deer are frequently spotted as they graze on available vegetation, well-adapted to winter conditions. Red fox and coyote are also active during winter, though they can be elusive. Observing tracks in the snow can provide clues to their presence, adding an exciting element to a winter visit to the park.

Another Way to See the Park

Before you visit the park, make a Rox Ride reservation. Roxborough State Park offers this as a complimentary guided tour on a five-passenger electric golf cart along the Fountain Valley Trail that gives you a new way to see the striking red-rock formations, expansive grassy meadows, and diverse wildlife while learning more from a ranger.

▶ Visiting Roxborough State Park in winter is great for avoiding crowds and has just as many spectacular views

◀ Mule deer often hang out together in shrubby underbrush

▲ Look down if you want to spot northern flickers—these woodpeckers tap into the ground looking for ants and other bugs

Golden Gate Canyon State Park

See some of Colorado's most iconic mammals or go leaf peeping at one of the largest aspen groves near the city.

Golden Gate Canyon State Park, located just a few miles west of downtown Golden, is a more than 12,000-acre park known for its sweeping views, rugged terrain, and rich ecosystems. With rolling hills, dense forests, and expansive meadows at elevations ranging from 7500 to over 10,000 feet, it's important to bring plenty of water and take your time if you aren't acclimated to the altitude.

The park features more than 35 miles of trails for hiking, biking, and horseback riding, accommodating all skill levels from easy and accessible paths to challenging routes with significant elevation gain. A popular easier hike is Raccoon Trail, a 2.5-mile loop that leads to Panorama Point—one of the park's most stunning overlooks. (If you don't feel up to hiking, you can also drive directly to this scenic spot!) Keep your eyes peeled on the trail, as animals are everywhere in Golden Gate Canyon State Park. Depending on the season, you might need to look out for black bear, mountain lion, moose, and coyote.

WHERE: 92 Crawford Gulch Rd., Golden, CO 80403
PARKING: Multiple parking lots.
DIFFICULTY: Easy to difficult, depending on trail.
FACILITIES: Restrooms at visitor center and some trailheads. Picnic areas at trailheads throughout park.
SPECIAL NOTES: Daily fee or state parks pass required for entry. No cell service in park.

To avoid conflicts with wildlife, stop by the visitor center to look at their sightings chart, review what animals are active during your visit, and educate yourself about how to engage with them if you do cross paths. Never try to approach a wild animal.

► Short-tailed weasels are small, agile predators known for hunting rodents and insects

▼ Beavers are active in the park's streams and ponds year-round, building dams that create vital wetland habitats

Birdwatchers will delight in seeing a variety of species, including golden eagle, red-tailed hawk, mountain bluebird, and even the occasional peregrine falcon. The park's forests are primarily composed of ponderosa pine and aspen trees, which provide seasonal color changes that enhance the park's beauty and make it a popular leaf-peeping destination every fall.

Go Big or Go Home

Golden Gate Canyon State Park is one of the few places near Denver where visitors can encounter Colorado's large mammals in their natural habitat. Among its diverse fauna, elk and mule deer stand out as some of the most prominent large animals and are often spotted on or near trails, grazing in open meadows or traveling through forested areas. Fall is rutting season, and the park is filled with the impressive, and sometimes terrifying, sounds of elk bugling as males compete for mates and establish dominance.

Mule deer, while slightly smaller, can often be spotted in the early morning or late evening. Known for their distinctive large ears (some would say they look like mules'), they browse on vegetation in meadows and wooded areas.

Even black bears roam the park. Though less frequently seen, these solitary animals are primarily active in spring and summer, foraging for berries, nuts, and insects. Look closely to see signs of their presence, such as tracks and claw marks, adding to the excitement of exploring this rich wildlife haven.

Aptly nicknamed, "Fat Bear Fall" is August through October of each year. Black bears will spend up to 20 hours each day eating in preparation for hibernation. A lot of bear and human conflicts occur during this time of year because food becomes more scarce. Protect yourself and bears by always properly disposing of food waste and always using bean canisters when camping.

Primo Leaf Peeping

Leaf peeping at Golden Gate Canyon State Park is a must-do fall experience. As aspens, cottonwoods, and other deciduous trees reach their peak color, they create a stunning palette of gold, orange, and red that contrasts beautifully with evergreen pines and the rugged terrain of the park.

Three main pigments are responsible for the gorgeous fall colors: carotenoids, anthocyanins, and chlorophyll. Carotenoids give us those beautiful yellows, oranges, and browns; anthocyanins are water-soluble pigments responsible for the rich reds and purples; and chlorophyll is the green pigment that's crucial for photosynthesis, helping plants convert sunlight into sugars, which trees store for winter.

Throughout the growing season, both chlorophyll and carotenoids are busy in the leaves. In summer, chlorophyll is constantly produced and broken down, making leaves look green. As fall approaches, shorter days trigger a process in leaves that seals off the veins, trapping sugars and promoting anthocyanin production. As the days get shorter, chlorophyll production slows down and eventually stops, revealing the vibrant carotenoids and anthocyanins underneath. Different trees bring their own flair to the autumn display—oaks might show off red and brown hues, while aspens turn that signature, stunning golden yellow.

▼ Raccoon, Mule Deer, and Beaver Trails are some of the best for leaf peeping, winding through areas where aspen groves and open meadows are particularly vibrant

TRIP 25

Eldorado Canyon State Park

Discover how the canyons of gold got their name at this state park.

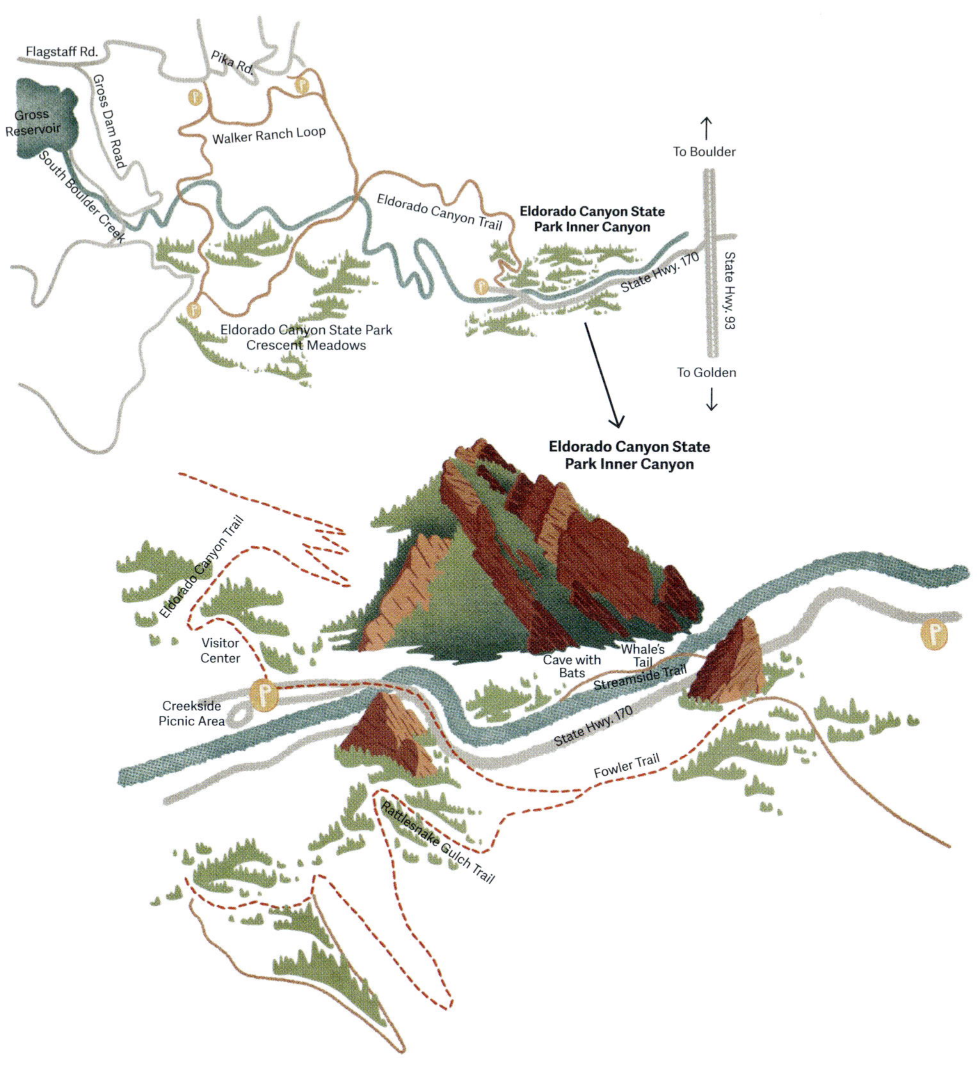

WHERE: 9 Kneale Rd., Eldorado Springs, CO 80025
PARKING: Small parking lot.
DIFFICULTY: Easy to moderate depending on chosen trail difficulty.
FACILITIES: Bathrooms at visitor center. Creekside picnic areas.
SPECIAL NOTES: Small parking lot fills quickly; take free shuttle during peak season. Timed reservations may be required for entry. Daily fee or state parks pass required for entry.

Eldorado Canyon State Park may be a bit of a drive from Denver, but the journey is worthwhile. With a free shuttle service available on weekends and during peak seasons, accessing the canyon is a breeze. South Boulder Creek, the park's main water feature, shaped the cliffs during the uplift of the Front Range. Additional tributary drainages include Rattlesnake Gulch, South Draw, Johnson Gulch, and an unnamed stream north of Johnson Gulch. Spanning about 1500 acres, the park is divided into two main areas: the Inner Canyon and Crescent Meadows, with elevations ranging from 5800 to 8800 feet.

Eldorado is one of the country's most sought-after outdoor climbing spots, and it's easy to see why. Towering cliffs offer breathtaking views and provide a thrilling challenge for climbers looking to push their limits and for hikers interested in canyon ecosystems. Whether you're a beginner or an experienced climber, the 500 technical routes ensure that you never run out of new terrain to explore.

▲ If you see something in the underbrush dart away quickly, it's probably a chipmunk seeking safety

◄ Asters are native wildflowers that add a pop of color to the grassland areas in the park

The varied ecosystems found in canyon environments, ranging from riparian areas along the creek to montane forests, support a range of plant and animal species, making it a fun spot to hike if you prefer trails that change their views. Rattlesnake Gulch Trail and Boulder Canyon Trail offer scenic views of the canyon and the surrounding foothills, with opportunities to spot wildlife like chipmunk, mule deer, red-tailed hawk, prairie rattlesnake, Steller's jay, bear, and bobcat.

Canyons create unique microclimates. Just a few feet apart, you can encounter a wide variety of plant species, from drought-tolerant xeric plants on sunlit slopes to moisture-loving vegetation thriving in cooler, shaded areas. This plant diversity supports numerous animal species that have adapted to these distinct environments.

Additionally, canyons shape local water flow and erosion patterns. Streams and rivers winding through them create fertile floodplains vital for sustaining plant life and providing smaller pools and wetlands crucial for amphibians and insects.

A Unique Relationship

Trees are often competitors for light and moisture, but sometimes they work together. You can see such a relationship between the paper birch and Douglas fir trees at Eldorado Canyon State Park. Paper birch can benefit neighboring Douglas firs by transferring carbon (in the form of sugars) through underground networks of ectomycorrhizal fungi. These beneficial fungi help create a symbiotic relationship where both the trees and fungi thrive. The fungi enhance tree root systems' ability to absorb water and essential nutrients, particularly phosphorus, while receiving carbohydrates and vitamins in return. This win-win relationship helps the trees get a little boost of energy, especially when they are shaded or stressed, and not only

◀ Golden eagles can be identified from below by their mostly black wing coloration with a white band on the tail

▲ Gold cobblestone lichen gets its common name because it resembles a cobblestone street

▼ The hops azure butterfly can usually be spotted mid-June to early July

helps individual trees survive, but also contributes to the overall health and resilience of the entire forest ecosystem.

HOPS AZURE BUTTERFLY

The hops azure butterfly, a rare and intriguing species, can be found in Eldorado Canyon State Park. It's characterized by its delicate, pale blue wings—the upper side of which is a soft blue, while the underside is a lighter, more mottled pattern. This coloration helps the butterfly blend into its surroundings, making it less noticeable to both predators and observers.

Wild hops found in the park are the host plant for its larvae, providing essential resources for caterpillars and making the conservation of this plant vital for the butterfly's survival.

Gold, Gold, Everywhere

The name "Eldorado" evokes images of gold, which is fitting, as the canyon cliffs appear to shimmer with a golden hue. Upon closer inspection, however, you'll discover that this color actually comes from the lichen that blankets the rock surfaces. Lichens are symbiotic organisms composed of fungi and algae. They play a crucial role in the ecosystem by colonizing rocky surfaces and contributing to soil formation. Common varieties include crustose lichen, which forms a tight, crusty layer on the rock; fruticose, which is more shrubby and forms upright colonies; and foliose, characterized by its leaf-like structures that can be easily peeled away. These lichens have adapted to the challenging conditions of high altitudes and fluctuating temperatures. Their vibrant hues—ranging from bright yellows and oranges to soft greens and grays—add a striking contrast and visual interest to the park's rugged landscape.

GOLDEN EAGLES GALORE

Every year, Eldorado Canyon State Park closes the Rattlesnake Gulch area on the south side of the canyon to protect nesting raptors. Golden eagles, cousins of the bald eagle, have dark brown feathers covering their entire bodies and a distinctive golden sheen on the back of their necks, which is particularly noticeable in the sunlight. Their expansive wingspan, which can reach up to 7.5 feet, allows them to soar effortlessly over the park's rugged landscapes and steep canyon walls.

ACKNOWLEDGMENTS

Thank you to Jefferson County Public Library, Denver Public Library, the Denver Museum of Nature and Science, Dinosaur Ridge, History Colorado, Colorado State University Extension, Jeffco Open Space, Denver Parks & Recreation, Colorado Parks and Wildlife, U.S. Fish and Wildlife Service, Colorado State Parks, National Park Service, and every location in the Field Trip section of this book. Please visit and support these places and institutions any way you can. They help keep our city's history alive.

A special thank you to Emily Crowley, Matt Macgee, and Amy Atwater for taking the time to share information and help me discover a side of Denver I didn't know about before. Huge thank yous to my incredible editors Naomi Ruiz, Andrew Keys, Matthew Burnett, and the entire team at Timber Press; you all helped make this book better than I could have ever imagined.

And an eternal thanks to cold-brew coffee, quiet library study rooms, and my mother. Without them, this book would not have been possible.

PHOTO AND ART CREDITS

Bluff Lake Nature Center, 172-173, 208
Felicia Brower, 15 (top), 25, 57 (right), 69, 80, 84, 194, 195, 196 (bottom), 204 (top), 206, 209–211, 224, 226, 227 (top), 229, 230, 233–236, 240, 254 (bottom), 297 (right),
Denver Museum of Nature and Science, 11 (top left), 33
Denver Public Library Special Collections, 20, 23
Alan Ford, 212
Jason Kann, 4, 14 (top), 15 (bottom), 53, 62 (top left), 248, 249, 284, 291, 294, 297 (left)
Michael Levine-Clark, 12–13, 73 (right), 182 (right), 215 (bottom), 286

Flickr
abbeyprivate, 115, 116
Adams, NPS, 149
Cecilia Alexander, 29, 95
Bill Badzo, 17–18
Heather Bell, USFWS, 60 (bottom right), 109
Seth Beres, USFWS, 265 (top right)
Jitze Couperus, 158, 187 (left)
Big Cypress National Park Service, 191 (right)
Jake Bonello, USFWS, 136
Gannon Castle, USFWS, 298 (top left)
Courtney Celley, USFWS, 27 (right), 65, 120, 121, 143, 277 (top left)
Paul Cryan, NPS, 150
Elisa Dahlberg, USFWS, 41 (left), 216 (top)
Gary Enslinger, USFWS, 277 (top right)
Laken Ewert, USFWS, 22 (right)
Jacob W. Frank, NPS, 122
Robyn Gerstenlager, USFWS, 71
Joanna Gilkeson, USFWS, 90, 97 (bottom right), 204 (bottom)
GlacierNPS, 129
Adam Grima, 97 (top)
Mick Hanan, USFWS, 44 (bottom)
Robb Hannawacker, 62 (bottom left), 74, 76, 85, 92 (right), 97 (left center), 99, 269, 264 (top left)
Andrew Hazen, 167
Marcie Hebert, USFWS, 75

Jan Helebrant, 14 (bottom), 36
Neal Herbert, 156
Dona Hilkey, 42
Ashton Hooker, NPS, 151
Jim Hudgins, USFWS, 165
Mark Hughes, 142
AJ—Angela James, USFWS, 205 (bottom)
Julia C. Johnson, USFWS, 187 (left)
Liz Julian, USFWS, 31, 147, 215 (top), 238 (left)
Dan Keck, 188
Tom Koerner, USFWS, 40 (right), 44 (top left), 47 (top), 48 (top), 52 (right), 83, 131, 138, 186, 191 (left), 201 (bottom), 239, 241 (left), 246, 254 (top), 292
Thibault Lefort, 241 (right)
Alan Levine, 270 (top left)
Krista Lundgren, USFWS, 250
M. Reed, NPS, 168
Mike Mauro, USFWS, 45 (top right)
Michael Menefree, Colorado National Heritage Foundation, 130
Ryan Moehring, USFWS, 201 (top), 214
Domingo Mora, 133
Kurt Moses, NPS, 113
Oregon Department Fish & Wildlife, 63 (bottom), 169,
Michael Rieger, FEMA, 61 (bottom left)
Roggio Wildlife, 52 (left)
Cortez Rohr, USFWS, 28
Jacqueline Russell, BLM Utah, 257
Alejandro Santillana, 97 (right center), 105, 108
Vic Schendel, USFWS, 56, 287
Alan Schmierer, 118, 140, 145, 157
Michael Schramm, USFWS, 141
Alex Schubert, USFWS, 160
Tina Shaw, USFWS, 64
Shenandoah National Park, 98
Shiva Shenoy, 244 (top)
Dana Nicole Smith, USFWS, 300–301
Grayson Smith, USFWS, 258 (top)
Scott Somershoe, USFWS, 125
Jennifer Soos, 128, 146
Cindy Souders, USFWS, 60 (top)
Carmen Sponseller, ODFW, 123
Bernard Spragg, 68

Jennifer Strickland, USFWS, 40 (left), 72
Sam Stukel, USFWS, 47 (bottom), 110, 119, 222, 277 (bottom)
Katie Theule, USFWS, 226 (bottom)
S&C Photography, 135, 154
Sanda Uecker, USFWS, 221 (top), 205 (top), 238 (right)
John K. Thorne, 15 (bottom)
tom00la, 66
Jill Utrup, USFWS, 57 (left)
U.S. Department of Agriculture, 71 (left), 87, 97 (bottom left)
U.S. Fish and Wildlife Service, 148, 152, 153
U.S. Forest Service, 41 (right)
USFS Pacific Northwest, 164
USFWS Midwest Region, 245
USFWS Mountain-Prairie Region, 22 (left), 27 (left), 86, 111
Watts, 144
Sheri Whala, USFWS, 51
White Sands National Park, 159
Wildlife Terry, 132
David Woolman, SCA, 112
Susan Young, 124

2.0 Generic
Andrea_44, 258 (bottom), 265
Jeffrey Beall, 136, 190, 192, 275 (bottom)
Mark Byzewski, 7, 48 (bottom), 182, 280, 281, 283
David Fulmer, 266–267
Judy Gallagher, 90, 97 (bottom right)
Brian Gratwicke, 8, 271 (top right)
isamiga76, 70
Michael Kirsch, 262, 263
Ron Knight, 264 (bottom)
Shelley Koerner, USFWS, 78
Larry Lamsa, 73 (left)
Jennifer Linnea, 11 (top right)
Adam Meek, 289 (top)
Chris M. Morris, 82
National Park Service, 77, 129, 191, 260,
pinoldy, 289 (bottom left)
Dave Ruske, 271 (bottom)
James St. John, 35, 252, 253 (bottom)
Andrey Zharkikh, 81
Robin Zebrowski, 11 (bottom)

INDEX

Felicia Brower is a Denver-based author with a penchant for plants and the natural world. She studied environmental policy and planning at Virginia Tech before becoming a writer and technical editor. When she's not in her garden, she's out on a hike keeping her eyes peeled for the plants and animals in this guide.